# In Search of God

# In Search of God

*God, Religious Scriptures & Proof of Divine Revelation*

## DR. MOHAMED GAD

iUniverse, Inc.
Bloomington

In Search of God
God, Religious Scriptures & Proof of Divine Revelation

iUniverse books may be ordered through booksellers or by contacting:

iUniverse
1663 Liberty Drive
Bloomington, IN 47403
www.iuniverse.com
1-800-Authors (1-800-288-4677)

ISBN: 978-1-4620-2448-3 (sc)
ISBN: 978-1-4620-2447-6 (hc)
ISBN: 978-1-4620-2705-7 (ebk)

Printed in the United States of America

iUniverse rev. date: 07/23/2011

DEDICATED TO THE PURSUIT OF KNOWLEDGE

ABOUT GOD

BECAUSE BEFORE I CAME INTO THIS WORLD

I WAS NOTHING

AND WHEN I CAME INTO THIS WORLD

I KNEW NOTHING

BUT HOPEFULLY BEFORE I LEAVE THIS WORLD

I WILL KNOW SOME THINGS

# CONTENTS

# Preface

*And Moses returned unto the LORD, and said, LORD, wherefore hast thou so evil entreated this people? why is it that thou hast sent me? (Exodus 5:22, King James Version)*

*For since I came to Pharaoh to speak in thy name, he hath done evil to this people; neither hast thou delivered thy people at all. (Exodus 5: 23, King James Version)*

*Then Pharaoh also called the wise men and the sorcerers: now the magicians of Egypt, they also did in like manner with their enchantments. (Exodus 7:11, King James Version)*

*For they cast down every man his rod, and they became serpents: but Aaron's rod swallowed up their rods. (Exodus 7:12, King James Version)*

*And he hardened Pharaoh's heart, that he hearkened not unto them; as the LORD had said. (Exodus 7:13, King James Version)*

Reading the above passages, we should concur that God only hardened Pharaoh's heart because he was evil and the hardening of his heart is what eventually led to his destruction. This is an important philosophical point because a superficial analysis would lead us to believe that our fates are predestined but clearly, Pharaoh had a choice to choose between good and evil yet he chose to follow the path of evil in the face of overwhelming evidence. The message is clear that if we turn our minds and hearts against God then God will harden our hearts against his path and this hardening will lead us to a path of self-destruction. Conversely, the passages below give a very different account of humility where the queen of Sheba accepted God's message.

*And when the queen of Sheba heard of the fame of Solomon concerning the name of the LORD, she came to prove him with hard questions. (1 Kings 10:1, King James Version)*

*And Solomon told her all her questions: there was not any thing hid from the king, which he told her not. (1 Kings 10:3, King James Version)*

*And the meat of his table, and the sitting of his servants, and the attendance of his ministers, and their apparel, and his cupbearers, and his ascent by which he went up unto the house of the LORD; there was no more spirit in her. (1 Kings 10:5, King James Version)*

*And she said to the king, It was a true report that I heard in mine own land of thy acts and of thy wisdom. (1 Kings 10:6, King James Version)*

No matter what our forefathers believed in we should open our hearts and minds to examine the facts and not be concerned with whether the ideas presented are pro Jewish, Christian or Islamic. Intellectual and spiritual advancement should compel us to overcome our emotions and not be buoyed or offended by certain ideas because these concepts support or question the faith we grew up with. Rather we should be more concerned whether the evidence presented is sound and factual meriting careful consideration without inciting emotional hysteria or accusations of biased penmanship.

The true spirit of learning should lead us to apply the same principles of the scientific method in studying religion where belief is based on reason and not where faith replaces reason. We must put aside our pride and follow the path of the queen of Sheba and not the path of Pharaoh. To quote the King James Version of the Bible: *But if from thence thou shalt seek the LORD thy God, thou shalt find him, if thou seek him with all thy heart and with all thy soul (Deuteronomy 4:29, KJV).*

A meaningful discussion about prophecy, Divine Revelation or religion would not be complete without commenting on the deeper philosophical questions of linking the revealed scriptures with respect to the purpose of creation, revelation, and subsequently the consequences of obedience or disobedience. In this endeavor, chapters on prayer and the hereafter are included. Before we try to understand the possible meaning of our existence, we must first ponder what obligates us to uncover the eternal message that may be hidden in Divine Revelation. Do we have a moral obligation to ourselves, our children and for the generations that follow to seek *"the Truth and nothing but the Truth so help me God"?*

إِنَّا عَرَضْنَا ٱلْأَمَانَةَ عَلَى ٱلسَّمَـٰوَٰتِ وَٱلْأَرْضِ وَٱلْجِبَالِ فَأَبَيْنَ أَن يَحْمِلْنَهَا وَأَشْفَقْنَ مِنْهَا وَحَمَلَهَا ٱلْإِنسَـٰنُ إِنَّهُۥ كَانَ ظَلُومًا جَهُولًا ۝

*We did indeed offer the Trust to the Heavens and the Earth and the Mountains; but they refused to undertake it, being afraid thereof: but man undertook it;—He was indeed unjust and unknowledgeable;—(Koran 33:72)*

According to the Koran God has given us a *"Trust"* (Koran 33:72), that we apparently chose to accept, the secret of which mankind cannot comprehend as we were not given the tools or knowledge to uncover this secret. The above verse suggests that at some point we must each individually have chosen to be born into this world. We should not be unjust to our souls and instead take the time to discover what may await us beyond this short journey of life.

وَإِذْ قَالَ رَبُّكَ لِلْمَلَـٰئِكَةِ إِنِّى جَاعِلٌ فِى ٱلْأَرْضِ خَلِيفَةً قَالُوٓاْ أَتَجْعَلُ فِيهَا مَن يُفْسِدُ فِيهَا وَيَسْفِكُ ٱلدِّمَآءَ وَنَحْنُ نُسَبِّحُ بِحَمْدِكَ وَنُقَدِّسُ لَكَ قَالَ إِنِّىٓ أَعْلَمُ مَا لَا تَعْلَمُونَ ۝

*Behold, thy Lord said to the angels: "I will create a vicegerent on earth." They said: "Wilt Thou place therein one who will make mischief therein and shed blood?—whilst we do celebrate Thy praises and glorify Thy holy (name)?" He said: "I know what ye know not." (Koran 2:30)*

Our impatience to know what we cannot possibly comprehend may lead us to deny that the wisdom of God is greater than our own. This in turn could result in a state of rebellion against God, where by being in a state of disbelief, there are no bounds to our transgressions. The biggest danger to our souls is our pride where like Satan we begin to reject God's authority, and begin to believe what is potentially evil as good. Like the angels, we are *unknowledgeable (Koran 2:30)* about God's plans so we cannot rationally use the excuse of ignorance as the basic tenet for our disobedience.

As the old adage goes there are two things sure in life, death and taxes. However, as we know some people may evade taxes but can we evade God even though He may at times seem detached? To Search for God may fulfill our intellectual curiosity but should we succeed in finding God then what may be expected of us? This passage from the *Old Testament* nicely summarizes what God expects of us:

*Let us hear the conclusion of the whole matter: Fear God, and keep his commandments: for this is the whole duty of man. (Ecclesiastes Qoh.12: 13)*

The fear of God is not just the fear of His anger but the realization that for all our actions we could be held accountable. We are generally driven by motivations and desires but in our quest for self-fulfillment, we may transgress the rights of others. A consequence of examining Divine Revelation is the attempt to define our relationship with God and our surroundings. As incredulous as it may seem all that God has deemed is that it would be well advised to heed, do good deeds and not die in disbelief.

There is a spiritual soul that needs to be nurtured but this must be done in a healthy manner leaving room for openness in discussion and objectivity. Comparative religion and cultures need to be taught in the public educational system to foster better understanding and tolerance. We can no longer afford to continue denying that religion and politics are not intertwined in the conscious or subconscious psyche of many peoples. We should not leave it solely to selective religious institutions, governments, libraries, bookstores or the mass media to shape our minds and attitudes. The greatest challenge of all times will be our willingness to seriously re-examine religion as without such examination the fabric of our societies may be torn apart. On the other hand, a changing morality that suites our times could leave our societies open to internal decay. This societal decay could permeate into every sphere of our lives affecting individual integrity, mental health, and the sense of social responsibility.

As humans, we all grow up with the beliefs and traditions of our forefathers that are nurtured during childhood, for better or worse, with ideas and rituals that shape our outlook toward others of different nationalities and traditions. As we seek to understand different belief systems we must not make assumptions or presuppositions that present day ritual or interpretations of scripture were the original intended meaning of the 'prophet' or revelations nor should we presuppose that other people of other faiths worship a different God or follow a religion that is a creation of a certain historical figure or persona. Rather we should examine the scripture in view of the possible authenticity of the message as whether it is truly from God. In this process, reason or logic not blind faith must prevail. We must ask can the revelation be truly from God and what 'proof' suggests that scripture is the 'word of God'.

However, in this process of discovery we cannot question the laws or Wisdom of God by trying to use our own intellect to explain that which God may not have explained. To exemplify this point we may speculate but not question God's system of reward or punishment as this is beyond our grasp.

Speculating on the rationale for commandments such as that which prohibits Jews and Muslims from eating pork, by invoking the risk of leishmaniasis is insufficient, as the sole purpose may be a Divine will to test obedience in preparation for a future higher purpose that we cannot presently comprehend. Similarly, when we try to fully understand Islamic inheritance laws we may be trying to question the equality or fairness of these laws for scripture does not explain the real rationale behind these laws. We may try to explain or understand certain laws but ultimately if we are to accept that scripture is divinely inspired we must accept that this is God's will or possibly another test of obedience.

Culture and religion are intertwined and identify who we are. Any challenge to our belief system may lead to uncertainty and instability and disturbs our psyche. We do not like changes to "our way of life" and the simple way to deal with such a threat is to shut out new ideas or try and impose our way of life on others. Fear of change allows emotions to override reasoning leading to bigotry and hatred. We may become passionate about our beliefs, refusing to examine or accept new ideas.

Fear plays on our emotions leading to a rush to judgment and cultivation of ignorant opinions about others. If we become aware of this human shortcoming we may begin to understand why history is replete with examples of religious strife. Hopefully, insight into our emotional psyche can help us change our attitudes towards others or ourselves inexplicable acceptance or rejection of certain belief systems.

In light of this argument we may better answer the question why did Moses leave Pharaoh's Egypt or why was Jesus crucified? Both Moses and Jesus presented a challenge to "a way of life" or a threat to the status quo. Similarly, the prophet Muhammad had the same effect on his people and was forced to leave his home in Mecca.

We cannot let blind faith, tradition or ritual, likes and dislikes become our guiding compass and cloud our judgment for this is what stirs emotions that becomes the potent mix which has driven a wedge between peoples throughout the times. Maybe all of us cannot learn to love one another, as might be expected in a utopian world, but at least we can come closer to first understanding ourselves so we may begin to understand each other. Tolerance thru understanding is the key to a brighter future for us and our children. Only the truth shall set us free but first we must have a true desire to seek it.

This latest edition of the book offers new as well as expanded chapters. Comparative analysis of Biblical and Koranic text with the view of demonstrating continuity of the Divine message is explored.

I wish to acknowledge and thank my parents and wife for their assistance, critique, patience and support. I also wish to give special credit to my teenage daughter for her redesign of the book cover.

# Introduction

The purpose of this book is an attempt to search for God. To search for God one must first ponder the existence of a supernatural force that explains the existence of the universe and the creation of man. Once one realizes that there is a higher intelligence that is responsible for our presence we should then be compelled by a sense of curiosity to find out if this supernatural omniscient and omnipotent God has left us to our own haphazard devices or has set up a blueprint, or roadmap, for us to follow. This should lead one to examine the revealed religions in a scholarly manner. To do so one must not confuse scripture with those who are followers of the faith. Followers as well as non-followers of a particular faith may entwine their own culture, superstitions, biases, fears and ignorance with the reality of the revelation and therefore misrepresent the truth of revealed scripture. Through omission, deception or dishonesty humans with certain motivations may distort certain truths or realities. If a lie is repeated often times it can take on lifelike qualities till we become convinced of its truth. To illustrate this point we ask did Jewish slaves build the *pyramids of Geiza*? In the 1956 movie *The Ten Commandments* and in the more recent 1998 animated movie *The Prince of Egypt* we are told that Jews built the Pyramids.

Abraham is the father of Isaac and Ishmael. According to recent discoveries at **Ebla,** as noted in the **National Geographic magazine** (*National Geographic, December 1978, page 736*), the true date of Abraham's existence is probably 2300 BC. *Ebla* was an ancient city in northwestern Syria sacked by the *Akkadian*s c. 2250 BC.

Historically, the Pyramids were built c.2560 BC. Therefore, the Jewish people, who are Abraham's descendents, were not around c.2560 BC. Short of a miracle or a re-writing of history it would seem improbable if not somewhat impossible that enslaved Jews built the *pyramids of Geiza.*

Joseph was thirty years old when he entered the service of Pharaoh King of Egypt *(Genesis 41:46 & 41:39-40, N IV)*. Joseph meets his brothers during the second year of the famine *(Genesis 45:6)* and at that time his father Jacob was 130 years old *(Genesis 47:7-9, N IV)*; by then Joseph is 39 years old as the seven years of plenty have ended and we are in the second year of the famine *(Genesis 41:53-4)*. Hence, when Joseph was born his father Jacob was 91 years old. Hence, Joseph probably figured prominently in Egypt for close to 80 years. Joseph died 110 years old *(Genesis 50:26)*.

Abraham was 100 years old *(Genesis 21:5, N IV)* when his son Isaac was born while Isaac was 60 years old when his son Jacob was born *(Genesis 25:26, NIV)*. Furthermore, as noted above, Jacob was 91 years old when Joseph was born. Hence, from the time Abraham was born till Joseph entered the service of Pharaoh there is a span of 281 years. As previously discussed, per *National Geographic Magazine*, Abraham lived around 2300 BC so Joseph was probably alive around 2000 BC.

The *Great Pyramid of Giza was probably* built circa 2560 BC for King Khufu *(Cheops)* (http://en.wikipedia.org/wiki/Great_Pyramid_of_Giza*)*. The etymology of the title Pharaoh, "*pr-Á3*", in hieroglyphs, means '*His Majesty'* and was first used as a title in 1550-1292 BC *(http://en.wikipedia. org/wiki/Pharaoh)*. Abram (Abraham) and Joseph lived well before 1550 BC when Egypt's rulers were called Kings yet the Bible relates both as living during the time when Pharaohs ruled Egypt *(Genesis 12:20 and 41:46)*.

The Bible *(Exodus 15:19)* and the *(Koran 10:75)* both concur that Moses lived during the time of Pharaohs. However, the Koran curiously reveals that Joseph lived during the rule of Egyptian Kings *(Koran 12:43, 12:72)* while the Bible states Joseph lived during the rule of Pharaohs *(Genesis 41:46)*. Hence, Prophet Muhammad could not have directly copied from the Bible and instead we must admit that the Koran quietly corrected a subtle yet blatant Biblical error.

*But the disbelievers say: "Naught is this but a lie which he has forged, and others have helped him at it." In truth it is they who have put forward an iniquity and a falsehood (Koran 25:4)*

*And they say: 'Tales of the ancients, which he has caused to be written: and they are dictated before him morning and evening" (Koran 25:5)*

**Ramses II** ruled during the 19th Dynasty (**1279-1212 BC**) and if we accept that he is the Pharaoh of the Exodus (supported by evidence later in this book) then based on Biblical literature this would suggest Joseph was present in Egypt around 1700 BC while Abraham was alive around 2000 BC. Rabbinic and Christian scholars are generally of the opinion that Abraham lived around 2000 BC. However, this would be in discordance with the aforementioned National Geographic (National Geographic, December 1978, page 736) reference but again would place Abraham as coming much later than the construction of the Pyramids that date back to 2560 BC. The word Pharaoh was 'first' used as a title in 1550-1292 BC and this would again leave Joseph as living during the time of Egyptian Kings and not Pharaohs. Furthermore, the Old Testament suggests, as we shall see below, that the Jews lived in Egypt approximately four hundred years placing Moses very close to the rule of Ramses II.

Moses was a Levite (Exodus 2:1& Exodus 6:13-20):

*And there went a man of the house of Levi, and took to wife a daughter of Levi. (Exodus 2:1)*

Abraham ⟶ Isaac ⟶ Jacob ⟶ **Levi** ⟶ **Kohath** ⟶**Amram** ⟶**Moses**

*Jacob (Israel) lived a hundred and forty-seven years (Genesis 47:28, NIV).*

Below we are told **Levi lived 137 years, Kohath 133 years, Amram 137 years**.

### Exodus 6

*And the LORD spake unto Moses and unto Aaron, and gave them a charge unto the children of Israel, and unto Pharaoh king of Egypt, to bring the children of Israel out of the land of Egypt. (Exodus 6:13, KJV)*

*And these are the names of the **sons of Levi** according to their generations; Gershon, and **Kohath**, and Merari: and the years of the life of Levi were an hundred thirty and seven years. (Exodus 6:16, KJV)*

*And the sons of Kohath; Amram, and Izhar, and Hebron, and Uzziel: and the years of the life of Kohath were an hundred thirty and three years. (Exodus 6:18, KJV)*

*And **Amram took him Jochebed his father's sister to wife; and she bare him Aaron and Moses**: and the years of the life of Amram were an hundred and thirty and seven years. (Exodus 6:20, KJV)*

This implies that the Jews lived in Egypt four long generations or approximately four hundred years from the time Joseph (who is Levi's brother) went to Egypt till the Exodus when Moses crossed the Red Sea.

This book is a compilation of different concepts derived from multiple sources. The author synthesizes these ideas in a lucid manner so that the reader may make his own conclusions. The main Biblical references, unless stated otherwise, are from the King James Version of the Bible. In this book the Koranic translation substitutes the word "God" for "Allah" as for some readers there is an implication that the Arabs have their "own" God. Similarly, we can illustrate that God in the Old Testament is referred to as Elohim, Shaddai, and Yahweh. The Hebrew word Elohim, is translated "God" throughout the first chapter of the book of Genesis. In Genesis 17:1 the "Almighty God" (Shaddai) is derived from the root *Shadad*, "to be strong or powerful." In Exodus 6:3, we read, *"I appeared unto Abraham, unto Isaac, and unto Jacob, by the name of God Almighty (Ail Shaddai), but by my name Jehovah (Yahweh) was I not known to them."* Yahweh (or Jehovah) means literally *"He who will be."*

The concept of multiple deities (in Arabic "alleha") was present in Arabia. Allah refers to the "Creator" making a clear distinction from other deities that may be worshipped. As known to pagan religions, there could be a god of war, a god of love, a god of rain, or a god of fire and the list is endless. In reality, the Arabic Christian Bible uses the word Allah. Allah is the Arabic word for God. In French, the word "Dieu" also has special significance. In England, a servant may have called his master "My Lord" but not likely "My God." Would it make sense to say that the French God is called "Dieu" or to say to an Arab Muslim your God 'Allah'?

Those who love knowledge for the sake of enlightenment should find this book engaging and refreshing. If we entertain, the concept that there is a God then the next logical question is did He (no gender intended) communicate to his creation or did He leave us to our own intuitions without a guide or compass? If we cannot answer this question then mankind will be in a dilemma whereby we are never certain if there are any absolute truths. The importance of finding answers to these questions will determine if the rule of man or the law of God should prevail. Does man or God determine what is right or wrong?

If our motto is "In God We Trust" should religion stay in or out of state affairs? The Turkish government for presumed economic reasons has recently decided to drop the death penalty so that their country may eventually meet criterion for joining the European Union. However, an economic giant like the U.S.A. does not have to bear such pressures and continues to uphold the death penalty. Is capital punishment good or bad and who is to decide?

مِنۡ أَجۡلِ ذَٰلِكَ كَتَبۡنَا عَلَىٰ بَنِىٓ إِسۡرَٰٓءِيلَ أَنَّهُۥ مَن قَتَلَ نَفۡسَۢا بِغَيۡرِ نَفۡسٍ أَوۡ

فَسَادٍ فِى ٱلۡأَرۡضِ فَكَأَنَّمَا قَتَلَ ٱلنَّاسَ جَمِيعٗا وَمَنۡ أَحۡيَاهَا فَكَأَنَّمَآ أَحۡيَا ٱلنَّاسَ

جَمِيعٗاۚ وَلَقَدۡ جَآءَتۡهُمۡ رُسُلُنَا بِٱلۡبَيِّنَٰتِ ثُمَّ إِنَّ كَثِيرٗا مِّنۡهُم بَعۡدَ ذَٰلِكَ فِى

ٱلۡأَرۡضِ لَمُسۡرِفُونَ ۝

*Because of that We ordained for the Children of Israel that **if anyone killed a person** not in retaliation of murder, or (and) to spread mischief in the land?* ***It would be as if he killed all mankind, and if anyone saved a life, it would be as if he saved the life of all mankind.*** *And indeed, there came to them Our Messengers with clear proofs, evidences, and signs, even then after that many of them continued to exceed the limits in the land (Koran 5:32)*

While in the Bible we find:

**Whoso killeth any person, the murderer shall be put to death** *by the mouth of witnesses: but one witness shall not testify against any person [to cause him] to die (Numbers 35:30, KJV).*

Can we declare the Ten Commandments as obsolete or are they a moral guidance for all times? Is religion the salvation of man or the cause of endless suffering due to wars? Would leaders like Napoleon Bonaparte, Adolf Hitler, and Joseph Stalin have not caused so much suffering for mankind if they had found God? Are declarations of holy wars or crusades motivated by abuses of power, bigotry, or greed? Does religion ultimately protect or destroy our human way of life? This book does not answer these issues but leaves the reader to ponder these questions. This writing only attempts to seek evidence for prophecy and the divine inspiration of scripture.

# God, Creation And Evolution

God and evolution for some are two different realms of thought that are considered diametrically opposed. When we see a table or a car we know that it could not have spontaneously evolved yet when we look at the glorious existence of our universe and life in all its forms some people refuse to acknowledge any possible role for a Supreme Creator and instead speak of evolution and Mother Nature as some sort of magical deities that run and transform all that we perceive. God is an entity that as humans we cannot fully conceptualize as He transcends time and all the constraints of the material world that we live in. Why not consider that God directs all evolutionary processes instead of the elusory notion of Mother Nature? To this end the argument will be put forth that there is overwhelming evidence for the existence of God. Afterwards we will contend that total evolution without guidance from a Higher Creator is impossible. The Creator of the universe and all life as we know it is the 'hidden hand' behind all evolutionary processes.

## BELIEVERS AND DISBELIEVERS

The human race is divided into believers and disbelievers. Some people believe in God while others do not. Some people believe in God yet not in Scripture. Belief in Scriptures may be partial or total; with some believing that Scriptures are God inspired but narrated by men while others believe that scriptures are entirely the word of God. Yet others maintain that Scriptures are only oral traditions and not God inspired. Disbelief is of varying degrees, encompassing a wide spectrum. In the English language, the terms agnostics and atheists are used to describe two extremes of disbelief. According to the Merriam Webster Dictionary, the definition

1

of agnosticism is a person who holds the view that any ultimate reality (as God) is unknown and probably unknowable; broadly, one who is not committed to believing in either the existence or the nonexistence of God or a god. Atheism is defined as a disbelief in the existence of a deity or the doctrine that there is no deity. So is the agnostic more reasonable than the atheist or is the agnostic also hanging in limbo by a different thread of disbelief? Why do the disbelievers only accept Evolutionary Theory without considering the concept of Creation or Intelligent Design?

There may be observations that lead us to question or doubt the veracity of an idea or concept. Certainly, we all question ourselves about the existence of God but whenever we question we should be wise in our questions and reasonable in the answers we seek. One's expectations for belief may require that we physically see God but in failing to do so one cannot infer that God does not exist. Personal experiences, although possibly real, cannot be easily translated as evidence to those who have not experienced them. Atheists claim that science disproves intelligent design but can never provide any conclusive science to support this view. This article will argue that to the unbiased astute observer there should be plenty of evidence for intelligent design or as religionists would say the presence of God. Deists maintain that they can observe God's manifestations in themselves as well as in all that surrounds them.

The proof for the existence of God may be indirect and requires reflecting on the intricacies of life forms as well as the complexities of the universe. Even Darwin, who is considered the father of modern day evolution, had doubts about his theories, mainly relating to the absence of intermediary forms although other interesting arguments and questions were raised. The presence of the Cambrian Explosion with the appearance of complex life forms over 540 million years ago or the paucity of intermediary forms for bats which have been preserved in the fossil records dating back to 54 million years ago are difficult for the total evolutionist to explain; evolutionists must rely on more theories to explain their fundamental theory of evolution.

Darwin remarked in his book, *The Origin of the Species*, that the complexity of the eye is difficult to explain using the concepts of evolutionary theories. How did the brain learn to integrate and interpret visual observations and process color perception? Thinking about the presence of beauty Darwin acknowledged that evolutionary theories played no role in explaining this phenomenon. The concept of survival of the fittest is one of the premises on which the foundation of evolution is based but this partial explanation only relates to life forms and not to the intricacies of the inanimate universe. The universe and earth which was necessary to support life as we know it must have followed an orderly transformation from an initial chaotic state that cannot be explained by Darwinian Theory. Our universe is directed, suspended or sustained by powerful forces that require a Supreme Creator or God. To this end we will present evidence in support of a hidden hand, intelligent design or as other realms would argue the forces of God.

Hence, atheists are not forthright when it comes to their doctrine as one may question if God exists but cannot produce evidence to support this claim. There is a difference between atheists and agnostics as the former is stubbornly certain of their doctrine of disbelief and the latter is disingenuously noncommittal. Endless probabilities with an intangible concept called Mother Nature and order from disorder are all unsustainable concepts that rely on whimsical wishful thinking. These concepts lack scientific bases and require a reliance on great leaps of faith.

The theory of Evolution is just a theory with limited evidence and scope. Microevolution not macroevolution is evident and plausible. Evolution and Creation do not have to be mutually exclusive concepts. For the Creationist the Sustainer of the universe is fully capable of setting in motion evolutionary forces that are self-adapting to changes in the environment. Differences in the human race are examples of transformations on the micro evolutionary scale. Microevolution may explain Asian, Black and White races or the development of bacterial resistance to antibiotics.

Apes and humans have strong genetic similarities but this does not prove evolutionary linkage. Where is the science that proves humans evolved from apes? All we have are imaginary artistic renderings of hunchbacks that straighten out into Homo sapiens. Maybe as some of those lucky and more fortunate apes become slightly more intelligent they thought they could see further by looking straight rather than looking downwards and hurting their backs. Even though the DNA of the chimpanzee is 98.4% identical to that of human DNA this fact does not mean that this similarity is due to evolutionary processes. To use a crude analogy a person who constructs one car model may use similar materials to construct a vastly more superior car model but this does not imply that natural selection was responsible for the evolution of the more superior car model. From the Creationist perspective what may be more interesting is the fact these two phenomenally different looking and functioning life forms only have a 1.6% genetic discordance. However, the assumption that genetic DNA is the sole determinant of all the variabilities in these two life forms would suggest that only genetic makeup or physical components determine all features of a living creature. For the religionist who accepts scripture as divinely inspired the spirit imparted by God, to all living humans, is a nonphysical entity that may have no relationship to genetic makeup.

Likewise, men and women have a strong genetic resemblance but that does not prove that one evolved from the other. Just because there is a human resemblance, we cannot scientifically prove that females evolved from males or vice versa. If we follow the evolutionary thought process then we should ponder if the male and female human species evolved separately or spontaneously. Evolution and Creation should not be considered mutually exclusive concepts or ideologies that deter believers or disbelievers from venturing into these two seemingly separate realms of thought. One may set up table to argue for Evolution, Mother Nature, chaotic origins, and the probabilities of random transformation of order from disorder versus Creation or Intelligent Design. Some atheists claim that science does not support Intelligent Design since they cannot 'see' the hand of God; however, Creationists maintain otherwise. The Creator is the intelligent force, creating order from disorder and setting in motion the micro evolutionary scheme.

How and when did the human procreative potential evolve? What created the attraction between males and females? Attraction of the different genders is necessary for procreation but which came first? Did gender identity develop before human attractive forces or did they develop spontaneously by chance? Did attraction develop before the development of procreative capabilities or did they both magically and simultaneously evolve? If your father were the very first Adam or your mother the very first Eve how many millions of years would Adam have to live before Eve spontaneously evolved so that they could have you? Yes, and who first programmed them then taught them how to conceive? The very first Adam and the very first Eve must have had simultaneous beginnings, coming together at the very same time and place to start to conceive.

Lets consider the intellectual capacity of the brain, perception of warm and cold sensations and our mental ability to process the dangers of each, manual dexterity with the sense of pressure applied on objects, pumping of the blood by our heart for every second we live, oxygen and carbon dioxide exchange via the lungs, filtering capacity of the kidney, the vocal cords and the ability to speak, the complexity of the ear and the ability to hear, the tongue and the ability to taste and enjoy food, the complexity of fetal reproduction, or other wonders such as regulatory genes that work to repair our body's cells.

All humans develop two sets of teeth, which meet the needs of a particular stage in their life, yet who is the Programmer who programmed our bodies thru this transformation? Only Intelligent Design can explain such a phenomenon and the burden of proof is on the atheist to prove otherwise or at least begin to accept the assessment that the believer is closer to the truth. Why do atheists wish to deny the presence of a Supreme Being or a Creator? The existence of God can be deduced whether we examine the intricacies of the universe or reflect on the simple to the most complex of life forms.

Darwinism is only a partial attempt to explain the transformation of life as we know it but cannot possibly explain the origin of life or the origin of this complex universe. Forces beyond observable science or laws of physics sustain the order found in the universe preventing planetary collision. God may be further explained in abstract terms as the alpha and omega or a Supreme Creator responsible for the presence of our material world yet transcending matter, time and space. Where matter or subsequent life forms come from is the alpha and where they end is the omega. Humans by definition are material, mortal, and finite in scope and therefore may have difficulties in accepting the presence of a nonphysical and eternal God. To assume our universe is the result of an uncontrolled Big Bang and subsequent Big Crunch, as the universe is presently expanding and will again collapse on itself, like a stretched elastic band, requires a big leap of faith. Who originated the Big Bang and from where did matter come from cannot be explained by a void; rather these phenomena depend on an alpha. All material things must have an alpha just as the very first Adam and the very first Eve. Emanating from God, the mover and shaker of our universe and the Creator of matter, time and space, is alpha, the beginning of times, and omega, the end of times.

The footprints of God are all around us. Entropy leads to disorder not order. The scientific evidence for the Big Bang theory and development of order from disorder resulting in our complex universe and beyond would require infinite probabilities. Left to chance disorder is the product of any set of probabilities. Entropy or chaos are the natural products of the Big Bang and should result in a disordered universe. The distance of the sun from the earth as well as the protective atmosphere around the earth, with the presence of the ozone layer, are vital for the creation and sustenance of life. The fine balance of planetary motion and the rotation of the earth give us night and day. The night gives us reprieve and rest from our long days. One would expect that a rational observer should find no plausible explanation, other than God, for our ordered universe.

There is no scientific evidence to explain how life or living organisms first evolved or how life could possibly transform from inanimate matter. Natural selection does not explain how life transformed from matter. The human body is made of atoms, and all our atoms come from the earth, yet we have characteristics that are distinctly different from soil or mud. What chance is there that if you spun some earthly particles together for eternity that on their own they would lead to some life form? Creation is a very rational concept for which there is every reason to accept and no reason to reject.

The atheist's views are not founded on sound logic or definitive scientific facts but rely on imaginary theories, half-baked truths, stretched beyond any reasonable science, and requiring fantastic imagination. These arguments are based on the premise of accepting complete evolution with unreasonable denial of the possibility of a Supreme Creator or Guiding Intelligence. The Evolutionary Theory is only a theory that cannot explain the origins of the universe, the origins of gender development or complexities of reproduction, physiological intricacies of human bodily organs, integration of the mind and body, the abilities of analytical thought, and as Darwin argued the development of vision or beauty.

Darwin's theories, with unverifiable intermediary forms, are sometimes accepted as facts rather than possible fiction. One may say that both arguments, at a minimum, are equally true but there can only be one eternal truth about the existence of God. One may have several hypotheses but eventually there is only one truth. If one comes across a table, chair or even a car can one conceive that with time any of these could have ever evolved? Everyone must decide for himself or herself about the truth of creation by looking at their own existence and the existence of their surroundings.

Evolutionary Theory depends on a tendency for the development of the more complex from the less complex, which is theoretically sustained by survival of the fittest, natural selection, or the ever-elusive concept of Mother Nature. However, with the millions of years of available fossil record there is a scarcity of intermediary forms or the presence of creatures halfway along the evolutionary path.

Since it is impossible to prove that God does not exist deists maintain that atheists are in no position to make definitive conclusions in support of their ideology. Hence, the self-professed scientific and logical atheists themselves are guilty of what they seemingly find distasteful in the deists. For atheists to accuse deists of being guilty of not being able to prove to them with the scientific proof that God exists belies the true fallacy in their arguments; because instead of proving their point or disproving the deists they firmly maintain their position without any proof. The atheist's claim of scientific support for their belief never materializes and instead they rely on theories that somehow take on lifelike qualities of definitive scientific facts.

Atheists sensing frustration in their quest to understand God's sense of purpose may well make foolish claims, as some authors have stated, that Mother Nature is playing a cruel joke. By evoking emotions of defiance and arrogance, thru fear and ridicule, these authors wish to turn the table on Mother Nature, the imaginary new foe. Whether such arguments are driven by bias or diabolical intent the end effect is the same. Playing on one's own or others fears or emotions, or capitalizing on human traits of defiance and anger can lead others to believe in eloquent yet distorted arguments. Believers accept, based on their interpretation of scripture, that they cannot fully comprehend the true meaning of creation, as this is part of God's plan or test. Because we see pain, suffering and injustice we may be disturbed but there is also happiness and goodness in our world. What we may observe, fear or perceive may taint our judgment in terms of what is fair or right but that should not lead us to deny the existence of God. Just because we cannot fully understand the purpose of certain outcomes, we should refrain from being impatient and questioning God's wisdom. Divine Purpose is partly in the realm of the unknown; believers in scriptures have faith that all will be revealed once we are resurrected into a new phase of existence.

Some atheists contend that religion is to blame for our ills. By finding fault with religious movements does not lend credence to the argument that the concept of God or religion is misguided. Humans are by nature fallible and make mistakes. These and other circuitous arguments partially fuel the atheist's refusal to consider the presence of the Creative forces or footprints that abound in our surroundings.

The ills of the world cannot be blamed on religion but rather on human conflicts that are driven by the pursuit of wealth, power, property and glory. Julius Caesar is famously quoted as saying, *"I came, I saw and I conquered"*. Similarly, Napoleon Bonaparte would not have pursued his adventures if they were not in pursuit of similar goals and desires. With some conflicts the forces of good, overcome evil as was witnessed during the American Civil War. The pillar of American civilization, which made the US great, is as the dollar bill states *"In God we trust"*.

Most death and destruction in this world was not caused by religious fanatics but rather by WW1 and WW11, which had nothing to do with religious conflicts. Was not Communism entrenched in atheist ideology? The Bolshevik Revolution had disastrous consequences hindering free thought by suppressing new and old ideas, killing free will and enterprise. Under the banner of Communism Lenin and Stalin were responsible for the killing and suffering of millions. Were not Lenin or Stalin just as arrogant and twisted, as religious zealots, in their logic and so certain of their own beliefs that they committed atrocities and tried to impose on the rest of the believing world their sordid views? Could it be the present day rampant alcoholism that is eroding the fabric of Russian society a result of years of atheist ideology where a bottle of vodka replaced the comfort of knowing that there is a God? Would it not be just as unfair if we blamed atheism for all the ills of Communist Mother Russia, as some would have us believe religion is to blame for all conflicts in our world?

However, did not ideologies such as Communism, racism or even fervent nationalism serve as basis to direct and control the masses? Any ideology can be used to control the masses and some atheists are guilty of promoting a material existence of sensual pleasures that diverts the masses away from God's spiritual guidance and commandments. Should we not try to search for a higher sense of purpose and meaningful existence rather than being guided by whimsical desires? The reality is that human conflict, differing ideologies and religion are a permanent part of humanity and we must come to terms with our fellow brethren in addressing these issues.

How can atheists find a purpose in life beyond a self-serving existence? Lying and cheating to achieve one's goals should be second nature to atheists as they are accountable to no one. The religious deists accept that there is a purpose in life with a quench for truth versus falsehood as they are accountable before God. Bernard Madoff, the financial wizard and his disingenuous pyramid or ponzie scheme, ruined the lives of many, by masterminding one of the greatest swindles in history, with no apparent sense of accountability to God. Only when the disbelievers allow themselves to discover the logical fallacies behind which atheism hides can they begin to examine other possibilities.

Reaching conclusions by observing the customs or outward behavior of the believer can be misleading; as behavior is tainted by a person's background or culture. Also, everyone is fallible but that does not mean one should completely discount someone's opinions just because they may have made some unintentional errors. Humans are sometimes guilty of clinging to unfounded beliefs or superstitions. Also, one should not let blind belief or trust in an author's eloquent diatribe, character assassination and ridicule deter one from examining if another person may be speaking some truth. Human emotions, preconceived ideas, prejudice, arrogance and blindly following a sorcerer's charismatic views may cloud our judgment, causing us to stumble and eventually leave us looking like blind fools. Even Pharaoh thru fear and ridicule kept his house in order, as did the charismatic Benito Mussolini and Adolf Hitler, till eventually reaching their very fateful ends.

## BELIEF IN SCRIPTURE

*"High above all is God, the King, the Truth! Be not in haste with the Qur'an before its revelation to thee is completed, but say, "O my Lord! advance me in knowledge" (Koran 20:114).*

Why do some people reject the concept that scripture could possibly be God inspired? Some atheists take pleasure in accusing deists of wishful thinking by believing in angels, heaven, hell and ancient fairytales. Some ideas may seem alien, such as entertaining the realm of the supernatural, spirits, angels and Satan. Yet, some people are willing to believe in the possibility of other life forms, UFOs and aliens without resorting to religion and are actively pursuing this type of research in the spirit of discovery. One may not initially grasp religion because it requires a serious effort as well as overcoming certain biases or preconceived ideas. 'Beware of the tales of the ancients' and 'preachers of doom and gloom' the ridiculing atheists would have one say. Scriptures must be read with an open mind. Religious scriptures state that at the beginning of time men lived hundreds of years. According to both the Bible (Genesis 9:29, King James Version) and the Koran (Koran 29:14) Noah lived 950 years. Human longevity probably gave us time to multiply; can the sciences or evolutionary theories refute this possibility?

The Koran states that the world was created in six days *"And certainly We created the heavens and the earth and what is between them in six days and there touched Us not any fatigue" (Koran 50:38)*. Yet, the Koran also speaks of a day that equals a thousand years *"He directs the whole affair from heaven to earth. Then it (affair) will again ascend to Him on a day whose length is a thousand years by the way you measure" (Koran 32:5)* and even fifty thousand years of our time *"The angels and the Spirit ascend to Him in a Day the measure whereof is fifty thousand years" (Koran 70:4)*. As we now know Einstein's theory of relativity can explain such phenomenon based on time, space and the speed of a moving object. Hence, our day is 24 hours long because of the speed of our rotating earth as it revolves around the sun. The Koran accepts the theory of relativity with varying measure of time. Our universe could very well be 15 billion years old or the earth 3.5 billion years old in terms of our time but this could be a meaningless time period for an observer in another frame of reference traveling at a different speed in another space. A similar argument can be made for the supposed evolutionary theory and that time in our sense of the word is immaterial to God. In a different frame of reference, the timeline for creation could be more or less, than what we perceive as real.

Numbers do not argue for or against the truth of anything as Christianity is the largest religion in the world but this does not necessarily lend credence to its absolute truth. Although some may say ignorance is bliss, the Christian World eventually revolted against the Church's intransigence and inflexibility of thought at a time when science was considered a threat to religion or the belief in God. The unfortunate outcome of this episode in history has been an over reliance on science to explain our existence and a complete distrust in the examination of religious scriptures as a source of prophetic revelation.

However, today Islam is the fastest growing religion in the world and this may lead one to consider that there may be a genuine truth that is unfolding. Similarly by observing the backwardness and violence we see today in the Muslim world one may not think that there is any credence to the religion of Islam; but if we reflect then we can see that these are the symptoms of illiteracy, ignorance, despair and frustration. Human emotion is better controlled with discipline and education; although for some, temperament and bigotry overrule. The splendor of Islamic Spain under the Moors or Turkish rule under Solomon the Magnificent should speak volumes to the unbiased observer at a time when religion, science and culture harmoniously coexisted for the benefit of society.

Religion is a bridge to God and this requires a dedicated and honest effort. Some people, in trying to explain any phenomenon, may make intentional or unintentional mistakes. Even scientists make honest mistakes and sometimes dishonest and deliberate errors to propagate their unfounded views and beliefs. Scientists are not gods and they sometimes fudge their data for nefarious purposes. Some atheists maintain that their assessments are based on solid science yet they have no real science to back up their views; rather they could have some preconceived ideas or beliefs to which they desperately wish to give some scientific credence. Not being able to prove with science their point of view, they may resort to half-baked truths and ridicule of their fellow man's views and beliefs. Likewise, religious fanatics mislead foolhardy unsuspecting impressionable people looking for leadership and a sense of purpose. Control by deception overrides logical reasoning to promote certain beliefs or dogma.

According to the Koran God bestowed His eternal Spirit upon Adam:

*"Behold! thy Lord said to the angels: "I am about to create humans, from of the essence of black mud fashioned in shape (Koran 15:28). When I have fashioned him and breathed into him of My spirit, fall ye down in prostration unto him" (Koran 15:29).*

Also from the Bible we quote:

*"And the LORD God formed man of the dust of the ground, and breathed into his nostrils the breath of life; and man became a living soul" (Genesis 2:7, KJV)*
*" Thou sendest forth thy spirit, they are created: and thou renewest the face of the earth (Psalm 104:30, KJV).*

In Islam the major difference between humans and angels is in humanity's ability to inflict harm as well as do well. Humans have free will with the choice to obey or disobey God whilst angels are obedient servants. In the English language when we speak highly of someone, we say he is an angel. In the Koran Satan is not a fallen angel but a Jinn, made of fire, unlike humans who are made from earth or clay. Jinn like humans are given free will and this is in variance with Christian doctrine that describes Satan as a fallen angel.

Even though life on earth is limited, by a physical death, the soul or spirit lives on and we are held accountable for our actions. Both the Bible and Koran warn of an endless torment for diabolical persons who are rotten to the core. For those imposters of Satan who rebel against God's Kingdom by arrogantly, knowingly and wrongfully rejecting and defying His covenants, the abyss is their final and permanent abode *(Isaiah 66:24 and Koran 4:168-169)*. These same people are so sadistic as to willfully inflict suffering on the rest of humanity. God imparted on us His eternal Spirit and with our physical resurrection will eventually send us on the paths of eternal salvation or damnation. Apparently, as God's Spirit is part of our eternal souls then accordingly the destinations are eternal. In Islam, it is possible for hell to be a temporary transition to heaven but the final eternal destination for all is either heaven or hell.

Science alone may help us find, but not explain, God. Only by examining Divine Revelation viz a viz prophetic revelation can we come to a true understanding of Divine Purpose or Will. Subsequently, the deist's acknowledgement of a belief system enables them to be at peace with God and their surroundings.

## Genetic makeup, Longevity and Marriage Laws

Factors such as cosmic radiation, environmental toxins such as fertilizers, man made radiation from diagnostic tests such as computerized tomography, gene mutations and pooling could all contribute to the degradation of mankind's genetic makeup. Spontaneous mutations, the overwhelming of genetic repair mechanisms and the development of autosomal recessive traits may have contributed to in an increased incidence of disease and a shortened life span for future generations.

*Altogether, Adam lived 930 years, and then he died.* (Genesis 5:5, New International Version)

**And all the days of Noah were nine hundred and fifty years**: and he died. (Genesis 9:29, King James Version)

وَلَقَدْ أَرْسَلْنَا نُوحًا إِلَىٰ قَوْمِهِۦ فَلَبِثَ فِيهِمْ أَلْفَ سَنَةٍ إِلَّا خَمْسِينَ عَامًا فَأَخَذَهُمُ ٱلطُّوفَانُ وَهُمْ ظَٰلِمُونَ ۞

*And verily we sent **Noah** (as Our messenger) unto his folk, and he continued with them for **a thousand years save fifty years;** and the flood engulfed them, for they were wrong-doers (Koran 29:14)*

*Altogether, Abraham lived a hundred and seventy-five years (Genesis 25:7, NIV)*

*Isaac lived a hundred and eighty years (Genesis 35:28, NIV)*

*Joseph, brother of Levi, lived 110 years old (Genesis 50:26)*

The above scriptural quotations reveal that the lifespan of prophets shortened with future generations. Adam lived 930 years, Noah 950 years, Abraham 175 years, Isaac 180 years and Joseph 110 years. Both the Old Testament and Koran suggest that Noah lived 950 years. The longevity of earlier human generations may have been due to a relatively superior genetic makeup and a scarcity of debilitating diseases.

*Amram married his father's sister Jochebed, who bore him Aaron and Moses. Amram lived 137 years.* (Exodus 6:20, New International Version)

*And the name of Amram's wife was Jochebed, the daughter of Levi, whom her mother bare to Levi in Egypt: and she bare unto Amram Aaron and Moses, and Miriam their sister (Numbers 25:59, KJV)*

We are told that Moses's father, Amram, married his paternal Aunt, Jochebed who is the daughter of Levi (Exodus 6:20, NIV & Numbers

25:59, KJV). Marriage laws changed with the progression of scriptural revelations. The children of Adam and Eve, Cain and Abel married their sisters and this was necessary for propagation of the human race.

A relative state of perfection in the genetic makeup of Adam and Eve would explain their children's low risk of inheriting negative genetic traits as well as the longevity of the first human generations. As the Bible confirms marrying ones siblings was permissible and so was marrying ones Aunt but each of these practices is no longer permissible religiously or culturally. Interestingly marrying one's cousin is permissible under Islamic laws and there has been no increased risk of negative genetic traits in the Islamic world.

## DARWINISM REVISITED

*To suppose that the eye* *with all its inimitable contrivances for adjusting the focus to different distances, for admitting different amounts of light, and for the correction of spherical and chromatic aberration,* **could have been formed by natural selection, seems, I freely confess, absurd in the highest degree.** *(***Charles Darwin***, The Origin of Species, VI, Difficulties of the Theory: Organs of Extreme Perfection and Complication, first paragraph).*

THE FOREGOING remarks lead me to say a few words on the protest lately made by some naturalists, against the utilitarian doctrine that every detail of structure has been produced for the good of its possessor. They believe that **many structures have been created for the sake of beauty, to delight man or the Creator** (but this latter point is beyond the scope of scientific discussion), or for the sake of mere variety, a view already discussed. **Such doctrines, if true, would be absolutely fatal to my theory.** (**Charles Darwin**, The Origin of Species, VI, Difficulties of the Theory: Utilitarian Doctrine, How Far True: Beauty, How Acquired, first paragraph).

*But just in proportion as this process of extermination has acted on an enormous scale, so must the number of intermediate varieties, which have formerly existed, be truly enormous.* **Why then is not every geological formation and every stratum full of such intermediate links?** *Geology assuredly does not reveal any such finely-graduated organic chain; and this, perhaps, is the most obvious and serious objection which can be urged against* *the theory. The explanation lies, as I believe, in the extreme imperfection of the geological record. (**Charles Darwin**, The Origin of Species, X, On the Imperfection of the Geological Record: On the Absence of Intermediate Varieties at the Present Day, first paragraph).*

*. . . I can answer these questions and objections only on the supposition that the geological record is far more imperfect than most geologists believe. (Charles Darwin, The Origin of Species, XV, Recapitulation and Conclusion, tenth paragraph)*

The above quotes, from *Charles Darwin's The Origin of Species (by permission from Bartleby.com)* should serve as good starting point for our present discussion. The evolutionary process between distinct life forms, over millions of years, would be expected to reveal ample evidence of transitional forms. The fossil or geological record seems adequate for the species but is lacking for the transitional forms so can we really blame this as an inadequacy or *"extreme imperfection"* of the geological record. Why is the fossil record lacking in primitive half formed predecessors?

There is a lack of hypothetical ancestors or transitional forms to explain variation of species such as found in fish, two legged creatures, or the development of a bird's feathered wings that are a prerequisite for flight. Natural selection does not explain how the DNA information necessary for wings to develop could realistically be transformed or guided by its own intuition. On the other hand why should we reject intelligent design by a Creator as rational explanation for this phenomenon? Intelligent design is a more logical explanation for variations of species than the random process of natural selection. Random processes are more likely to result in chaotic events that produce disorder or unintelligent design. To develop any meaningful life form *"natural selection"* requires the assistance of *"intelligent"* selection.

However, we should also note that the observation of evolutionary processes, such as bacterial resistance to antibiotics, does not preclude the presence of a guiding force or *"intelligent design."* Bacterial mutation in this instance is a beneficial mutation supportive of "survival of the species" but we could also contend that this is more aptly described as *"intelligent selection"* rather than *"natural selection."* Determining the specific genetic DNA code that dictates each specific stage of *"natural selection"* is only part of the puzzle. However, we must also ask how and wherefrom the

DNA code that determines natural selection came about. To simply say that "*survival of the species*" requires natural selection does not explain what brought about the genetic code that dictates survival of the species by "*natural selection.*" This positive entity called "*natural selection*" would need to have a genetic code of its own that would be capable of self–monitoring, continually improving and outdoing itself by performing self-adaptation. The biggest myth is that the presence of evolution somehow disproves the presence of God.

Many life forms appear fully formed in the fossil record. However, the "*missing link*" between many life forms and their presumed ancestors remains elusive. Perhaps the supposed intermediary forms are now extinct but should we not have ample evidence of preserved intermediary links? We would expect to find boundless numbers of intermediary forms, for each known species, in the fossil record to explain evolutionary processes that supposedly formed and progressed over millions of years. Somehow, we can manage to find ample evidence of certain fossil records and not of others. Even though dinosaurs are extinct, we have ample fossil records in many museums. There are 527 genera of dinosaurs so far discovered. However, bats, the only flying mammals, making up to 20% of the mammalian species, are a good example of a species lacking intermediary forms in the fossil record. During the *Cambrian age,* there is the sudden appearance of complex life forms without ancestry in a period known as the *Cambrian explosion.*

Determining which species qualify as transitional forms and where they fit into lineages is really a matter of speculation and debate. Presuming that most evolutionary processes developed over millions of years this does not necessarily confer sequential evolutionary processes unless we are there to observe and confirm each transitional stage. Similarities between species may suggest but by no means prove evolutionary linkage. Also if we consider the complexity of the single cell as the building block of life or the transformation of inorganic to organic life form we have further insurmountable hurdles to overcome in terms of evolutionary theory as "*natural selection*" and "*survival of the fittest*" are concepts that cannot be utilized to explain such phenomenon. Similarly, **the simultaneous** development of human male and female life forms necessary for propagation and preservation of the species cannot possibly be explained by the process of intermediary forms as the human, having no mechanism to reproduce, would have long ago become extinct before this evolutionary process could bring itself to natural fruition. The guiding force of a supreme being to explain these gaps in the creation of life is the missing link that explains intelligent design.

Atheists have to believe that evolution is the only major force working in nature to explain life, as to consider otherwise would open other possibilities they do not wish to contemplate. All atheists must be evolutionists but the converse does not hold. A person may accept some instances of evolutionary phenomenon and still believe in God. Atheists, by accepting evolutionary theory as the major force in nature, believe that that they have sufficient proof to reject God's existence. Atheists are not intellectually honest by denying the existence of God, because the best anyone may postulate is to question the presence of God. Once an atheist crosses this bridge and leaves this state of denial then the concept of God can easily become within the realm of their beliefs. Subsequently by examining religious scripture, one may attempt to find the missing link that connects us to the Creator.

## EVOLUTION OF APES FROM HUMANS?

You ask 'evolution of apes from humans'? But think again and ask why not? Possibly we are missing the intermediary forms. Who says it had to be 'evolution of humans from apes'? Maybe in the old days, there was a survival advantage to being an ape; when humans were still too stupid to feed themselves and defenseless against wild animals that roamed our wilderness. If you think this line of reasoning is silly then please read on as you may find that a similar line of reasoning can leave one quite bemused.

The article "Gene regulation separates humans from apes: study" last updated Wed, 14 Nov 2007 (http://www.abc.net.au/news/newsitems/200603/s1587605.htm) notes the findings of a group of researchers led by Yoav Gilad, an assistant professor of genetics at the University of Chicago:

*"What sort of changes in the environment or lifestyle would drive such a rapid shift in the expression of genes—in this case the liver—in humans and no other primate?"* **Associate professor Gilad speculates that the answer could lie in the acquisition of fire, one of the fundamental differences**

**between humans and animals.** *"No other animal relies on cooked food,"* associate professor Gilad said.

## Gene regulation

The notion that gene regulation in the liver evolved because humans discovered fire and hence cooked food as Yaov Gilad claims sounds very scientific don't you all agree? One does not know where people get ideas from and what scientific methods are used to substantiate this postulate. The only problem is that cooked food could have caused some irreparable damage to the liver before its regulatory genes evolved and if the liver was not damaged then we had a good liver to start with. I wonder why these intelligent apes did not learn from us and start cooking their food with fire too. Maybe we need to feed those apes some cooked food as probably they would like that too; then we can also see if their livers will change their regulatory genes so one day they can become humans too.

## Gene Mutation Linked To Cognition Is Found Only In Humans

*"a certain form of neuropsin, a protein that plays a role in learning and memory, is expressed only in the central nervous systems of humans"*

*"Gene sequencing revealed a mutation specific to humans that triggers a change in the splicing pattern of the neuropsin gene, creating a new splicing site and a longer protein. Introducing this mutation into chimpanzee DNA resulted in the creation of type II neuropsin."*

The above is quoted from the article "Gene Mutation Linked To Cognition Is Found Only In Humans" as published in Science Daily, May 9, 2007 (*http://www.sciencedaily.com/releases/2007/05/070508072829.htm*).

One may ask did someone interfere with or remove this type type II neuropsin from human brains to see what happens to our learning and memory? Without doing so then, we really do not know its role. How about interfering with some other genes that we think don't have any bearing on learning or memory; could we not be pleasantly surprised by some unexpected findings? A supposed "mutated" gene introduced into the chimpanzee DNA resulted in type II neurosporin but we will be impressed when these chimpanzees develop a higher level of cognition. The basic and flawed assumption is that we have a "mutated" gene as opposed to a God "implanted" gene. Supposedly, when a chimpanzee gene somehow managed to mutate into a more useful gene the first humans came about yet somehow this only happened to one or a few lucky chimpanzees. One might have expected that random mutations most likely would have long ago resulted in extinction of species before we would get a human from a chimpanzee. I wonder when someone will tell us why we look so much prettier than those poor and ugly chimpanzees or maybe I should rephrase and say which gene mutation caused humans to turn into chimpanzees? When these scientists can prove to us that this gene is definitely a mutated as opposed to a God implanted gene then maybe we can take them more seriously. However, if we wish to accept at face value theses hypothetical explanations then we can believe in anything we please.

## EVOLUTION WITHOUT CREATION?

Mother nature the mother of all mothers discovers that life without sight is not so bright. So life form discovers that eyes which give us sight are a wonderful asset, but . . . dust gets in your eyes . . . ah, says Mother nature let's evolve some eyelids, another wonderful asset, but . . . the eyelids rub against the eyes giving a gritty sensation . . . ah, says Mother nature, how about some lubricating solution? Mother nature ever so wise and evolution ever so bright. Then another million years pass by to evolve a pair of lacrimal glands to lubricate the eyes so that we may have a clearer view. Random chaos with order from disorder? Think again dear Darwin, think again.

## TOTAL EVOLUTION?

Which came first, the ability to hear or to speak? Speech relies on air pressure provided by the lungs, pulse output by the vocal cord while hearing is dependent on the external auditory canal, middle and inner ear. Speech impediments may result from a cleft lip, cleft palate or vocal cord disorders not to mention if you are in heart failure you can't catch your breath or let alone make full sentences. And how about the brain that controls or directs our speech and processes all the information we hear? Did the brain's speech and hearing centers come first or later? Did the eye come first or the ability for the brain to process what we see? How about the liver that metabolizes what we eat or the kidneys that filter the metabolites of what we consume?

Did the desire and pleasure of tasting, eating and drinking come first or did the liver and the kidneys? How do the liver and kidneys always know what to do and do it right each time?

We must ponder did creatures that learned to walk, swim or fly accidentally do so on their own or was there a supernatural guiding force. Did the immune system with all its complexity and ability to fight infections magically evolve on its own? What is behind the *"intelligence"* that regulates and instructs gene repair mechanisms? Who or what is responsible for *"human intelligence"* with its subsequent great innovations in the last two centuries? What makes us think? How could spontaneous mutations, which are sometimes responsible for cancer and therefore generally detrimental, explain evolution? How about regulatory genes that repair mutations? Is evolution without creation the biggest myth of our times? Who is this god called evolution? Is the human attempt to cling onto the evolutionary theory the result of deceitful wishful thinking, arrogance and a false belief that we are our own gods and therefore accountable to nobody but our own desires?

# CREATION

The Old Testament suggests that God, after creating the world in six days rested on the seventh day and was then refreshed. However, the Koran states that fatigue did not *"touch"* God.

## EXODUS

*It is a sign between me and the children of Israel for ever: for in six days the LORD made heaven and earth, and **on the seventh day he rested**, and was refreshed. (**Exodus** 31:17)*

وَلَقَدْ خَلَقْنَا ٱلسَّمَـٰوَٰتِ وَٱلْأَرْضَ وَمَا بَيْنَهُمَا فِى سِتَّةِ أَيَّامٍ وَمَا مَسَّنَا مِن

لُّغُوبٍ ﴿٣٨﴾

*And certainly We created the heavens and the earth and what is between them in six days and **there touched Us not any fatigue**. (**Koran** 50:38)*

The following verse besides suggesting that our universe was created by the Big Bang also mentions that every living thing is made of water.

أَوَلَمْ يَرَ ٱلَّذِينَ كَفَرُوٓاْ أَنَّ ٱلسَّمَـٰوَٰتِ وَٱلْأَرْضَ كَانَتَا رَتْقًا فَفَتَقْنَـٰهُمَا

وَجَعَلْنَا مِنَ ٱلْمَآءِ كُلَّ شَىْءٍ حَىٍّ أَفَلَا يُؤْمِنُونَ ﴿٣٠﴾

*Do not the Unbelievers see that the heavens and the earth were joined together, before we clove them asunder? **We made from water every living thing.** Will they not then believe? (Koran 21:30)*

The creation of man as described in the Old Testament Books of Genesis (Genesis 2:7) and Job suggests that man is made of clay and the spirit of God (Job 33:4 & 33:6). Clay is defined as mud or wet soil (earth). All of the constituents of the human body such as oxygen, carbon, hydrogen, nitrogen, calcium, iron, potassium, sulfur, chromium, cobalt, copper, fluorine, zinc, tin, selenium are from the earth. How was it known that the human was made of earth or clay? Was this Old Testament belief based on God, the theory of Creation or the theory of Evolution? The Koran similarly and correctly describes the human as made of clay and water (see below). The human body is 60% water by weight. The Koran also notes that God breathed his spirit into man.

*And **the LORD God formed man of the dust of the ground**, and breathed into his nostrils the breath of life; and man became a living soul (Genesis 2:7).*

*The spirit of God hath made me, and **the breath of the Almighty hath given me life**. (Job 33:4)*

21

*Behold, I am according to thy wish in God's stead:* **I also am formed out of the clay.** *(Job 33:6)*

وَإِذْ قَالَ رَبُّكَ لِلْمَلَٰٓئِكَةِ إِنِّى خَٰلِقٌۢ بَشَرًا مِّن صَلْصَٰلٍ مِّنْ حَمَإٍ مَّسْنُونٍ

(٢٨)

*Behold!* thy **Lord said to the angels: "I am about to create humans, from of the essence of black mud** fashioned in shape.* (Koran 15:28)*

فَإِذَا سَوَّيْتُهُۥ وَنَفَخْتُ فِيهِ مِن رُّوحِى فَقَعُوا۟ لَهُۥ سَٰجِدِينَ (٢٩)

*When I have fashioned him and **breathed into him of My spirit,** fall ye down in prostration unto him."* (Koran 15:29)*

قَالَ لَمْ أَكُن لِّأَسْجُدَ لِبَشَرٍ خَلَقْتَهُۥ مِن صَلْصَٰلٍ مِّنْ حَمَإٍ مَّسْنُونٍ (٣٣)

*He (Satan) said: "I am not one to prostrate myself to human whom Thou hast of created the essence of black mud* fashioned in shape. (Koran 15.33)*

إِذْ قَالَ رَبُّكَ لِلْمَلَٰٓئِكَةِ إِنِّى خَٰلِقٌۢ بَشَرًا مِّن طِينٍ (٧١)

*Behold, thy Lord said to the angels, I am about to create man from clay (Koran 38.7)*

وَهُوَ ٱلَّذِى خَلَقَ مِنَ ٱلۡمَآءِ بَشَرًا فَجَعَلَهُۥ نَسَبًا
وَصِهۡرًا وَكَانَ رَبُّكَ قَدِيرًا ۝

*And He (God) has **created humans from water,** then He has made for him blood relationship and marriage relationship, and your Lord is powerful. (Koran 25:54)*

وَٱللَّهُ خَلَقَ كُلَّ دَآبَّةٍ مِّن مَّآءٍ فَمِنۡهُم مَّن يَمۡشِى عَلَىٰ بَطۡنِهِۦ وَمِنۡهُم مَّن
يَمۡشِى عَلَىٰ رِجۡلَيۡنِ وَمِنۡهُم مَّن يَمۡشِى عَلَىٰٓ أَرۡبَعٖ يَخۡلُقُ ٱللَّهُ مَا يَشَآءُ إِنَّ
ٱللَّهَ عَلَىٰ كُلِّ شَىۡءٍ قَدِيرٌ ۝

*And God has created every animal from water: of them there are some that creep on their bellies; some that walk on two legs; and some that walk on four. God creates what He wills for verily God Has power over all things. (Koran 24:45)*

ثُمَّ سَوَّىٰهُ وَنَفَخَ فِيهِ مِن رُّوحِهِۦ وَجَعَلَ لَكُمُ ٱلسَّمۡعَ وَٱلۡأَبۡصَٰرَ
وَٱلۡأَفۡـِٔدَةَ قَلِيلٗا مَّا تَشۡكُرُونَ ۝

*Then He made him complete and breathed into him of His spirit, and He gave you hearing and sight and hearts; little is it that you give thanks. (Koran 32:9)*

# Old And New Testament Prophesies

In this section we will examine Biblical Prophecy as pertaining to scriptural predictions of the future coming of a person in the form of a prophet. Fulfillment of prophecy is one of the main foundations on which Divine Revelation reaches out to our intellect so that we may have a firm basis for our beliefs. Prophecy of the coming of a prophet helps determines if someone who claims inspiration from God is a fraud or true prophet. By definition a prophet is one who utters Divine Will. If someone who claims communication from God fits the description in a prophecy then we need to examine the oral or written message that this person has revealed. If these prophecies are true then this should lead us suspect that there is a genuine continuity of the prophetic tradition and that the basis of Scripture is Divine Inspiration. Hence, we are able to establish linkage between the Old and New Testament prophecies leading to Prophet Muhammad and the Koran. Interestingly in the tradition of prophecy all Major Prophets stem from Abraham and the Middle East.

الَّذِينَ يَتَّبِعُونَ الرَّسُولَ النَّبِيَّ الْأُمِّيَّ الَّذِى يَجِدُونَهُ مَكْتُوبًا عِندَهُمْ فِى التَّوْرَىٰةِ وَالْإِنجِيلِ يَأْمُرُهُم بِالْمَعْرُوفِ وَيَنْهَىٰهُمْ عَنِ الْمُنكَرِ وَيُحِلُّ لَهُمُ الطَّيِّبَٰتِ وَيُحَرِّمُ عَلَيْهِمُ الْخَبَٰئِثَ وَيَضَعُ عَنْهُمْ إِصْرَهُمْ وَالْأَغْلَٰلَ الَّتِى كَانَتْ عَلَيْهِمْ فَالَّذِينَ ءَامَنُوا بِهِۦ وَعَزَّرُوهُ وَنَصَرُوهُ وَاتَّبَعُوا النُّورَ الَّذِى أُنزِلَ مَعَهُۥٓ أُوْلَٰئِكَ هُمُ الْمُفْلِحُونَ ۝

*"Those who follow the Apostle, the unlettered prophet, whom they find mentioned in their own Scriptures, in the Torah and the Gospel . . "* (Koran 7:157).

24

Sir William Muir, British Orientalist and Scholar, author of books on Islam, questioned the authenticity of the above Koranic verse. *(Sir William Muir, K.C.S.I., LL.D. The Coran: Its Composition And Teaching; And The Testimony It Bears To The Holy Scriptures, Society for Promoting Christian Knowledge, London, England, 1878, 239 pages).* In the Second Part of the book there is a section titled *Testimony of the Coran to the Scriptures of the Old and New Testaments.* Sir Muir's inability to find the relevant passages, in the Old and New Testaments, which would verify verse V11-157 led him to question the Divine revelation of the Koran. The above verse implies that the old scriptures foretold of the coming of prophet Muhammad. To quote **Sir William Muir** directly from a section titled Testimony To The Holy Scriptures, page 225:

*"**Mahomet** very often, in the Corân, **refers to those who held the Scriptures** in their hands **as witnesses in favour of his mission**. It is **alleged that their Divine books contained evidence in his favour**, that their contents corresponded with the Corân, **that the honest and enlightened interpreters of their prophecies recognized him and his Revelation**, and rejoiced in the recognition. (**VII**, XIII, XV, XXXV, XXXIX, XLV, . . .)".*

This section is a compilation of references found in the *authorized King James Version of 1611* pertaining to the coming of a prophet who fits the description of the prophet Muhammad. The *King James Version (KJV)*, a relatively authentic translation of the Bible, was available to Sir William Muir. The *New International Version (NIV)* and other updated Versions of the Bible have some changes, which might cause some difficulties for the reader in following some of the arguments put forth. Besides, *Sir William Muir,* a British subject, familiar with the authorized *KJV* would not have objected to using this version of the Bible for the purposes of the following discussion. If for the purposes of this discussion a version other than the *KJV* is used then the author will also attempt to reference the *KJV* for comparison.

Before we embark on this discussion it may be useful to understand *prophet Muhammad's* familiarity with Old Testament scriptures. One could think of no better source than Rabbi Abraham Geiger's 1883 book *Judaism and Islam (translated by FM Young, 1896).* On page seventeen (second section of the first division), of ***Rabbi Abraham Geiger's*** book we find the title: *Could Muhammad borrow from Judaism? And if so* *how was such borrowing possible for him?* From page seventeen we quote *"The possibility of borrowing from Judaism lay for Muhammad, partly in the knowledge which might be imparted to him by word of mouth through intercourse with the Jews, and partly in personal knowledge of their Scriptures;* **while allowing him the first source of information, we must deny him the second.** *"*Therefore Rabbi Geiger acknowledges that Muhammad, the prophet of Islam, had *no personal knowledge* of the *Old or New Testament* scriptures.

# ABRAHAM, ISHMAEL AND ISAAC

*Genesis, Exodus, Leviticus, Numbers, and Deuteronomy* are the first five books of the Hebrew Scriptures. These five books that contain the laws of God, as bestowed on Moses, are also referred to as the *Torah*. The key to understanding the *Judeo-Christian* and *Islamic* origins or continuum lies in the Book of Genesis, the first book of the Pentateusch or Old Testament scriptures. Abram, meaning the exalted father, had his name changed by God to Abraham, meaning a father of many nations. Abraham fathered Ishmael the father of the Arab nation and then Isaac the father of the Jewish nation. Ishmael and Isaac both fathered twelve sons. As we shall discuss the two most important sons of Ishmael as relating to Biblical prophecies are Tema and Kedar.

GENESIS 16

*And Sarai Abram's wife took* **Hagar** *her maid the Egyptian, after Abram had dwelt ten years in the land of Canaan, and gave her to her husband Abram* **to be his wife**. *(Genesis 16:3)*

*And the angel of the LORD said unto her, Behold, thou [art] with child, and shalt bear a son, and* shalt call his name Ishmael; because the LORD hath heard thy affliction. *(Genesis 16:11)*

*And Hagar bare Abram a son: and* Abram called his son's name, which Hagar bare, Ishmael. *(Genesis 16:15)*
　　*And Abram [was] fourscore and six years old, when Hagar bare Ishmael to Abram. (Genesis 16:16)*

## GENESIS 17

*And when Abram was ninety years old and nine, the LORD appeared to Abram, and said unto him, I [am] the Almighty God; walk before me, and be thou perfect. (Genesis 17:1)*

*And I will make my covenant between me and thee, and will multiply thee exceedingly. (Genesis 17:2)*

*And Abram fell on his face: and God talked with him, saying, (Genesis 17:3)*

*As for me, behold, my covenant [is] with thee, and thou shalt be a father of many nations. (Genesis 17:4)*

*Neither shall thy name any more be called Abram, but thy name shall be Abraham; for a father of many nations have I made thee. (Genesis 17:5)*

*And I will make thee exceeding fruitful, and I will make nations of thee, and kings shall come out of thee. (Genesis 17:6)*

*And I will establish my covenant between me and thee and thy seed after thee in their generations for an everlasting covenant, to be a God unto thee, and to thy seed after thee. (Genesis 17:7)*

*And I will give unto thee, and to thy seed after thee, the land wherein thou art a stranger, all the land of Canaan, for an everlasting possession; and I will be their God. (Genesis 17:8)*

*And God said unto Abraham, Thou shalt keep my covenant therefore, thou, and thy seed after thee in their generations. (Genesis 17:9)*

*This [is] my covenant, which ye shall keep, between me and you and thy seed after thee; Every man child among you shall be circumcised. (Genesis 17:10)*

*And ye shall circumcise the flesh of your foreskin; and it shall be a token of the covenant betwixt me and you. (Genesis 17:11)*

*And he that is eight days old shall be circumcised among you, every man child in your generations, he that is born in the house, or bought with money of any stranger, which [is] not of thy seed. (Genesis 17:12)*

*He that is born in thy house, and he that is bought with thy money, must needs be circumcised: and my covenant shall be in your flesh for an everlasting covenant. (Genesis 17:13)*

*And the uncircumcised man child whose flesh of his foreskin is not circumcised, that soul shall be cut off from his people; he hath broken my covenant. (Genesis 17:14)*

*And God said unto Abraham, As for Sarai thy wife, thou shalt not call her name Sarai, but Sarah [shall] her name [be]. (Genesis 17:15)*

*And I will bless her, and give thee a son also of her: yea, I will bless her, and she shall be [a mother] of nations; kings of people shall be of her. (Genesis 17:16) Then Abraham fell upon his face, and laughed, and said in his heart, Shall [a child] be born unto him that is an hundred years old? And shall Sarah, that is ninety years old, bear? (Genesis 17:17)*

*And Abraham said unto God, O that Ishmael might live before thee! (Genesis 17:18)*

*And God said, Sarah thy wife shall bear thee a son indeed; and thou shalt call his name Isaac: and I will establish my covenant with him for an everlasting covenant, [and] with his seed after him. (Genesis 17:19)*

*And as for Ishmael, I have heard thee: Behold, I have blessed him, and will make him fruitful, and will multiply him exceedingly; twelve princes shall he beget, and I will make him a great nation. (Genesis 17:20)*

*But my covenant will I establish with Isaac, which Sarah shall bear unto thee at this set time in the next year. (Genesis 17:21)*

*And he left off talking with him, and God went up from Abraham. (Genesis 17:22)*

*And Abraham took Ishmael his son, and all that were born in his house, and all that were bought with his money, every male among the men of Abraham's house; and circumcised the flesh of their foreskin in the selfsame day, as God had said unto him. (Genesis 17:23)*

*And Abraham [was] ninety years old and nine, when he was circumcised in the flesh of his foreskin. (Genesis 17:24)*

*And Ishmael his son [was] thirteen years old, when he was circumcised in the flesh of his foreskin. (Genesis 17:25)*

## GENESIS 21

*And the LORD visited Sarah as he had said, and the LORD did unto Sarah as he had spoken. (Genesis 21:1)*

*For Sarah conceived, and bare Abraham a son in his old age, at the set time of which God had spoken to him. (Genesis 21:2)*

*And Abraham called the name of his son that was born unto him, whom Sarah bare to him, Isaac. (Genesis 21:3)*

*And Abraham circumcised his son Isaac being eight days old, as God had commanded him. (Genesis 21:4)*

*And Abraham was an hundred years old, when his son Isaac was born unto him. (Genesis 21:5)*

*And Sarah said, God hath made me to laugh, [so that] all that hear will laugh with me. (Genesis 21:6)*

*And she said, Who would have said unto Abraham, that Sarah should have given children suck? For I have born [him] a son in his old age. (Genesis 21:7)*

*And the child grew, and was weaned: and Abraham made a great feast the [same] day that Isaac was weaned. (Genesis 21:8)*

*And Sarah saw the son of Hagar the Egyptian, which she had born unto Abraham, mocking. (Genesis 21:9)*

*Wherefore she said unto Abraham, Cast out this bondwoman and her son: for the son of this bondwoman shall not be heir with my son, [even] with Isaac. (Genesis 21:10)*

*And the thing was very grievous in Abraham's sight because of his son. (Genesis 21:11)*

*And God said unto Abraham, Let it not be grievous in thy sight because of the lad, and because of thy bondwoman; in all that Sarah hath said unto thee, hearken unto her voice; for in Isaac shall thy seed be called. (Genesis 21:12)*

*And also of the son of the bondwoman will I make a nation, because he [is] thy seed. (Genesis 21:13)*

*And Abraham rose up early in the morning, and took bread, and a bottle of water, and gave [it] unto Hagar, putting [it] on her shoulder, and the child, and sent her away: and she departed, and wandered in the wilderness of Beersheba. (Genesis 21:14)*

*And the water was spent in the bottle, and she cast the child under one of the shrubs. (Genesis 21:15)*

*And she went, and sat her down over against [him] a good way off, as it were a bowshot: for she said, Let me not see the death of the child. And she sat over against [him], and lift up her voice, and wept.(Genesis 21:16)*

*And God heard the voice of the lad; and the angel of God called to Hagar out of heaven, and said unto her, What aileth thee, Hagar? Fear not; for God hath heard the voice of the lad where he [is]. (Genesis 21:17)*

*Arise, lift up the lad, and hold him in thine hand; for I will make him a great nation. (Genesis 21:18)*

*And God opened her eyes, and she saw a well of water; and she went, and filled the bottle with water, and gave the lad drink. (Genesis 21:19)*

*And God was with the lad; and he grew, and dwelt in the wilderness, and became an archer. (Genesis 21:20)*

*And he dwelt in the wilderness of Paran: and his mother took him a wife out of the land of Egypt. (Genesis 21:21)*

*Lift up thine eyes unto the high places, and see where thou hast not been lien with. In the ways hast thou sat for them, as the* Arabian in the wilderness; *and thou hast polluted the land with thy whoredoms and with thy wickedness (Jeremiah 3:2).*

Till today the Bedouin Arabs dwell in the desert wilderness.

GENESIS 25

*Now these [are] the generations of Ishmael, Abraham's son, whom Hagar the Egyptian, Sarah's handmaid, bare unto Abraham: (Genesis 25:12)*
*And* these [are] the names of the sons of Ishmael, *by their names, according to their generations: the firstborn of Ishmael, Nebajoth; and* Kedar, *and Adbeel, and Mibsam, (Genesis 25:13)*
*And Mishma, and Dumah, and Massa, (Genesis 25:14)*
*Hadar, and* Tema, *Jetur, Naphish, and Kedemah: (Genesis 25:15)*
*These [are] the sons of Ishmael, and these [are] their names, by their towns, and by their castles; twelve princes according to their nations.(Genesis 25:16)*

In *Genesis*, first book of the Old Testament, we find that *Isaac* is a son of *Abraham (Genesis 25:11)*. We know that *Ishmael* was *Abraham's* firstborn *(Genesis 17 and 21);* so how could it be that *Isaac* is referred to as *Abraham's* only son *(Genesis 22:2 and Genesis 22:16)?* Could it be possible that a scribe took it upon himself to swap *Isaac* for *Ishmael*?

*And it came to pass after these things, that God did tempt Abraham, and said unto him, Abraham: and he said, Behold, [here] I [am]. (Genesis 22:1)*
*And he said, Take now thy son,* thine only [son] Isaac, *whom thou lovest, and get thee into the land of Moriah; and offer him there for a burnt offering upon one of the mountains which I will tell thee of. (Genesis 22:2)*

Lest it be said otherwise we reaffirm that **Ishmael is a son of Abraham:**

*Then Abraham gave up the ghost, and died in a good old age, an old man, and full [of years]; and was gathered to his people. (Genesis 25:8)*

*And* his sons *Isaac and Ishmael buried him in the cave of Machpelah, in the field of Ephron the son of Zohar the Hittite, which [is] before Mamre; (Genesis 25:9)*

## THE TWELVE JEWISH TRIBES

Isaac's son Jacob, also known as Israel, *(Genesis 32:28)* fathered twelve sons that became known as the twelve tribes *(Genesis 49:28)*. Dan and Gad were several of his sons to be born of maids; they were original founding members of the twelve tribes:

*And she gave him Bilhah her handmaid to wife: and Jacob went in unto her. (Genesis 30:4)*
*And Bilhah conceived, and bare Jacob a son. (Genesis 30:5)*
*And Rachel said, God hath judged me, and hath also heard my voice, and hath given me a son: therefore called she his name Dan. (Genesis 30:6)*

*And Zilpah Leah's maid bare Jacob a son. (Genesis 30:10)*
*And Leah said, A troop cometh: and she called his name Gad (Genesis 30:11)*

*. . Now the sons of Jacob were twelve: (Genesis 35:22)*
*The sons of Leah; Reuben, Jacob's firstborn, and Simeon, and Levi, and Judah, and Issachar, and Zebulun: (Genesis 35:23)*
*The sons of Rachel; Joseph, and Benjamin: (Genesis 35:24)*
*And the sons of Bilhah, Rachel's handmaid; Dan, and Naphtali: (Genesis 35:25)*
*And the sons of Zilpah, Leah's handmaid; Gad, and Asher: these [are] the sons of Jacob, which were born to him in Padanaram. (Genesis 35:26)*

Hence, four of the twelve Jewish tribes are descendants of maids. Likewise by the same logic *Ishmael*, son of *Sarah's* maid *Hagar*, is also a legitimate son of *Abraham. Ishmael* is also referred to as a son of *Abraham (Genesis, chapter 25:12). Hagar* bore *Abram* a son *Ishmael (Genesis16: 15).*

The sons of Ishmael peopled the north and west of the Arabian Peninsula, and eventually formed the chief element of the Arab nation, the wandering Bedouin tribes. *(Smith, William, Dr., Smith's Bible Dictionary, 1860)*.

According to Easton's Bible Dictionary Ishmael died at the age of one hundred and thirty-seven years, but where and when are unknown *(Genesis 25:17)*. He had twelve sons, who became the founders of so many Arab tribes or colonies, the *Ishmaelites*, who spread over the wide desert spaces of Northern Arabia from the Red Sea to the Euphrates *(Genesis 37:25,27,28; 39:1)*. *(M.G. Easton M.A., D.D., Illustrated Bible Dictionary, Third Edition, published by Thomas Nelson, 1897)*.

In *Genesis chapter 17:5* God changed *Abram's* name to *Abraham "father of many nations"*. **God promises Ishmael** *"a great nation"(Genesis 17:20, 21:18)*. Ishmael is referred to as having twelve princes.

God's nations are spiritual nations not just nations of might, power, or numbers. To pursue the fulfillment of this prophecy we need to remember the names of two of the **sons of *Ishmael*,** one is **Kedar** *(Genesis 25:13)*, **and** the other is **Tema** *(Genesis 25:15)*. Also note that **the names of the sons of *Ishmael*** became the names of their towns *"* . . . by their *towns* and *castles"* (Genesis 25:16). *Tema* may refer to an Oasis north of Medina *(J. Hastings Dictionary of the Bible)*. To view the location of Tema during Isaiah's time please refer to the map at the end of the book. Arabia

## Tema In History

Arabia Antica Antica a portal for Pre-Islamic Arabian studies conducted by the University of Pisa, *(http://arabiantica.humnet.unipi.it/)* has a link to a map of Arabia showing the location of Tayma *(http://arabiantica.humnet.unipi.it/index.php?id=929)*. The Columbia Encyclopedia, Sixth Edition, 2001-07 *(http://www.bartleby.com/65/x-/X-TemaSAr.html)* notes that Tema is a variant spelling of Tayma, Saudi Arabia. The online Encyclopædia Britannica informs us that the Neo—Babylonian king Nabonidus left Babylonia around 552 BC to reside in Taima (oasis of Tayma' is in the northern Hejaz or northern Arabia) extending his power as far as Yathrib (modern day Medina). *(http://www.britannica.com/eb/topic-584926/Tayma)*

The association of *Kedar* with Arabia is made in the book of Ezekiel:

**Arabia, and all the princes of Kedar**, *they occupied with thee in lambs, and rams, and goats: in these [were they] thy merchants. (Ezekiel 27:21)*

The association of *Kedar* with tents is made in the *Psalms and Song of Solomon:*

*Woe is me, that I sojourn in Mesech, [that] I dwell in the* **tents of Kedar** *(Psalms 120:5)*

*I [am] black, but comely, O ye daughters of Jerusalem, as* **the tents of Kedar**, *as the curtains of Solomon. (Song of Solomon 1:5)*

The association of Arabs with tents:

*It shall never be inhabited, neither shall it be dwelt in from generation to generation: neither shall the* **Arabian pitch tent** *there; neither shall the shepherds make their fold there. (Isaiah 13:20)*

The association of *Kedar* with the House of God is made in Isaiah *(Isaiah 60:7):*

All the flocks of Kedar shall be gathered together unto thee, *the rams of Nebaioth shall minister unto thee: they shall come up with acceptance on mine altar,* and I will glorify the house of my glory. *(Isaiah 60:7)*

One may also find reference to **Kedar** in the Davis Dictionary of the Bible *(Presbyterian Church, 1980), International Standard Bible Encyclopedia (A.S. Fulton), and Smith's Bible Dictionary (Pelgrave).*

According to *Easton's Dictionary of the Bible, Kedar* is the name for the nomadic tribes of Arabs, the Bedouins generally *(Isaiah 21:16; 42:11; 60:7; Jeremiah 2:10; Ezekiel 27:21),* who dwelt in the north-west of Arabia. They lived in black hair-tents *(Song of Solomon Cant 1:5). (M.G.*

*Easton M.A., D.D., Illustrated Bible Dictionary, Third Edition, published by Thomas Nelson, 1897).* These black tents were made out of goat hair.

*Smith's Bible Dictionary* relates that the tribe of *Kedar* seems to have been one of the most conspicuous of all the *Ishmaelite* tribes, and hence the rabbins call the Arabians universally by this name. *(Smith, William, Dr. Smith's Bible Dictionary, c1860).*

The *Ishmaelites* as a people are mentioned in *1 Chronicles and the Psalms:*

*Over the camels also [was] Obil the* Ishmaelite: *and over the asses [was] Jehdeiah the Meronothite (1 Chronicles 27:30).*

The tabernacles of Edom, and the **Ishmaelites;** of Moab, and the Hagarenes; *(Psalms 83:6)*

**Ishmael** dwelt in the wilderness of **Paran** *(Genesis 21:21).* Finally before we move on to the book of *Isaiah* where *Kedar* and *Tema* will again be mentioned in fulfillment of God's prophecies, we will examine two short references in the Bible which prophesize the impending arrival of a "*. . . holy one from Paran*" **(Habakkuk 3:3).** "*God coming from Teman and the holy one from Paran*"(Habakkuk 3:3).

A line in the Book of Jubilees (20:13) mentions that the descendants of Abraham's son by Hagar, Ishmael, as well as his descendants by Keturah, became the "Arabians" or "Arabs". The 1st century Jewish historian Josephus similarly described the descendants of Ishmael (i.e. the Ishmaelites) as an "Arabian" people. He also calls Ishmael the "founder" (κτίστης) of the "Arabians". *(http://74.125.95.132/search?q=cache:jCus53BDeKcJ:en. wikipedia.org/wiki/Abraham+lot+nephew+of+abraham+islam&cd=1&hl=e n&ct=clnk&gl=us)*

**Book of Jubilees 20:13**

**The Dwelling-places of the Ishmaelites and of the Sons of Keturah (xx. 12-13)**

And Ishmael and his sons, and the sons of Keturah and their sons, went together and dwelt from Paran to the entering in of Babylon in all the land which is towards the East facing the desert. And these mingled with each other, and their name was called Arabs, and Ishmaelites. (http://www.sacred-texts.com/bib/jub/jub45.htm)

R.H. Charles, the translator, a distinguished academic Biblical scholar, concluded that Jubilees was a version of the Pentateuch, written in Hebrew, parts of which later became incorporated into the earliest Greek version of the Jewish Bible, the Septuagint. (The Book of Jubilees (translated by R. H. Charles, Society for Promoting Christian Knowledge, London, 1917, http://www.sacred-texts.com/bib/jub/index.htm#contents)

Muslims believe that God revealed to the prophet *Muhammad*, in the form of direct recitations, a book known as the Koran. The first verse of the Koran was revealed to prophet *Muhammad* in Mecca as a command *"Read" (Koran, 96:1-5)* and this pattern of revelation repeated itself, in Mecca and Medina, over twenty years until the revelation was complete, and God commanded prophet *Muhammad* to say, *"today we have perfected your religion"*.

During the early days of the message persecution of Muslims was common and unbearable forcing prophet *Muhammad* and his followers to flee from Mecca to Medina. Medina's inhabitants were more hospitable and supportive allowing prophet *Muhammad* to defeat the pagan Meccans at the battle of Badr in the second year of Hijra (i.e. the second year of the flight from Mecca to Medina).

Within years prophet *Muhammad* made a victorious and bloodless return to Mecca with an army of **ten thousand men** *(Page 400, Chapter 24, Life of Prophet Muhammad, by Dr. Muhammad Hussein Haykal, ISBN 089259-002-5, Library of Congress Catalog Card Number 76-4661)*, destroying the idols in Mecca and again restoring the Ka'aba as a monotheistic house of worship which till today unites followers in a yearly pilgrimage that symbolizes their belief in the Oneness of God. Muslims believe that the prophet *Abraham* and *Ishmael* built a house of worship at Mecca that eventually through the centuries became transformed into a house of idol worship. During the pilgrimage to Mecca Muslims retrace Hagar's footsteps, in her search for water to help quench the thirst of her son, drinking from the well that sprung at God's command to save *Ishmael* from imminent death. This ritual retraces one of history's memorable journeys reaffirming God's covenant with Ishmael. The Hebrew word

**Ishmael** translated into English **means *"God hears"*.** Muslims and Jews observe their covenant with God by circumcising their male offspring.

*Awake, awake; put on thy strength, O Zion; put on thy beautiful garments, O Jerusalem, the holy city: for henceforth there shall no more come into thee the uncircumcised and the unclean. (Isaiah 52:1, KJV)*

## JACOB'S (ISRAEL) PROPHECY

Abraham's Grandson thru Isaac was Jacob (Israel). Israel originally in Hebrew is "Yisrael." Yisrael is thought to mean, "He has striven with God." Levi, Joseph and Judah are brothers and sons of Jacob (Israel). As discussed in the introduction Moses descended from the tribe of Levi. However, the ancestry of Jesus can be linked back to King David and Judah.

Abraham⟶ Isaac ⟶Jacob ⟶ Judah ⟶⟶⟶ David ⟶Solomon⟶⟶⟶ Jesus

One arrow represents one generation while several arrows signify multiple generations. (http://www.newadvent.org/cathen/06410a.htm)

وَوَهَبْنَا لَهُۥٓ إِسْحَٰقَ وَيَعْقُوبَ وَجَعَلْنَا فِى ذُرِّيَّتِهِ ٱلنُّبُوَّةَ وَٱلْكِتَٰبَ وَءَاتَيْنَٰهُ أَجْرَهُۥ فِى ٱلدُّنْيَا ۖ وَإِنَّهُۥ فِى ٱلْءَاخِرَةِ لَمِنَ ٱلصَّٰلِحِينَ ۝

*And We gave (Abraham) Isaac and Jacob, and caused the prophethood and the book to remain in his seed, and We granted him his reward in this world, and in the hereafter he will most surely be among the good. (Koran 29:27)*

The Koran confirms that the prophetic lineage will continue the furthest through Jacob. The law and the Ten Commandments via Moses serve as a constant reminder to mankind's obligations towards God and towards each other. Moses was the Great Grandson of Levi and although an extremely important prophet the long prophetic lineage throughout the centuries continued thru Jacob and not his brother Levi.

*And **Jacob called unto his sons, and said,** Gather yourselves together, that I may tell you [that] which shall befall you in the last days. (Genesis 49:1, KJV)*

*The scepter shall not depart from Judah, nor a lawgiver from between his feet, until Shiloh come; and unto him [shall] the gathering of the people [be]. (Genesis 49:10, KJV).*

*And Jacob called his sons, and said, Gather yourselves together, and I will tell you what will befall you at the end of days. (Genesis 49:1, Darby Version of 1890)*

*The scepter will not depart from Judah, Nor the lawgiver from between his feet, Until Shiloh come, And to him will be the obedience of peoples. (Genesis 49:10, Darby Version of 1890).*

In Eaton's Bible Dictionary *Shiloh* generally is understood as denoting the Messiah, *"the peaceful one"*, as the word signifies (Genesis 49:10). However, one may argue that prophet Muhammad certainly brought "peace" and managed to unite the warring Arab tribes while only chaos ensued for the Jewish peoples during and after the life of Jesus. The Vulgate Version translates the word, *"he who is to be sent"*, in allusion to the Messiah; the Revised Version, margin, *"till he come to Shiloh."* (M.G. Easton M.A., D.D., Illustrated Bible Dictionary, Third Edition, published by Thomas Nelson, 1897).

Jacob, a Jewish prophet, prophesizes that Jewish spiritual leadership and law would remain with the Jewish nation till Shiloh (*"he who is to be sent"*) a non-Jew arrives; then this non Jewish Prophet would become the new spiritual leader of the peoples. Jesus himself being a Jew could not be Shiloh. The only known prophet thru non-Jewish lineage is the Arab descendent from Ishmael known as Prophet Muhammad. The universal Muslim greeting is *'alsalam alikum'* which is translated as "peace be upon you". Also the people did not obey Jesus but they ultimately obeyed Prophet Muhammad in his very lifetime *"**And to him will be the obedience of peoples**". (**Genesis 49:10, Darby Version of 1890**).*

# MOSES'S PROPHECY

وَرُسُـــلًا قَـــدۡ قَصَصۡنَٰهُـــمۡ عَلَيۡـــكَ مِـــن قَبۡـــلُ وَرُسُـــلًا لَّـــمۡ
نَقۡصُصۡهُـــمۡ عَلَيۡـــكَ وَكَـــلَّمَ ٱللَّـــهُ مُوسَـــىٰ تَكۡلِيمٗا ﴿١١٤﴾

*Of some apostles We have already told thee the story; of others We have not; and to Moses God spoke direct; (Koran 4:164)*

### And **the LORD spake unto Moses, saying**, *(Leviticus 12:1)*

Now we will return to the Old Testament, book of **Deuteronomy**, where God thru *Moses* prophesizes of things to come. In Deuteronomy we read,

*"I will raise them up a Prophet from among their brethren, like unto thee, and will put my words in his mouth; and he shall speak unto them all that I shall command him." (Deuteronomy 18:18).*
*"And it shall come to pass, [that] whosoever will not hearken unto my words which he shall speak in my name, I will require [it] of him." (Deuteronomy 18:19).*

We should note that Christian scholars interpret this prophecy as referring to the coming of Jesus Christ, but

*"... from among their brethren ..."*
cannot mean from amongst the Jewish peoples since God is not addressing a single Jew but is addressing the Jewish nation. Also it should be emphasized that this revelation did not say "from amongst your descendants." The brethren of the *Israelites* (descendants of Abraham thru Isaac) are the Ishmaelites (descendants of Abraham thru Ishmael). Jesus, to the dismay of some Christian scholars, should be excluded from this prophecy, as he is a Jew from the lineage of Isaac. In the *New American Standard Bible* "their brethren" has become "from among their countrymen" but the *KJV* as well as the *Jewish Publication Society's 1917 edition of the Hebrew Bible in English (http://www. mechon-mamre.org/e/et/et0518.htm)* maintains the phrase "from among their brethren".

38

*". . . like unto thee . . ."*

The above quotation foretells the likeness of the prophet to Moses. **Prophet Muhammad like Moses had a natural birth, and death.** They both married. Jesus had an unnatural birth and death; he also never married. Muhammad and Moses had dual functions as prophets and **statesmen bringing to humanity a code of laws**, delivered from God, which till today are present in the Koran and Torah (Old Testament) respectively. Jesus did not bring a code of laws and never became a statesman. Both prophet Muhammad and Moses **went into forced migration only to triumph in their very lifetimes**, whereas Jesus never did.

*". . . put my words in his mouth . . ."*

*The first* revealed verse in the Koran is verse 96:1 *"Read in the name of thy Lord who createth"(Koran 96:1)*. In the Old Testament we find the almost identical phrase " . . . ***words which he shall speak in my name . . ."*** *(Deuteronomy 18:18)*. Every "Surah" or chapter in the Koran begins with the words, *"**In the name of God**, the Beneficent, the Merciful"*. Muslims believe that the Koranic revelation from God was sent to the prophet Muhammad via the Archangel Gabriel over a period of twenty years. The sequential arrangement of the verses in the Koran does not reflect the sequence of revelation. The Arabic word *"El Koran"*, derived from the root word *"read"* literally means *"the readable Book"*.

## LORD SHINED FROM MOUNT PARAN

In the Old Testament, book of ***Deuteronomy***, we read:

*And this is the blessing, wherewith **Moses** the man of God blessed the children of Israel before his death. (Deuteronomy 33:1).*
*And he **said**, The Lord came from Sinai, and rose up from Seir unto them; he shined forth from **mount Paran**, **and he came with ten thousand of saints: from his right hand went a fiery law for them** (Deuteronomy 33:2).*

The Lord coming from Sinai refers to *Moses (see Exodus l9: 18-20)*. In the Bible we are told that Esau (Edom), the brother of Jacob dwelt in Seir (Genesis 36: 6-8). Seir may refer to the village of Sa'ir near Jerusalem an area from which God sent his message thru Jesus. Mount Paran may refer to the Mountain in Mecca where prophet Muhammad received his first revelation from God via the Archangel Gabriel.

Ishmael is associated with Paran. As we noted above, *"Ishmael dwelt in the wilderness of Paran" (Genesis 21:21)*. Prophet Muhammad entered Mecca with an army of *ten thousand* men *delivering a fiery law*. Prophet *Muhammad* made a victorious and bloodless return to Mecca with an army of *ten thousand men (Page 400, Chapter 24, Life of Prophet Muhammad, by Dr. Muhammad Hussein Haykal, ISBN 089259-002-5, Library of Congress Catalog Card Number 76-4661)*. The only historical figure who could fulfill the criterion of a descendant from *Ishmael*, and bring a law so comprehensive that it governs such diverse issues as moral conduct, matrimonial obligations, financial transactions, and spiritual commitments to God, can be no other than prophet Muhammad and the religion of Islam.

*A prayer of Habakkuk the prophet* upon *Shigionoth. (Habakkuk 3:1)*
*O LORD, I have heard thy speech, and was afraid:* *O LORD, revive thy work in the midst of the years*, *in the midst of the years make known; in wrath remember mercy. (Habakkuk 3:2)*
*God came from Teman, and the Holy One from mount Paran. Selah. His glory covered the heavens, and the earth was full of his praise. (Habakkuk 3:3).*

Could Teman refer to Tema or Medina and mount Paran again refer to the mountains surrounding the valley of Mecca or Kedar? This point will become clearer in the following chapter dealing with Tema and Kedar in the nighttime prophecy of Isaiah. God's coming from Teman may refer to the force of ten thousand saints that entered Mecca under the leadership of prophet Muhammad on his return from Medina or Teman.

# ISAIAH'S (ISAIAS) PROPHECY

*Isaias* is thought to mean *"God is salvation."* Isaiah (*Isaias*) was a prophet who lived in the 8ᵗʰ century BC Kingdom of Judah and advised the Israelites to obey God. This was the period prior to the Jewish people being exiled to Babylon; culminating in what is otherwise known as the diaspora or scattering of the Jewish people. According to the Rabbinic literature, Isaiah was a descendant of King David and Judah (*http://en.wikipedia.org/wiki/Isaiah*).

Abraham⟶ Isaac ⟶Jacob ⟶ Judah ⟶⟶⟶ David ⟶Solomon⟶⟶⟶ Isaiah⟶⟶⟶ Jesus

The key to understanding the prophecies in the Old Testament's Book of Isaiah is found in the Book of Genesis. Now that the relevant passages of the Book of Genesis have been discussed we can begin to explore two crucial chapters in the Book of Isaiah.

## ISAIAH 21

*For thus hath the Lord said unto me, Go, set a watchman, let him declare what he seeth. (Isaiah 21:6)*

*And* **he saw** *a chariot [with] a couple of horsemen, a chariot of asses, [and]* **a chariot of camels***; and he hearkened diligently with much heed: (Isaiah 21:7)*

*". . . stand continually upon the watchtower in the* **daytime** *. . ."* *(Isaiah 21:8)*

*And, behold, here cometh a chariot of men, [with] a couple of horsemen. And he answered and said, Babylon is fallen, is fallen; and all the graven images of her gods he hath broken unto the ground. (Isaiah 21:9,* **KJV***)*

In the *Douay-Rheims* version of the *Roman Catholic Bible* we find an English translation of *Isaiah 21:7* that is probably more accurate and true to the original text than the *KJV*. This conclusion will become more apparent during the unraveling of this prophecy. According to the Catholic Church the *Douay-Rheims* Version was published by 1610 after being translated from the *Latin Vulgate* (and compared with the Hebrew and Greek texts).

*For thus hath the Lord said to me: Go, and set a watchman: and whatsoever he shall see, let him tell. (Isaiah 21:6)*
*And* he saw a chariot with two horsemen, a rider upon an ass, and a rider upon a camel: *and he beheld them diligently with much heed. (Isaiah 21:7)*
*And a lion cried out: I am upon the watchtower of the Lord, standing continually by day: and I am upon my ward, standing whole nights. (Isaiah 21:8)*
*Behold this man cometh, the rider upon the chariot with two horsemen, and he answered, and said: Babylon is fallen, she is fallen, and all the graven gods thereof are broken unto the ground. (Isaiah 21:9,* Douay-Rheims Version*)*

The early or **"*daytime*"** *(Isaiah 21:8)* prophecies are:

The *fall of Babylon* is related to a *chariot with two horsemen (Isaiah 21:9)*

*Jesus* is the *rider on the ass. (John 12:15)* and *(Matthew 21:5)*

(1) Isaiah was a prophet in the 8th century BC Kingdom of Judah. Judah, fell in 586 B.C to the Babylonian King Nebuchadnezzar. However, in 539 BC Cyrus the Great of Persia conquered Babylon. This period was a respite for the Jewish peoples from the tribulations of the exile to Babylon as confirmed by the Biblical passages below.

*Now in the first year of **Cyrus king of Persia**, that the word of the LORD by the mouth of Jeremiah might be fulfilled, the LORD stirred up the spirit of Cyrus king of Persia, that he made a proclamation throughout all his kingdom, and put it also in writing, saying, (Ezra 1:1, KJV)*
**Thus saith Cyrus king of Persia, The LORD God of heaven hath given me all the kingdoms of the earth***; and he hath charged me to build him an house at Jerusalem, which is in Judah. (Ezra 1:2, KJV)*

**That saith of Cyrus, He is my shepherd***, and shall perform all my pleasure: even saying to Jerusalem, Thou shalt be built; and to the temple, Thy foundation shall be laid. (Isaiah 44:28, KJV)*

***Thus saith the LORD to his anointed, to Cyrus****, whose right hand I have holden, to subdue nations before him; and I will loose the loins of kings, to open before him the two leaved gates; and the gates shall not be shut; (Isaiah 45:1, KJV)*

*(2) "And **Jesus, when he had found a young ass, sat thereon; as it is written,** "(John 12:14)*

*"Fear not, daughter of Sion: behold, thy King cometh, sitting on an ass's colt." (**John 12:15**)*

*All this was done, that it might be fulfilled which was spoken by the prophet, saying, (Matthew 21:4)*

*Tell ye the daughter of Sion, Behold, thy King cometh unto thee, meek, and sitting upon an ass, and a colt the foal of an ass. (**Matthew 21:5**)*

*And the disciples went, and did as Jesus commanded them, (Matthew 21:6)*

(3) Then as we shall see the latter or *"nighttime"* prophecy *(Isaiah 21:11)* will reveal that Muhammad is the *rider on the camel.*

*". . . Watchman what of the night? . . ." (Isaiah 21:11)*

*". . . The burden upon Arabia." (Isaiah 21:13)*

*". . . The inhabitants of the land of Tema brought water to him that was thirsty, they prevented with bread him that fled . . ." (Isaiah 21:14)*

*For they fled from the swords, from the drawn sword, and from the bent bow, and from the grievousness of war. (Isaiah 21:15)*

*For thus hath the Lord said unto me, Within a year, according to the years of an hireling, and all the glory of Kedar shall fail: (Isaiah 21:16)*

*And the residue of the number of archers, the mighty men of the children of Kedar, shall be diminished: (Isaiah 21:17)*

## ISAIAH 42

*Behold my servant, whom I uphold; mine elect, [in whom] my soul delighteth; I have put my spirit upon him: he shall bring forth judgment to the Gentiles. (Isaiah 42:1)*

*He shall not cry, nor lift up, nor cause his voice to be heard in the street.
(Isaiah 42:2)*

*A bruised reed shall he not break, and the smoking flax shall he not quench:
he shall bring forth judgment unto truth. (Is. 42:3)*

*He shall not fail nor be discouraged, till he have set judgment in the earth: and
the isles shall wait for his law. (Isaiah 42:4)*

*Thus saith God the LORD, he that created the heavens, and stretched them
out; he that spread forth the earth, and that which cometh out of it; he that
giveth breath unto the people upon it, and spirit to them that walk therein:
(Isaiah 42:5)*

*I the LORD have called thee in righteousness, and will hold thine hand, and
will keep thee, and give thee for a covenant of the people, for a light of the
Gentiles; (Isaiah 42:6)*

*To open the blind eyes, to bring out the prisoners from the prison, [and] them
that sit in darkness out of the prison house. (Isaiah 42:7)*

*I [am] the LORD: that [is] my name: and my glory will I not give to another,
neither my praise to graven images. (Isaiah 42:8)*

*Behold, the former things are come to pass, and new things do I declare: before
they spring forth I tell you of them. (Isaiah 42:9)*

*Sing unto the LORD a **new** song, [and] his praise from the end of the earth,
ye that go down to the sea, and all that is therein; the isles, and the inhabitants
thereof. (Isaiah 42:10)*

*Let the wilderness and the cities thereof lift up [their voice], the villages [that]
Kedar doth inhabit: let the inhabitants of the rock sing, let them shout from
the top of the mountains. (Isaiah 42:11)*

*Let them give glory unto the LORD, and declare his praise in the islands.
(Isaiah 42:12)*

*The LORD shall go forth as a mighty man, he shall stir up jealousy like
a man of war: he shall cry, yea, roar; he shall prevail against his enemies.
(Isaiah 42:13)*

*I have long time holden my peace; I have been still, [and] refrained myself:
[now] will I cry like a travailing woman; I will destroy and devour at once.
(Isaiah 42:14)*

*I will make waste mountains and hills, and dry up all their herbs; and I will
make the rivers islands, and I will dry up the pools. (Isaiah 42:15)*

*And I will bring the blind by a way [that] they knew not; I will lead them
in paths [that] they have not known: I will make darkness light before them,*

and crooked things straight. These things will I do unto them, and not forsake them. (Isaiah 42:16)
They shall be turned back, they shall be greatly ashamed, that trust in graven images, that say to the molten images, Ye [are] our gods. (Isaiah 42:17)
Hear, ye deaf; and look, ye blind, that ye may see. (Isaiah 42:18)
Who [is] blind, but my servant? Or deaf, as my messenger [that] I sent? Who [is] blind as [he that is] perfect, and blind as the LORD'S servant? (Isaiah 42:19)
Seeing many things, but thou observest not; opening the ears, but he heareth not. (Isaiah 42:20)
The LORD is well pleased for his righteousness' sake; he will magnify the law, and make [it] honourable. (Isaiah 42:21)
But this [is] a people robbed and spoiled; [they are] all of them snared in holes, and they are hid in prison houses: they are for a prey, and none delivereth; for a spoil, and none saith, Restore. (Isaiah 42:22)
Who among you will give ear to this? [who] will hearken and hear for the time to come? (Isaiah 42:23)
Who gave Jacob for a spoil, and Israel to the robbers? Did not the LORD, he against whom we have sinned? For they would not walk in his ways, neither were they obedient unto his law. (Isaiah 42:24)

Before we proceed perhaps one might reflect that this prophecy coincides with God being displeased with the Jewish nation that had sinned and did not follow God's ways. Maybe for this reason the scepter departs from Judah *(Genesis 49:10)* and is passed unto the Gentiles.

To summarize, the nighttime prophecy comes after the daytime (or initial) prophecy and will bring:

" . . . *bring judgment to the Gentiles* . . ." *(Isaiah 42:1)*—this prophet will bring judgment to the non-Jewish people of Kedar.

"He shall not fall nor be discouraged, till he have set judgment in the earth and the Isles shall wait for his law." *(Isaiah 42:4)*—complete success for this prophet is guaranteed.

*"give thee for* a covenant of the people, *for* a light of the Gentiles;" *(Isaiah 42: 6)*—a covenant and light for the Gentiles or non Jewish people of *Kedar*, fulfillment of God's covenant with the descendants of *Ishmael*.

" . . . *former things are come to pass, and new things do I declare* . . ." *(Isaiah 42:9)—new revelation declared by God*.

" . . . *Sing unto the Lord a new song* . . ." *(Isaiah 42:10)*—implies a rhythmical or song like revelation whose distinction could be a new or different language.

*"Let the wilderness and the cities thereof lift up their voice, the villages that Kedar doth inhabit; let the inhabitants of the rock sing, let them shout from the top of the mountains." (Isaiah 42:11)—the people of Kedar will adopt this new religion and recite this new revelation.*

*And* the residue of the number of archers, the mighty men of the children of Kedar, shall be diminished: *(Isaiah 21:17)*—the people of *Kedar (Mecca)* who had caused this prophet and his followers to flee to *Tema (Medina)* not only are defeated but also embrace this religion or new song.

" . . . *The Lord . . . will magnify the law* . . ." *(Isaiah 42:20)—i.e. God will expand the law*.

To pursue this prophecy, in the *Book of Isaiah,* we will start with *chapter 21* and where necessary refer to *chapter 42*.

" . . . *stand upon the watchtower in the daytime* . . ." *(Isaiah 21:8)*

" . . . *watchman what of the night?* . . ." *(Isaiah 21:11)*

These above statements suggest a prophetic dream, which foretells of things yet to come.

" . . . *The burden upon Arabia." (Isaiah 21:13)*

The people of Arabia will take responsibility for establishing this religion or fulfilling God's commands. This implies placement of a religious burden upon Arabia since it would seem logical that this would be the kind of burden that God would place upon nation.

"... *The inhabitants of the land of* Tema *brought water to him that was thirsty, they prevented with bread him that fled* ..." *(Isaiah 21:14)*

Again one cannot help but wonder at the analogy of prophet Muhammad and his followers fleeing from his enemies at *Mecca (Kedar)* to *Medina (Tema)* where they received food and water. As we have just mentioned two of the **sons of Ishmael** are **Kedar** *(Genesis 25:13)*, and **Tema** *(Genesis 25:15)*. *Tema* may refer to an Oasis north of Medina *(J. Hastings Dictionary of the Bible)*. Also note that **the names of the sons of Ishmael became the names of their towns** "... by their *towns* and *castles" (Genesis 25:16)*. The association of *Kedar* with Arabia is also made in the *book of Ezekiel (Ezekiel 27:21)*.

"... *within a year* ... *all the glory of* Kedar *shall fail." (Isaiah 21:16)*—Historically, the pagans of Mecca *(Kedar)* were defeated in the second year of Hijra at the *battle of Badr.*

"... *bring judgment to the Gentiles* ..." *(Isaiah 42:1)*

"... *former things are come to pass, and new things do I declare...*" *(Isaiah 42:9)*

"... *The Lord* ... *will magnify the law* ..." *(Isaiah 42:20)*

*Jesus* did not come to change the law of *Moses* but to fulfill it. Also *Jesus*, a Jew, brought his message to the *Jews* unlike *Muhammad* who brought his message to the non-Jews or Gentiles magnifying the law and declaring new things.

The quotation, "... *Sing unto the Lord a new song* ..." *(Isaiah 42:10)* may suggest new language, such as Arabic, that is different than the languages of old (Hebrew and Aramaic). The Koran is recited in songlike or rhythmic Arabic when performing the five daily prayers.

"*He shall not fall nor be discouraged, till he have set judgment in the earth: and the Isles shall wait for his law. (Isaiah 42:4)*

Succeed he did indeed. Islam spread to all civilizations, eventually reaching as far as Spain in the Western world, China in the Far East, well as the Isle of Indonesia. *[the Isles shall wait for his law. (Isaiah 42:4)]*.

*Let the wilderness and the cities thereof lift up their voice, the villages that Kedar doth inhabit; let the inhabitants of the rock sing, let them shout from the top of the mountains. (Isaiah 42:11)*

This prophecy foretells **(1) the defeat of the people of *Kedar*** (Mecca) *[Isaiah 21:16]* **(2) their rejection of the false idolatrous religion of their forefathers** "*. . . They shall be greatly ashamed, that trust in graven images, that say to the molten images, ye are our gods." (Isaiah 42:17)* **and (3) their subsequent acceptance of Islam** *as they too* **sing** *(Isaiah 42:11) a new song (Isaiah 42:10) unto their Lord.*

The Koran has it's own unique style, a musical like tempo, not found in Arabic prose or poetry. "*. . . Sing unto the Lord a new song . . .*"*(Isaiah 42:10)*. As a matter of fact God, in the Koran, challenges all of mankind to write a verse, which has the style of the Koranic text. The Aza'an or call to prayer is made from hilltops or tall minarets on top of Mosques.' . . . *let them shout from the top of the mountains.' (Isaiah 42:11).*

In the Old Testament *book of Zephaniah* there is an obscure reference to a new language of revelation from God: "***For then I will turn to the people a pure language, that they may call upon the name of the Lord, to serve him with one consent.***" *(Zephaniah 3:9).*

# PARACLETE (PARAKLETOS)

## INTRODUCTION

*And **Jacob called his sons**, and said, Gather yourselves together, and **I will tell you what will befall you at the end of days**. (Genesis 49:1, Darby Version of 1890).*

***The scepter will not depart from Judah, Nor the lawgiver from
between his feet, Until Shiloh come, And to him will be the obedience
of peoples.*** *(Genesis 49:10,* ***Darby Version of 1890****).*

The reader may recall Jacob's prophecy, in the section titled JACOB'S
PROPHECY, which foretold the coming of a non-Jewish prophet called
**Shiloh** *(Prince of Peace)*. Could this be a reference to the *"prince of this
world"* as mentioned below in *John 14:30:*

*Ye have heard how I said unto you, I go away, and come [again] unto you. If ye
loved me, ye would rejoice, because I said, I go unto the Father: for **my Father
is greater than I**. (John 14:28)*
*And now I have told you before it come to pass, that, when it is come to pass,
ye might believe. (John 14:29)*
*Hereafter I will not talk much with you: for the prince of this world cometh,
and hath nothing in me. (John 14:30, KJV)*

This concept of a non-Jewish prophet is reiterated below in *Matthew
21:43* as again it is foretold that the Kingdom of God will be given
to a different nation (the *Ishmaelites* or Arabs *viz a viz* the prophet
*Muhammad*). Also we may recall that Abraham was promised to be a *father
of many nations (Genesis 17:5)* and *Ishmael* was promised *a great nation
(Genesis 21:13)*.

*Jesus saith unto them, Did ye never read in the scriptures, The stone which
the builders rejected, the same is become the head of the corner: this is the
Lord's doing, and it is marvellous in our eyes? (Matthew 21:42)*
*Therefore say I unto you, The kingdom of God shall be taken from you,
and given to a nation bringing forth the fruits thereof. (Matthew 21:43)*
*And whosoever shall fall on this stone shall be broken: but on whomsoever
it shall fall, it will grind him to powder. (Matthew 21:44, KJV).*

*The stone [which] the builders refused is become the head [stone] of the corner.
(Psalms 118:22).*

*And many other things blasphemously spake they against him. (Luke 22:65)*
*And as soon as it was day, the elders of the people and the chief priests and the
scribes came together, and led him into their council, saying, (Luke 22:66)*

*Art thou the Christ? tell us. And he said unto them, If I tell you, ye will not believe: (Luke 22:67)*
*And if I also ask [you], ye will not answer me, nor let [me] go. (Luke 22:68)*
*Hereafter shall the Son of man sit on the right hand of the power of God. (Luke 22:69)*
*Then said they all, Art thou then the Son of God? And he said unto them, Ye say that I am. (Luke 22:70)*
*And they said, What need we any further witness? for we ourselves have heard of his own mouth. (Luke 22:71)*

Jesus says that he is *the* "Son of man" *(Luke 22:69)* and denies being *"the Son of God"* by saying *"**Ye say that I am**" (Luke 22:70)*. Jesus was accused of a false claim (a blasphemy) and for this reason was crucified.

## THE PARACLETE

*But **that the word may be fulfilled which is written in their law**: They hated me without cause. (John 15:25)*
But when the Paraclete cometh, *whom I will send you from the Father, the* Spirit of truth, *who proceedeth from the Father,* he shall give testimony of me. *(John 15:26,* Douay-Rheims*)*.

*But I told you not these things from the beginning, because I was with you. And now* I go to him that sent me, *and none of you asketh me: Whither goest thou? (John 16:5)*
*But because I have spoken these things to you, sorrow hath filled your heart. (John 16:6)*
*But I tell you the truth: it is expedient to you that I go: for if I go not,* the Paraclete *will not come to you; but if I go, I will send him to you. (John 16:7)*
*And when he is come, he will convince the world of sin, and of justice, and of judgment. (John 16:8)*
*Of sin: because they believed not in me. (John 16:9)*
*And of justice: because I go to the Father; and you shall see me no longer. (John 16:10)*
*And of judgment: because the prince of this world is already judged. (John 16:11)*

*I have yet many things to say to you: but you cannot bear them now. (John 16:12)*

*But when he, the* Spirit of truth, *is come,* he will teach you all truth. *For he shall not speak of himself;* but what things soever he shall hear, he shall speak; *and the things that are to come, he shall shew you. (John 16:13,* Douay-Rheims)

**Parakletos** is a Greek word meaning **advocate or intercessor** (*Davis Dictionary of the Bible*). The word *paraclete* is not to be found in the *KJV* of the Bible as it is replaced by the word Comforter. The *paraclete* as described in John 15:26 and John 16:13 is referred to as: (1) *Spirit of truth* (2) one who *will teach all truth* (3) speaks *only what he hears (not what he sees i.e. this is not a vision) and (3) he will convince the world of sin, and of justice, and of judgment.* According to this description it would not be unreasonable to conclude that the *paraclete* is a human such as prophet Muhammad *for the paraclete speaks, teaches and convinces the world of sin, justice and judgement.*

Jesus stated that the *"prince of this world"* will come after he departs:

*Hereafter I will not talk much with you: for the prince of this world cometh, and hath nothing in me. (John 14:30, KJV)*

According to the above statement and description the reader would agree that the *"**prince of this world**"* is unlikely to be Jesus. Could the *paraclete* be referring to *"that prophet"* as mentioned in our previous discussion?

*And this is the record of John, when the Jews sent priests and Levites from Jerusalem to ask him, Who art thou? (John 1:19)*

*And he confessed, and denied not; but confessed, I am not the Christ. (John 1:20)*

*And they asked him, What then? Art thou Elias? And he saith, I am not.* Art thou that prophet? *And he answered, No. (John 1:21, KJV)*

*"That prophet"* is clearly not *Jesus Christ.* Hence, we must ask does the prophet foretold in *Deuteronomy 18:18* or the passages previously discussed from the *Book of Isaiah* best fit this long awaited prophet?

# THAT PROPHET

## MATTHEW

In the New Testament, *Gospel of Matthew*, Jesus says, "*. . . kingdom to be given to **a nation** that will bring the fruit thereof*" *(Matthew 21:43).*
*Therefore say I unto you, The kingdom of God shall be taken from you, and given to a nation bringing forth the fruits thereof. (Matthew 21:43)*
*And whosoever shall fall on this stone shall be broken: but on whomsoever it shall fall, it will grind him to powder. (Matthew 21:44)*
*And when the chief priests and Pharisees had heard his parables, they perceived that he spake of them. (Matthew 21:45)*
*But when they sought to lay hands on him, they feared the multitude, because they took him for a prophet. (Matthew 21:46, KJV)*

Jesus like the previous prophets was Jewish so we are left wondering which new nation, other than the Jewish nation (which largely rejected Jesus) would receive the Kingdom of God.

## LUKE

*And **many** other **things blasphemously spake they against him**. (Luke 22:65)*
*And as soon as it was day, the elders of the people and the chief priests and the scribes came together, and led him into their council, saying, (Luke 22:66)*
*Art thou the Christ? tell us. And he said unto them, If I tell you, ye will not believe: (Luke 22:67)*
*And if I also ask [you], ye will not answer me, nor let [me] go. (Luke 22:68)*
*Hereafter shall the* Son of man *sit on the right hand of the power of God. (Luke 22:69)*
Then said they all, Art thou then the Son of God? And he said unto them, Ye say that I am. (Luke 22:70)
*And they said, What need we any further witness? for we ourselves have heard of his own mouth. (Luke 22:71, KJV)*

Since Jesus knew his fate *"nor let me go" (Luke 22:68)* what would he lose if he admitted that he was, in the Trinitarian sense, *"the Son of God"*. Could the above literal accusation of Jesus truly being the *"son"* of God be the blasphemy (profanity) that was spoken against him? By Jesus replying, *"Ye say that I am"* to the question *"Art thou then the Son of God?"* would indicate that he is not the Son of God *(Luke 22:71)*.

## JOHN

In the New Testament's *Gospel of John*, after *John the Baptist* denies that he is Christ one is even more perplexed with his denial of being . . ."*that prophet*" . . . *(John 1:20-21)*.

*And this is the record of John, when the Jews sent priests and Levites from Jerusalem to ask him, Who art thou? (John 1:19)*
*And he confessed, and denied not; but confessed, I am not the Christ. (John 1:20)*
*And they asked him, What then? Art thou Elias? And he saith, I am not. Art thou that prophet? And he answered, No. (John 1:21, KJV)*

Could the learned priests and *John the Baptist* have been referring to the prophecies that we have thus far been discussing?

# BACA (MECCA)

إِنَّ أَوَّلَ بَيْتٍ وُضِعَ لِلنَّاسِ لَلَّذِى بِبَكَّةَ مُبَارَكًا وَهُدًى لِّلْعَٰلَمِينَ ۝

*Verily, the first House (of worship) appointed for mankind was that at **Baca** (Mecca), full of blessing, and guidance for the entire world. (Koran 3:96)*

There is one reference to *'Baca'* in the Koran. Baca is another word for Mecca. We also find, in the Psalms of David, a pilgrimage made to a house of worship called Baca .

## PSALMS (84:2-10)

(To the chief Musician upon Gittith, A Psalm for the sons of Korah.) How amiable [are] thy tabernacles, O LORD of hosts! (Psalms 84:1)

*My soul longeth, yea, even fainteth for the courts of the LORD: my heart and my flesh crieth out for the living God. (Psalms 84:2)*

*Yea, the sparrow hath found an house, and the swallow a nest for herself, where she may lay her young, [even] thine altars, O LORD of hosts, my King, and my God. (Psalms 84:3)*
*Blessed [are] they that dwell in thy house: they will be still praising thee. Selah. (Psalms 84:4)*
*Blessed [is] the man whose strength [is] in thee; in whose heart [are] the ways [of them]. (Psalms 84:5)*

*[Who] passing through the valley of Baca make it a well; the rain also filleth the pools. (Psalms 84:6)*
*They go from strength to strength, [every one of them] in Zion appeareth before God. (Psalms 84:7)*
*O LORD God of hosts, hear my prayer: give ear, O God of Jacob. Selah. (Psalms 84:8)*
*Behold, O God our shield, and look upon the face of thine anointed . (Psalms 84:9)*
*For a day in thy courts [is] better than a thousand. I had rather be a doorkeeper in the house of my God, than to dwell in the tents of wickedness. (Psalms 84:10, KJV)*

**Blessed is the man** *whose strength is in you;* **Who have set their hearts on a pilgrimage.** *(Psalms 84:5,* **World English Bible***)*
*Passing through the valley of Weeping, they make it a place of springs.*
*Yes, the autumn rain covers it with blessings.*
*(Psalms 84:6, World English Bible)*

*How lovely your dwelling, O LORD of hosts!* (Psalms 84:2, **New American Bible, United States Conference of Catholic Bishops**)

*Happy are those who find refuge in you, whose hearts are set on pilgrim roads. (Psalms 84:6,* **New American Bible, United States Conference of Catholic Bishops)**
*As they pass through the Baca valley, they find spring water to drink. Also from pools the Lord provides water for those who lose their way. (Psalms 84:7,* **New American Bible, United States Conference of Catholic Bishops)**

Could the weeping refer to Hagar trying to find water for her son Ishmael?

*And she went, and sat her down over against [him] a good way off, as it were a bowshot: for she said, Let me not see the death of the child. And she sat over against [him], and lift up her voice,* **and wept** *(Genesis 21:16, KJV).*
*And God heard the voice of the lad; and* **the angel of God called to Hagar out of heaven,** *and said unto her, What aileth thee, Hagar? fear not; for God hath heard the voice of the lad where he is. (Genesis 21:17, KJV).*
**Arise, lift up the lad,** *and hold him in thine hand;* **for I will make him a great nation.** *(Genesis 21:18, KJV).*
*And God opened her eyes, and* **she saw a well of water;** *and she went, and filled the bottle with water, and gave the lad drink (Genesis 21:19, KJV).*
*And* **God was with the lad;** *and he grew, and dwelt in the wilderness, and became an archer. (Genesis 21:20, KJV).*
*And* **he dwelt in the wilderness of Paran:** *and his mother took him a wife out of the land of Egypt. (Genesis 21:21, KJV).*

The Koran maintains that *Abraham* and *Ishmael* built a House of Worship at the valley of Mecca *(Baca)* which is surrounded by the Sirat mountains.

As is noted in the above Bible versions, of the Psalms of David, *Baca* is referred to as a site of pilgrimage, where there is spring water to drink (well of Zamzam) and a House of God. The other famous House of God is that of Solomon's Temple in Jerusalem in whose direction Muslims initially prayed. Subsequently, the Koran commanded a change in the direction of prayer towards the direction of Mecca *(Koran 2:143).*

$$\text{وَإِذْ جَعَلْنَا ٱلْبَيْتَ مَثَابَةً لِّلنَّاسِ وَأَمْنًا وَٱتَّخِذُوا۟ مِن مَّقَامِ إِبْرَٰهِۧمَ مُصَلًّى}$$

$$\text{وَعَهِدْنَآ إِلَىٰٓ إِبْرَٰهِۧمَ وَإِسْمَٰعِيلَ أَن طَهِّرَا بَيْتِيَ لِلطَّآئِفِينَ وَٱلْعَٰكِفِينَ}$$

$$\text{وَٱلرُّكَّعِ ٱلسُّجُودِ ﴿١٢٥﴾}$$

*And (remember) when We made the House (the Kabah at Mecca) a focal point for mankind and a place of safety. And take you (people) the Maqam (place) Abraham as a place of prayer, and* **We commissioned Abraham and Ishmael that they should purify My House** *(the Kabah at Mecca) for those who are circumambulating it, or staying (Itikaf), or bowing or prostrating themselves (there, in prayer). (Koran 2:125)*

$$\text{وَإِذْ يَرْفَعُ إِبْرَٰهِۧمُ ٱلْقَوَاعِدَ مِنَ ٱلْبَيْتِ وَإِسْمَٰعِيلُ رَبَّنَا تَقَبَّلْ مِنَّآ إِنَّكَ}$$

$$\text{أَنتَ ٱلسَّمِيعُ ٱلْعَلِيمُ ﴿١٢٧﴾}$$

*And (remember)* **As Abraham and (his son) Ishmael were raising the foundations of the House** *(the Kabah at Mecca), (saying), "Our Lord, accept this from us. Verily! You are the Hearer, the Omniscient." (Koran 2:127)*

# The Trinity

The only major difficulty that now arises and must be thoughtfully tackled is the character of Jesus. To the Jews the historical Jesus was a person, to the Trinitarian Christians a Son of God and to the Muslims a human prophet. The confusion about the character of Jesus is what divides the three major world religions and one is tempted to ask was this by accident or part of a plan to test each individual believer's true loyalty to God versus loyalty to country, tribe or family. Curiously our world has been polarized by the problems of the Middle East whether one examines the status of Jerusalem or the interactions of the Christian, Muslim, or Jewish peoples over the years. Also the Middle East commands our attention given the world's dependence on oil. Is this all part of a Divine Master plan to bring the peoples of the world to interact? Will the world be able to overcome these differences avoiding collusion or collision? Can the world instead work towards a course of reconciliation? The concept of the *Trinity* is the most difficult idea to discern. The questions relating to this concept that one should pose are (1) Is it possible? (2) Is it probable? and (3) Is it plausible?

## ONE GOD

To the Jews the Old Testament clearly says God is ONE: *Hear, O Israel: The LORD our God [is]* **one** *LORD: (Deuteronomy 6:4).*

In *Hosea* God says that he is not man "*I [am] God, and not man*".

*I will not execute the fierceness of mine anger, I will not return to destroy Ephraim: for* I [am] God, and not man; *the Holy One in the midst of thee: and I will not enter into the city.*
*(Hosea 11:9)*

*Have we not all* one father? *hath not* one God *created us? why do we deal treacherously every man against his brother, by profaning the covenant of our fathers? (Malachi 2:10)*

To the Moslems and Jews God is ONE.

# JESUS IS GOD?

*And at the ninth hour Jesus cried with a loud voice, saying, Eloi, Eloi, lama sabachthani? which is, being interpreted, My God,* **my God,** *why hast thou forsaken me? (Mark 15:34, KJV)*

*And about the ninth hour Jesus cried with a loud voice, saying, Eli, Eli, lama sabachthani? that is to say, My God,* my God, *why hast thou forsaken me? (Matthew 27:46, KJV)*

The above two verses reveal that *Jesus* is: (1) not God and (2) not co-equal with God. The *Jesus of Matthew 27:46 and Mark 15:34* is not omniscient as he questions God's wisdom and clearly acknowledges that he is less than God by saying *"my"* God.

# ONLY BEGOTTEN SON?

*For God so loved the world, that he gave* **his only begotten Son**, *that whosoever believeth in him should not perish, but have everlasting life.* **(John 3:16**, *KJV)*

*For God so loved the world that he gave* his only Son, *so that everyone who believes in him may not perish but may have eternal life.* (John 3:16, *New Revised Standard Version—NRSV)*

The word *"begotten"* has been removed from the NRSV. Furthermore if *John 3:16* in the NSRV is accepted as a genuine statement how could Jesus be God's only son when Adam is also a son of God *(Luke 3:38)*.

*Which was the son of Enos, which was the son of Seth, which was the son of* **Adam**, *which was the* **son of God**. *(Luke 3:38, KJV)*.

Also,

*Now there was a day when the* sons of God *came to present themselves before the LORD, and Satan came also among them. (Job 1:6)*

*For as many as are led by the Spirit of God, they are the* sons of God. *(Romans 8:14)*

*For whereas they would not believe any thing by reason of the enchantments; upon the destruction of the firstborn, they acknowledged this people to be the* **sons of God**. *(Wisdom of Solomon 18:13)*

**Jesus (Isa) is like Adam** *(Koran 3:59)*

Jesus (Isa) is like Adam (Koran 3:59) implies they are both humans of unnatural births. Could the fact that we find both Adam and Jesus equally mentioned (25 times) in the Koran also imply a creative likeness? This observation appears to take on more significance in view of the fact the Koran stating that God "keeps a count of all things"(Koran 72:28)? The word Isa is found 27 times using a search engine but only 25 references to Isa are actual text as two are in explanatory brackets (Koran 4:157 and 4:159). Search Adam and he is also found 25 times. (*http://quod.lib.umich. edu/k/koran/simple.html*)

Again for verification:

*http://www.2muslims.com/cgi-bin/hadith/quran/quran.cgi*

Enter the word **Adam** or **Jesus** and scroll to the bottom and will get a count of 25 for each.

*. . . and **He keepeth count of all things*** (Koran 72:28)

# SPIRIT OF GOD

According to the Old Testament passages quoted below The *Spirit of God* refers to (1) that which God imparts to us while we live, *(Exodus 31:3)* (2) that which God taketh when we die, *(Ecclesiastes 12:7)* (3) has components of wisdom and understanding, *(Exodus 31:3)* and (4) the character of which we know not *(Ecclesiastes 11:5)*.

*And Pharaoh said unto his servants, Can we find [such a one] as this [is],* a man in whom the Spirit of God [is]*? (Genesis 41:38)*

And I have filled him with the spirit of God, in wisdom, and in understanding, and in knowledge, *and in all manner of workmanship, (Exodus 31:3)*

*And when they came thither to the hill, behold, a company of prophets met him; and the* Spirit of God came upon him, and he prophesied among them *(1 Samuel 10:10)*

*As* thou knowest not what [is] the way of the spirit, *[nor] how the bones [do grow] in the womb of her that is with child: even so thou knowest not the works of God who maketh all. (Ecclesiastes 11:5).*

*Then shall the dust return to the earth as it was: and* the spirit shall return unto God who gave it. *(Ecclesiastes 12:7)*

*Cast me not away from thy presence; and take not thy* holy spirit *from me. (Psalms 51:11)*

*Then he remembered the days of old, Moses, [and] his people, [saying], Where [is] he that brought them out of the sea with the shepherd of his flock? where [is] he that put his* Holy Spirit *within him?(Isaiah 63:11)*

However, the *Spirit of God* somehow takes on more mystical qualities and significance in the form of a *Trinitarian* God. The Koran states that God bestows or *breathes* His *Spirit* into His creation at the time of completion *(Koran 15:29, 32:9, 38:72)*, God used the Holy Spirit to reveal or communicate Koranic scriptures to prophet *Muhammad (Koran 16:101-102)* and also *"strengthened" Jesus* with the *Holy Spirit (Koran 2:87, 2:253, 5:110)*.

# SONS OF GOD

*"Son of God"* in the form of the Trinitarian God the term has a special significance. However, humans are referred to as *"sons of God"*:

*That the* sons of God *saw the daughters of men that they [were] fair; and they took them wives of all which they chose. (Genesis 6:2)*

*Again there was a day when the* sons of God *came to present themselves before the LORD, and Satan came also among them to present himself before the LORD. (Job 2:1)*

*He answered and said, Lo, I see four men loose, walking in the midst of the fire, and they have no hurt; and the form of the fourth is like the* Son of God. *(Daniel 3:25)*

The real problems with the *Trinity* are (1) it contradicts the concept of the ONE God in the *Old Testament*, (2) implies that God is the author of confusion since while God is ONE He is also Three, (3) when *Christ* was crucified there was no God for three days (4) and that God allows himself to be sacrificed by some of his most worthless creation *(Pontius Pilate)* to forgive previous and future generations of mankind. Is God not capable of forgiveness without performing the ultimate sacrifice? How could previous generations before *Christ* be saved if they had no chance to believe in a concept they knew nothing about?

If God is immortal than how could it be that he has a son who has mortal attributes? If God has a son then he has been given human attributes and loses his godliness. Conversely, a son has the powers of God the father and could even challenge him. Hence we would be set us up for the concept of many Gods. The problem with belief is that many humans lack the ability to accept an abstract God and must humanize the God that they wish to believe in. Humans have a desire to touch and feel their God leading to artistic renderings of *Jesus Christ* and the *Virgin Mary*.

The Koran is clear on the concept of God:

قُلْ هُوَ ٱللَّهُ أَحَدٌ ۝

*Say "He is God, (the) One.*

ٱللَّهُ ٱلصَّمَدُ ۝

*The Self-Sufficient Master*

لَمْ يَلِدْ وَلَمْ يُولَدْ ۝

*"He begets not, nor was He begotten*

وَلَمْ يَكُن لَّهُۥ كُفُوًا أَحَدٌ ۝

*"And there is none co-equal or comparable unto Him."(Koran 112: 1-4)*

وَقُلِ ٱلْحَمْدُ لِلَّهِ ٱلَّذِى لَمْ يَتَّخِذْ وَلَدًا وَلَمْ يَكُن لَّهُۥ شَرِيكٌ فِى ٱلْمُلْكِ وَلَمْ يَكُن لَّهُۥ وَلِىٌّ مِّنَ ٱلذُّلِّ وَكَبِّرْهُ تَكْبِيرًا ۝

*And say: "All the praises and thanks be to God, Who has not begotten a son (nor an offspring), and Who has no partner in (His) Dominion, nor He is low to have a helper, protector or supporter. And magnify Him with all the magnificence". (Koran 17:111)*

*Never did God take to Himself a son, and never was there with him any (other) god— in that case would each god have certainly taken away what he created, and some of them would certainly have overpowered others; glory be to God above what they describe (Koran 23: 91)*

In the Bible we also read:

*Jesus saith unto her, Touch me not; for I am not yet ascended to my Father: but go to my brethren, and say unto them, I ascend unto my Father, and your Father; and [to] my God, and your God. (John 20:17, KJV)*

The above statement leaves one with the impression that Jesus does not raise himself to a level equal to God but is rather similar to us mortal humans. This is certainly far removed from those who try to proclaim that Jesus is the Son of God.

*And certain men which came down from Judea taught the brethren, [and said], Except ye be circumcised after the manner of Moses, ye cannot be saved. (Acts 15:1, KJV)*
*When therefore Paul and Barnabas had no small dissension and disputation with them, they determined that Paul and Barnabas, and certain other of them, should go up to Jerusalem unto the apostles and elders about this question. (Acts 15:2, KJV)*

The above quotation reveals the uncertainty in the early *Christian Church* about which *Old Testament* commandments to keep and which to abrogate. Yet in the Book of Matthew *Jesus* proclaims:

*Think not that I am come to destroy the law, or the prophets: I am not come to destroy, but to fulfill. (Matthew 5:17)*
*For verily I say unto you, Till heaven and earth pass, one jot or one tittle shall in no wise pass from the law, till all be fulfilled. (Matthew 5:18)*
*Whosoever therefore shall break one of these least commandments, and shall teach men so, he shall be called the least in the kingdom of heaven: but whosoever shall do and teach [them], the same shall be called great in the kingdom of heaven. (Matthew 5:19, KJV)*

Muslims and Jews continue to follow the ordinance of circumcision. Interestingly, the *United Nations World Health Organization (WHO) & UNAIDS* as of 2006 are promoting circumcision to battle the AIDS epidemic as this reduces the risk of heterosexuals acquiring AIDS by 60% *(www.unaids.org)*.

## BORN AGAIN CHRISTIANS?

Could *John 3:3* be interpreted as that no man can see the kingdom of God before his resurrection? The catchy phrase of the *"born again"* Christians that is attributed to the KJV is no longer found in the NRSV.

*Verily, verily, I say unto thee, except a man be **born again**, he cannot see the kingdom of God. (John 3:3, Authorized King James Version)*

*Very, truly, I tell you, no one can see the kingdom of God without being* born from_above. *(John 3:3, New Revised Standard Version)*

## THE ANOINTED ONE

Some people think that Christ *"the anointed one"* is an exclusive designation. However, the examples below reveal otherwise:

*Thus saith the LORD to his anointed, to Cyrus, whose right hand I have holden, to subdue nations before him; and I will loose the loins of kings, to open before him the two leaved gates; and the gates shall not be shut; (Isaiah 45:1)*

*The Spirit of the Lord GOD [is] upon me; because the LORD hath anointed me to preach good tidings unto the meek; he hath sent me to bind up the brokenhearted, to proclaim liberty to the captives, and the opening of the prison to [them that are] bound; (Isaiah 61:1)*

## FATHER, THE WORD & THE HOLY GHOST "ARE ONE"?

*For there are three that bear record in heaven, the Father, the Word, and the Holy Ghost: **and these three are one**. (1 John 5:7, King James Version) And there are three that bear witness in earth, the Spirit, and the water, and the blood: and these three agree in one. (1 John 5:8, King James Version)*

*There are three that testify: (1 John 5:7, New Revised Standard Version) the Spirit and the water and the blood, and these three agree. (1 John 5:8, New Revised Standard Version)*

The difference in the translations is obvious and should need no further explanation. In the NRSV we are no longer told that the Father, the Word, and the Holy Ghost *"Are One"*.

# I AND THE FATHER "ARE ONE"?

*"I and the Father are one"* (John 10:30, KJV) does not necessarily have to be interpreted as meaning that the Jesus and the Father are of the same substance but could also mean that they are unified in purpose. Jesus in the subsequent verses was about to be stoned to death for uttering these words, but then explained, with reference to the old scriptures, that God Himself has called other people *'gods' (John 10:34, NIRV)*. In support of this claim the New International Reader's Version of the Bible makes direct reference to *(Psalm 82:6)*. In essence Jesus is saying *"I am not God"* and therefore is personally discounting the present day Trinitarian interpretation of the words *"I and the Father are one"*.

**Psalm 82:6**

*I have said, **Ye are gods; and all of you are children of the most High**. (Psalm 82:6 KJV)*

**John 10:30**

*I and my Father are one. (John 10:30, KJV)*
*Then the Jews took up stones again to stone him. (John 10:31, KJV)*

*Jesus answered them, Many good works have I shewed you from my Father; for which of those works do ye stone me? (John 10:32, KJV)*

*The Jews answered him, saying, For a good work we stone thee not; but for blasphemy; and because that thou, being a man, makest thyself God. (John 10:33, KJV)*

*Jesus answered them, Is it not written in your law, I said, Ye are gods? (John 10:34, KJV)*

*If he called them gods, unto whom the word of God came, and the scripture cannot be broken; (John 10:35, KJV)*

*Say ye of him, whom the Father hath sanctified, and sent into the world, Thou blasphemest; because I said, I am the Son of God? (John 10:36, KJV)*

# FATHER AND SON

By definition, a son has the qualities of his father, the daughter of her mother or the children of their parents. Hence, if the father is a mortal being then the son is a mortal being. Likewise, if for a moment we are willing to accept that Pharaoh was divine, as indeed clever Pharaoh suggested to his subjects, then the Son of Pharaoh should be divine. But if a Divine Father is Eternal how does one accept that His Son could be a mortal and Die? Also how could we accept that the Son and the Father are One (John 10:30, KJV) or as some would say that Jesus is Lord, if the Father is Greater than the Son (John 14:28, KJV)?

**I and my Father are one.** (John 10:30, King James Version)

*Ye have heard how I said unto you, I go away, and come [again] unto you. If ye loved me, ye would rejoice, because I said, I go unto the Father: for my **Father is greater than I.*** (John 14:28, KJV)

Using rational thought processes or reason one has no recourse but to question the validity of such logical inconsistencies. How could we accept the incomprehensible logic of a half mortal half divine being that is neither fully mortal nor fully divine?

If the Father is greater than the Son (John 14:28, KJV) then the relationship of the Father and Son is not as equals but rather that of God the Father being Divine and Eternal while the Son, a mortal being, a product of a miraculous Virgin Birth. As Mother Mary was mortal then we would expect her son to have a similar fate. In John 10:30 the Father and the Son are not one in essence but rather the narrator, figuratively speaking, was probably implying a oneness of purpose.

## WHATEVER HAPPENED TO HELL, HEAVEN OR SIN?

Let us imagine a story of a father who had two sons called Judas and Jim. Poor old Judas could not do anything without committing a sin while Jim was an exemplary son who did not know how to sin. The father admonished his son Judas to be good like his sinless son Jim. The father warned his son Judas, and even threatened with hell. Then the father seeing no hope for change in his son Judas planned forgiveness for all of his sins. The father thought that it would not serve justice to punish his son Judas and spare his son Jim, as he loved his son Judas just as much as his Jim. So somehow he decided to punish his other son Jim. The good son Jim reluctantly obeyed his father and took the blame for all of Judas's sins. Judas knowing that he would not be punished decides to help out his father in punishing Jim. Judas reassures all his other siblings and friends not to worry about sinning, as Jim has thoroughly suffered for their collective sins. Then we are compelled to believe in this account of the story to avoid burning in hell—with no chance of forgiveness for all of our sins. Can you imagine a more wonderful story about a loving father and redemption from sin? To take this story a little further can you imagine a loving father who would have no second thoughts in allowing his favorite son to be tortured and humiliated to save you and me? This account of the story about the father of Judas and Jim would not be condonable by most people unless we wish to accept a father who is sadistic beyond belief.

Surely as God prevented Abraham from killing his son he would not orchestrate such a horrific death for Jesus whom He sent to mend the ways of His wayward flock. Only a crucifixion with common criminals for the mobs to cheer might have been needed by the Romans and King Herod to keep the peace. Even the Biblical account of the story suggests that Jesus was not such a willing participant in the crucifixion scheme.

**Matthew 27:45-46 (King James Version):**

*Now from the sixth hour there was darkness over all the land unto the ninth hour (Matthew 27:45).*
*And about the ninth hour Jesus cried with a loud voice, saying, Eli, Eli, lama sabachthani? that is to say, My God, my God, why hast thou forsaken me? (Matthew 27:46).*

*Jesus, when he had cried again with a loud voice, yielded up the ghost (Matthew 27:50).*

مَا ٱتَّخَذَ ٱللَّهُ مِن وَلَدٍ وَمَا كَانَ مَعَهُ مِنْ إِلَٰهٍ إِذًا لَّذَهَبَ كُلُّ إِلَٰهٍ بِمَا خَلَقَ وَلَعَلَا بَعْضُهُمْ عَلَىٰ بَعْضٍ سُبْحَٰنَ ٱللَّهِ عَمَّا يَصِفُونَ ۝

*And their saying: "We killed Christ Jesus the son of Mary, the Apostle of God";—but **they killed him not, nor crucified him, but so it was made to appear to them, and those who differ therein are full of doubts, with no (certain) knowledge, but only conjecture to follow**, for of a surety they killed him not:—(Koran 4:157)*

عَٰلِمِ ٱلْغَيْبِ وَٱلشَّهَٰدَةِ فَتَعَٰلَىٰ عَمَّا يُشْرِكُونَ ۝

*Knower of the Invisible and the Visible and Exalted be He over all the partners they attribute to Him. (Koran 23:92)*

وَإِنَّ هَٰذِهِۦ أُمَّتُكُمْ أُمَّةً وَٰحِدَةً وَأَنَا۠ رَبُّكُمْ فَٱتَّقُونِ ۝

*And verily **this Brotherhood of yours is a single Brotherhood**, and I am your Lord and Cherisher: so keep your duty unto Me. (Koran 23:52).*

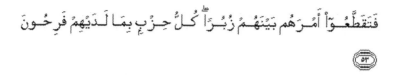

*But they (mankind) have broken their religion among them into sects, each party rejoicing in its tenets (Koran 23:53).*

*But leave them in their confused ignorance for a time (Koran 23:54).*

## GOD INCARNATE?

Before Jesus was born there could have been no Trinity, as the Old Testament does not discuss the existence of Jesus before his miraculous birth to the Virgin Mary. When Jesus was crucified and dead for three days there obviously could be no Trinity. Therefore, the Triune God concept could only exist during the life of Jesus and possibly after his resurrection. We are asked to believe that God created the confusing concept of the Trinity—where the true nature of Jesus cannot be explained. The Gospels did not explain the Triune nature of Jesus. The Church, but not God, has advised people to use faith, rather than reason, to accept this mysterious phenomenon. The truth requires logical analysis whereas faith only requires unquestionable acceptance. A raging debate led to convening the Council of Nicea in 325 AD where the concept of the Trinity was initially formalized during the reign of Constantine the Great.

Why would God have to perform a sacrifice to forgive us our sins? What happened to the concept of a simple pardon? Why couldn't God just forgive us by simply commuting our sentence if he so desired? Why would God allow one of His most worthless creations, Judas Iscariot to have the honor of performing the ultimate sacrifice? Symbolic human sacrifices vis a vis Abraham or real animal sacrifices vis a vis the Jews in the Old Testament were performed by honorable and God fearing people—not cowards and traitors.

The symbolic sacrifice where God commanded Abraham to sacrifice his son was a test of faith that is meant as an eternal message to humanity—our faith in God in one way or another will also be put to the test. Even if humanity is asked to obey God's seemingly incomprehensible commands God reassures us that He would never burden us with impossible tasks. The journey of life is meant to strengthen our faith in God for a higher purpose beyond this life. How unjust it would have been if God had allowed Abraham's son to be a sacrificed. Similarly how could God allow Jesus to bear our sins and become a sacrificial lamb? Animal sacrifices such as lambs in particular situations are not only a symbolic act of gratitude and appreciation towards our Provider but are also eaten as a form of sustenance. But what kind of spiritual sustenance could we as humans extract if God had truly sanctioned and condoned the sacrifice of Jesus vis a vis a crucifixion? According to the Biblical account Jesus questions the moment of his own crucifixion.

*And about the ninth hour Jesus cried with a loud voice, saying, Eli, Eli, lama sabachthani? that is to say, My God, my God, why hast thou forsaken me? (Matthew 27:46, KJV)*

Were we to accept that this momentous occasion was meant for the redemption of the collective soul of all humanity how can we be led to believe that Jesus would be kept in darkness about his role in this most significant of Divine decrees?

As Adam and Eve, Abraham, Isaac, Moses, David and Solomon did not preach the Trinity, the crux of a present day belief system, then did God really plan to be God Incarnate? How will God judge the generations that knew nothing about the Trinity especially when a present day belief system claims that there is no salvation without belief in a Triune God? Could the concept of a Triune God have not been propagated to scare the Jews and disbelievers of their times into following an institutionalized system or new world order purporting that there is only one road to salvation?

In the New Testament, Jesus did not explicitly say that he is God. Jesus did not even preach the Trinity in the Gospels. Or would someone maybe have us believe that it was part of a divine master design for Jesus not to directly and clearly respond to the questions posed to him in the Gospel of Luke-

**And many other things blasphemously spake they against him.**
And as soon as it was day, the elders of the people and the chief priests
and the scribes came together, and led him into their council, saying,
**Art thou the Christ? tell us.** *And he said unto them, If I tell you, ye will
not believe:*
*And if I also ask [you], ye will not answer me, nor let [me] go.*
*Hereafter shall the* **Son of man** *sit on the right hand of the power of
God.*
**Then said they all, Art thou then the Son of God? And he said unto
them, Ye say that I am.**
*And they said, What need we any further witness? for we ourselves have
heard of his own mouth. (Luke 22:65-71, KJV)*

Possibly Jesus refused to acknowledge that he was Christ because he
knew that his fate was sealed. The etymology of the word Christ literally
means the anointed one. (Etymology: Middle English Crist, from Old
English, from Latin Christus, from Greek Christos, literally, anointed).
Anointment is the application of oil for a sacred rite, divine election, or
consecration (to devote irrevocably to the worship of God by a solemn
ceremony—consecrate comes from com+ sacrare—Anglo-French sacrer).
Jesus knew that the *"chief priests"* were not willing to accept that he was a
prophet or the anointed one. Interestingly the Jews are still awaiting the
Messiah (savior). Jesus proceeds to describe himself as the *"Son of man"*
and not *"the Son of God"*.

The above encounter between Jesus and the chief priests, and scribes
could have been a golden opportunity for Jesus to testify to the world
about his supposed real identity. Jesus could have simply proclaimed that
he was a Triune God and then maybe no human could challenge the
authenticity of the Trinitarian concept. Was Jesus so afraid of his fate that
he dared not admit he was a Triune God? Probably the real *"blasphemy"*
was that the establishment wished to accuse Jesus of being a Triune
God (*"for we ourselves have heard of his own mouth"*) and therefore have
reasonable justification to crucify him alongside common criminals. The
word blasphemy means disrespect or irreverence to that which is sacred.
The only crime that Jesus, like prophets before him, committed was to
attempt and purify a corrupted people who followed their own selfish
desires rather than obey God's commandments.

Jesus would not even acknowledge the basic tenant of modern day Christianity that he was the Son of God and simply replied, *"Ye say that I am" to* the question, *"Art thou then the Son of God?"* **Also in the preceding verse Jesus had just described himself as the** *"Son of man"* **and not the** *"Son of God".*

Why did not Jesus while on the cross proclaim that he was here to die for our sins (and also that if we did not believe in the Triune God then there would be no salvation and we would perish)? Rather we are told in the Books of Mark and Matthew:

*And at the ninth hour Jesus cried with a loud voice, saying, Eloi, Eloi, lama sabachthani? which is, being interpreted, My God,* ***my God, why hast thou forsaken me?*** *(Mark 15:34, KJV)*

*And about the ninth hour Jesus cried with a loud voice, saying, Eli, Eli, lama sabachthani? that is to say, My God, my God, why hast thou forsaken me? (Matthew 27:46, KJV)*

One may also argue that Jesus in his human moment of doubt, as we all have moments of doubt, had a normal human fear of death as well as possibly a sense of an unaccomplished mission. However, we must remember that our death in this world, as difficult as it may seem, is a necessary transition for our resurrection. Resurrection into a new life is a covenant that God has made with his human creation just as God made and kept a covenant with the Jews, as mentioned in the Old Testament, as well as the Koran, that after they had become scattered all over the earth that they would then be gathered from all the nations to the land of Israel. Just as Abraham had faith to follow God's inscrutable decree to sacrifice his beloved son God is asking all humanity to have faith that the burdens of this life are part of a price that we must pay to earn the rights of passage—resurrection to a higher purpose and life eternal. Adam learned that the only shortcut to the gift of eternal life is thru obedience to God and not to our selfish desires. The symbolic eternal message of God through Adam's fall from heaven is that we will surely fall or fail unless we try to follow God's proscribed path to eternal salvation.

These stories of Adam and Abraham when interpreted literally make a good bedtime story but the deeper meaning is in the universal message that God is sending to all humanity—unwavering obedience to the supreme

Creator. Hence, God will only bestow honor on those who are worthy of his grace.

*And (We said): O Adam! Dwell you and your wife in the garden; so eat from where you desire, but do not go near this tree, for then you will be of the unjust. (Koran 7:19)*

*So We said: O Adam! This is an enemy to you and to your wife; therefore let him not drive you both forth from the garden so that you should be unhappy; (Koran 20:117)*

*But the devil made an evil suggestion to him; he said: O Adam! Shall I guide you to the tree of immortality and a kingdom that decays not? (Koran 20:120)*

*Then they both ate of it, so their evil inclinations became manifest to them, and they both began to cover themselves with leaves of the garden, and Adam disobeyed his Lord, so his life became evil (to him).(Koran 20:121)*

The tree of immortality is only assured by obeying God and not our own desires. Also lest not forget the destructive power of sibling jealousy/rivalry as with Cain and Abel or Joseph's eleven brothers. If we rebel like Noah's people, Lot's people, or Pharaoh then there will only be ignominy. A covenant with the Jews at the time of Moses was made conditional on resisting evil and for this they were delivered from Egypt to the land of Israel. Also if we try to resist temptation like the prophet Joseph *(Koran 12:24-29)* or the Virgin Mary *(Koran 66:12)* then as with their example we shall have a life of bliss in this world and the hereafter.

Jesus, unlike Jonas, had more faith and trust in God by not wavering or avoiding his responsibilities even at the moment of a seemingly horrible death. Jesus had a degree of faith whereby, unlike some of his disciples, he did not deny or betray God in the mission with which he was entrusted. Jesus like Abraham worked and lived for a noble cause and higher purpose that transcended the material temptations and distractions of a fleeting life. The spiritual core of these two great personalities is the essence of all scripture as their selfless sacrifice to God and humanity was their resounding achievement. Their legacy is one of exemplary humility and obedience to God.

Without critical examination of established belief systems then humanity will not move forward in understanding the superficial differences that divide us and thus leading to endless bigotry, hatred and suffering. There is nothing better than fear of the misunderstood or unknown to stir greedy and even down trodden peoples and societies to horrid atrocities that are committed under banners of nationalism or religion.

To some religion is an expedient belief system that fills a spiritual void, and is reinforced by social customs and traditions. Like an inherited heirloom some people are willing to believe in seemingly priceless belief systems with which they become so emotionally attached that they cannot depart.

# SEPTUAGINT LXX

Introduction to the Septuagint LXX by Sir Lancelot C.L. Brenton:

*The earliest version of the Old Testament Scriptures which is extant, or of which we possess any certain knowledge, is the translation executed at Alexandria in the third century before the Christian era: this version has been so habitually known by the name of the SEPTUAGINT, that the attempt of some learned men in modern times to introduce the designation of the Alexandrian version (as more correct) has been far from successful.*

**Introduction to the Septuagint LXX: Greek and English by Sir Lancelot C.L. Brenton, published by Samuel Bagster & Sons, Ltd., London, 1851**

Jewish scholars argue that the original Greek Septuagint from 300 to 200 B.C. only refers to the Pentateuch or first five books of the Old Testament. The Septuagint was translated from earlier Hebrew text that no longer exists. The Masoretic text is much newer and based on later Hebrew writings derived from Latin dating from about 600 to 900 A.D. The Septuagint and Masoretic texts have some similarities with some of the Hebrew Dead Sea scrolls. The Dead Sea Scrolls are dated to have been written during a period spanning from 300 BC to 68 AD.

## ISAIAH (ESAIAS) CHAPTER 7

*Therefore the Lord himself shall give you a sign; behold,* **a virgin shall conceive** *in the womb, and shall bring forth a son,* **and** *thou shalt* **call his name Emmanuel.** *(Isaiah (Esaias) 7:14, Septuagint)*

*Therefore the Lord Himself shall give you a sign: behold,* **the young woman shall conceive,** *and bear a son, and shall* **call his name Immanuel.** *(Isaiah 7:14, Today's New International Version)*

'Today's New International Version' or the 'Hebrew Bible' uses *"young woman"* instead of *"virgin"* as a possible translation for *Isaiah 7:14*. Also Jewish scriptures prefer *"young woman"* to dispel the possibility of a virgin birth. The virgin birth is only meant to strengthen the prophecy when it occurs rather than signify any special status of divinity. Adam had no mother or father and therefore it would be presumptuous to assume that Adam has any divine or supernatural status because of his 'supernatural birth'. *The Greek word "Parthenos" as found in the Septuagint is* commonly translated "virgin" by Christian scholars and *"young woman"* by Jewish scholars. However, in the Hebrew or Masoretic Text, the Hebrew word "alma" is translated "a young girl". The Koranic version relates the story as that of a virgin birth.

*"Emmanual" (Isaiah Chapter 7:14)* means *'God is with us'* which to Trinitarian Christian theologians would suggest that Jesus is God. However, this reference does not state that God is human or one of three or that Jesus is the 'son of God.' Rather a simple figurative expression could be inferred rather than the rigid literal interpretation that is so forcefully propagated. Surely God could have clarified this prophecy so that a clear reference to the Trinity and 'God Incarnate' would be unquestionable. Unfortunately, selective reasoning may argue any viewpoint to a senseless end.

## ISAIAH 9:6 (King James Version)

*For unto us a child is born, unto us a son is given: and the government shall be upon his shoulder:* **and his name shall be called Wonderful, Counsellor, The mighty God, The everlasting Father, The Prince of Peace.** *(Isaiah 9:6, King James Version)*

## ISAIAH 9:6 (Septuagint)

*For a child is born to us, and a son is given to us, whose government is upon his shoulder:* **and his name is called the Messenger of great counsel:** *for I will bring peace upon the princes, and health to him.* (**Isaiah 9:6, Septuagint**)

Trinitarian Christian theologians would argue, using the King James Version of the Bible, that Isaiah 9:6 is a reference to the coming of Jesus and that Jesus is 'God'. The only problem is that in the Trinitarian sense Jesus is not 'God' but is the 'son of God'. Also, the English translation of the Greek Septuagint does not lend credence to this concept, as this messenger is not described as *"The mighty God, The everlasting Father"* but only as *"the Messenger of great counsel"*.

# JESUS, JONAH & THE WHALE

*Jonas* is the Greek form of *Jonah (Easton's Bible Dictionary).* In the *Book of Matthew* Jesus is quoted as saying:

*But he answered and said unto them, An evil and adulterous generation seeketh after a sign; and there shall no sign be given to it, but* **the sign of the prophet Jonas: (Matthew 12:39) For as Jonas was three days and three nights in the whale's belly; so shall the Son of man be three days and three nights in the heart of the earth.** *(Matthew 12:40)*
*The men of Nineveh shall rise in judgment with this generation, and shall condemn it: because they repented at the preaching of Jonas; and, behold, a greater than Jonas [is] here. (Matthew 12:41,KJV)*

While Jesus presumably *"died"* for three days and three nights the analogy with the passages in the book of Jonah does not support this concept, as Jonas was not *"dead"* for three days and three nights. *"Then* **Jonah prayed unto the LORD his God out of the fish's belly,***"(Jonah 2: 1).*

## JONAH I

*Now the word of the LORD came unto Jonah the son of Amittai, saying, (Jonah 1:1)*
*Arise,* go to Nineveh, *that great city, and cry against it; for their wickedness is come up before me. (Jonah 1:2)*
But Jonah rose up to flee *unto Tarshish from the presence of the LORD, and went down to Joppa; and he found a ship going to Tarshish: so he paid the fare thereof, and went down into it, to go with them unto Tarshish from the presence of the LORD. (Jonah 1:3)*
*But the LORD sent out a great wind into the sea, and there was a mighty tempest in the sea, so that the ship was like to be broken. (Jonah 1:4)*
*Then the mariners were afraid, and cried every man unto his god, and cast forth the wares that [were] in the ship into the sea, to lighten [it] of them. But Jonah was gone down into the sides of the ship; and he lay, and was fast asleep. (Jonah 1:5)*
*So the shipmaster came to him, and said unto him, What meanest thou, O sleeper? arise, call upon thy God, if so be that God will think upon us, that we perish not. (Jonah 1:6)*
*And they said every one to his fellow, Come, and let us cast lots, that we may know for whose cause this evil [is] upon us. So they cast lots, and the lot fell upon Jonah. (Jonah 1:7)*
*Then said they unto him, Tell us, we pray thee, for whose cause this evil [is] upon us; What [is] thine occupation? and whence comest thou? what [is] thy country? and of what people [art] thou? (Jonah 1:8)*
*And he said unto them, I [am] an Hebrew; and I fear the LORD, the God of heaven, which hath made the sea and the dry [land]. (Jonah 1:9)*
*Then were the men exceedingly afraid, and said unto him, Why hast thou done this? For the men knew that he fled from the presence of the LORD, because he had told them. (Jonah 1:10)*

*Then said they unto him, What shall we do unto thee, that the sea may be calm unto us? for the sea wrought, and was tempestuous. (Jonah 1:11)*

*And he said unto them, Take me up, and cast me forth into the sea; so shall the sea be calm unto you: for I know that for my sake this great tempest [is] upon you. (Jonah 1:12)*

*Nevertheless the men rowed hard to bring [it] to the land; but they could not: for the sea wrought, and was tempestuous against them. (Jonah 1:13)*

*Wherefore they cried unto the LORD, and said, We beseech thee, O LORD, we beseech thee, let us not perish for this man's life, and lay not upon us innocent blood: for thou, O LORD, hast done as it pleased thee. (Jonah 1:14)*

So they took up Jonah, and cast him forth into the sea*: and the sea ceased from her raging. (Jonah 1:15)*

*Then the men feared the LORD exceedingly, and offered a sacrifice unto the LORD, and made vows. (Jonah 1:16)*

*Now the LORD had prepared a great fish to swallow up Jonah. And Jonah was in the belly of the fish three days and three nights. (Jonah 1:17, KJV)*

## JONAH 2

*Then Jonah prayed unto the LORD his God out of the fish's belly, (Jonah 2:1)*

*And said, I cried by reason of mine affliction unto the LORD, and he heard me; out of the belly of hell cried I, [and] thou heardest my voice. (Jonah 2:2)*

*For thou hadst cast me into the deep, in the midst of the seas; and the floods compassed me about: all thy billows and thy waves passed over me. (Jonah 2:3)*

*Then I said, I am cast out of thy sight; yet I will look again toward thy holy temple. (Jonah 2:4)*

*The waters compassed me about, [even] to the soul: the depth closed me round about, the weeds were wrapped about my head. (Jonah 2:5)*

*I went down to the bottoms of the mountains; the earth with her bars [was] about me for ever: yet hast thou brought up my life from corruption, O LORD my God. (Jonah 2:6)*

*When my soul fainted within me I remembered the LORD: and my prayer came in unto thee, into thine holy temple. (Jonah 2:7)*

*They that observe lying vanities forsake their own mercy. (Jonah 2:8)*

*But I will sacrifice unto thee with the voice of thanksgiving; I will pay [that] that I have vowed. Salvation [is] of the LORD. (Jonah 2:9)*

*And the LORD spake unto the fish, and it vomited out Jonah upon the dry [land]. (Jonah 2:10, KJV)*

# ORIGINAL SIN

Christian doctrine preaches that every human is born in a state of sin. *Original sin* is also known as *hereditary sin* or *birth sin*. Christians believe that the idea of original sin is born from *Adam* and *Eve's* original sin or *fall*. The concept whereby the *crucifixion of Jesus* is deemed necessary for the forgiveness of our sins is based on Christianity's concept of original sin. The proceeding *New Testament* quotations illustrate the aforementioned concept of *crucifixion*.

*In this was manifested the love of God toward us, because that **God sent his** only begotten **Son into the world, that we might live through him**. (1 John 4:9)*

*I am crucified with Christ: nevertheless I live; yet not I, but Christ liveth in me: and the life which I now live in the flesh I live by the faith of **the Son of God**, who loved me, and **gave himself for me**. (Galations 2:20)*

However, original sin was unknown to Moses and is unknown to Judaism. The Old Testament does not support the concept of original sin. According to the Old Testament Book of Ezekiel, *(Ezekiel 18:19-20 and 18:30)* we are all judged based on the consequences of our own actions. The learned Rabbis and Jews of the Old Testament times were not waiting for a Savior who would die for their sins.

*"Yet you ask, 'Why does the son not share the guilt of his father?' Since the son has done what is just and right and has been careful to keep all my decrees, he will surely live. (Ezekiel 18:19)*

*The soul who sins is the one who will die. **The son will not share the guilt of the father**, nor will the father share the guilt of the son. The righteousness of the righteous man will be credited to him, and the wickedness of the wicked will be charged against him. (Ezekiel 18:20)*

*"Therefore, O house of Israel, I will judge you, each one according to his ways, declares the Sovereign LORD. Repent! Turn away from all your offenses; then sin will not be your downfall." (Ezekiel 18:30)*

Hence, to the Jews there is no concept of original sin or a need for God to sacrifice a son to forgive us our sins. Also, in Islam, there is no concept of original sin and individuals are judged based on their deeds. God forgives Adam and Eve after they repent *(Koran 2:37)*.

فَتَلَقَّىٰٓ ءَادَمُ مِن رَّبِّهِۦ كَلِمَٰتٍ فَتَابَ عَلَيۡهِ إِنَّهُۥ هُوَ ٱلتَّوَّابُ ٱلرَّحِيمُ ﴿٣٧﴾

*"Then Adam received from his Lord words (of revelation), and He relented toward him. Lo! He is the relenting, the Merciful." (Koran 2:37)*

قُلۡ أَغَيۡرَ ٱللَّهِ أَبۡغِى رَبًّا وَهُوَ رَبُّ كُلِّ شَيۡءٍۚ وَلَا تَكۡسِبُ كُلُّ نَفۡسٍ إِلَّا عَلَيۡهَاۚ وَلَا تَزِرُ وَازِرَةٌ وِزۡرَ أُخۡرَىٰۚ ثُمَّ إِلَىٰ رَبِّكُم مَّرۡجِعُكُمۡ فَيُنَبِّئُكُم بِمَا كُنتُمۡ فِيهِ تَخۡتَلِفُونَ ﴿١٦٤﴾

*"Say: Shall I seek another than God for Lord, when He is Lord of all things?* **Each soul earneth only on its own account,** *nor doth any laden bear another's load. Then unto your Lord is your return and He will tell you that wherein ye differed." (Koran 6:164)*

## COUNCIL OF NICEA

**Arius** was a Christian who **believed in One God** and did not accept the Trinitarian concept. His followers known as Arians did not believe that Jesus could logically co-exist with God. Constantine the Great died believing in One God.

In 325 A.D. The Nicene council decided that Arius was to be banished by Constantine the Great. But Emperor Constantine reconsidered and decided to recall Arius. On the day of his return Arius mysteriously died. Constantine the Great accepted Arianism and banished Athanasius, the Trinitarian, who was a proponent of God the Incarnate, to exile. Constantine's son Constantius followed Arian Christianity. However, eventually the Council of Nicea, that Constantine the Great had convened and later rejected, became the defining moment of Christianity, as we know it today.

Other debatable topics include the *'hidden'* books or *apocrypha*. *The Gospel of Barnabas* is one of these books apparently quoted by Iranaeus. *The Gospel of Barnabas* is mentioned in the Gelasian Decree and the List of Sixty Books.

**Nestorianism** is a belief that Christ consisted of **two separate persons**, one human and one divine. Nestorius, c.386–451 A.D., Patriarch of Constantinople, did not recognize that the Virgin Mary was the mother of God since this would compromise Jesus Christ's divinity.

The **Council of Chalcedon** in 451 A.D. defined Jesus Christ to be **one person** in two perfect **natures**, one divine (Son of God) and one human (Son of Mary). The two natures of Jesus (divine and human) were united as the single person of the Trinity.

The **Monophysites**, rejected this Chalcedonian definition and affirmed that there was *'one nature'*. Monophysite churches are still found today; the Coptic Orthodox Church of Egypt is a Monophysite Church. Derived from Greek *'monos'* means *'one'* and *'physis'* means *'nature'* is the belief that Christ has only one nature.

## POPE HONORIUS I

Pope Honorius I (625–638 A.D.) was anathematized or denounced after his death by the Sixth Ecumenical Council, the Third Council of Constantinople, in 680–681 A.D. Pope Honorius I was condemned as a heretic because he disputed a doctrinal question relating to God the incarnate. Although the Catholic Church believes otherwise it would seem that Papal infallibility, which is usually guided by the Holy Spirit, somehow went wrong.

يَـٰٓأَهۡلَ ٱلۡكِتَـٰبِ لَا تَغۡلُواْ فِى دِينِكُمۡ وَلَا تَقُولُواْ عَلَى ٱللَّهِ إِلَّا ٱلۡحَقَّ إِنَّمَا ٱلۡمَسِيحُ عِيسَى ٱبۡنُ مَرۡيَمَ رَسُولُ ٱللَّهِ وَكَلِمَتُهُۥٓ أَلۡقَىٰهَآ إِلَىٰ مَرۡيَمَ وَرُوحٌ مِّنۡهُ فَـَٔامِنُواْ بِٱللَّهِ وَرُسُلِهِۦ وَلَا تَقُولُواْ ثَلَـٰثَةٌ ٱنتَهُواْ خَيۡرًا لَّكُمۡ إِنَّمَا ٱللَّهُ إِلَـٰهٌ وَٰحِدٌ سُبۡحَـٰنَهُۥٓ أَن يَكُونَ لَهُۥ وَلَدٌ لَّهُۥ مَا فِى ٱلسَّمَـٰوَٰتِ وَمَا فِى ٱلۡأَرۡضِ وَكَفَىٰ بِٱللَّهِ وَكِيلًا ۝

*O people of the Book do not exceed the limits in your religion, nor say of God aught but the truth. The Messiah Jesus son of Mary, was a Messenger of God and His Word, which He bestowed on Mary and a spirit created by Him; so believe in God and His Messengers.* **Say not: "Three (trinity)" Cease, it is better for you.** *For God is One God, Glory be to Him above having a son. To Him belongs all that is in the heavens and all that is in the earth. And God is All Sufficient as a Disposer of affairs. (Koran 4:171)*

## EPISTLE TO THE HEBREWS

The *Epistle to the Hebrews* in the *New Revised Standard Version (NRSV 1989 A.D.)* of the Bible is entitled *"Letter to the Hebrews"* while in the *Authorized King James Version (1611 A.D.)* it is entitled *"The **Epistle of Paul** the Apostle to the Hebrews."* The religious scholars of the *NRSV* probably decided to leave out Paul as the definitive author of the Epistle to the Hebrews as it is well known that its *"language and style vary in many particulars from the grammatical form of the other letters of Paul"(Catholic Encyclopedia).* Throughout history the authorship of the Epistle to the Hebrews has been debated.

# CALVINISM AND UNITARIANISM

## CALVINISTS

**John Calvin** (1509–64) spread the idea that salvation could only be achieved thru the grace of a Trinitarian God. Good works did not matter and crimes would be forgiven as long as reason was substituted with blind faith in the Trinity.

## UNITARIANS

**Jospeh Priestly** (1733–1804) rejected the Trinity and was persecuted for his ideas having to leave England and immigrate to the United States where he was welcomed. He wrote a book called History of Corruptions of Christianity (1782) where he believed Greek thought corrupted the original teachings of Christianity. Unitarians reject the Trinity or that Jesus is God as he never proclaimed, "I am God" and instead believe Jesus is human. John Priestly was also a chemist who isolated and described the properties of carbon dioxide, nitrous oxide (laughing gas), and oxygen. He invented soda pop and discovered that India gum could be used to erase lead pencil marks. John Adams, the second president of the United States, attended his sermons and rejected the Trinity. Jared Sparks a Unitarian contemporary of John Adams was president of Harvard. Unitarians could not accept that three are one, and one is three; and yet that the one is not three, and the three are not one. Likewise, Thomas Jefferson who wrote the Declaration of Independence and was the third president of the United State did not accept the Trinity and edited a new Christian Bible called the Jefferson Bible. Unitarians and Unitarian Churches are still present to this day.

# MITHRAISM AND ZOROASTRIANISM

*Then he said unto me, Have you seen this, O son of man?* ***Turn yet again and you will see greater abominations than these*** *. . . at the door of the temple of the Lord, between the door of the altar, were twenty five men, with* *their backs toward the temple of the Lord and their faces toward the east, and* **they worshipped the sun toward the east** *(Ezekiel 8:15-16, KJV).*

When Constantine the Great became Emperor, the main religion of the Roman Empire was **Mithraism**. The mythical birth date of the solar **sun god Mithra** was December 25. The feast of Sol Invicta (the unconquered sun) was honored by Roman soldiers on December 25 at the end of the winter solstice (shortest day of the year). December 25 was called Brumalia, dies natalis solis invicti or birthday of the unconquered sun. This lengthening of the day represented a victory of light over darkness. The day of the sun, **Sunday (Deis Solis)**, was a day of rest. The Sun god was minted on Roman coins, during the reign of Constantine the Great, with the Latin inscription SOLI INVICTO COMITI (To the invincible sun, a companion).

Christmas and Sunday were not a Church holidays during the time of the apostles. Constantine the Great in his attempt to consolidate these two main religions of his time created harmony in the land by continuing to observe December 25 as a major holiday and Sunday as a day of rest. Mithra originated with the Persians and is also mentioned in the Hindu scripture the Vedas. Later on Mithra survived in the **Zoroastrian** religion of Persia. In contrast, the Egyptian Orthodox *'Coptic'* Christians and the Russian Orthodox Church celebrate the birth of Jesus Christ on January 7.

## PAUL (SAUL)

*Saul or Shaul* is the Jewish name of *St. Paul or Paul. Saul (Paul)* was a member of a Jewish sect called the *Pharisees (Acts 26:5).*

*My manner of life from my youth, which was at the first among mine own nation at Jerusalem, know all the Jews; (Acts 26:4)*
*Which knew me from the beginning, if they would testify, that after the most straitest sect of our religion I lived a* Pharisee. *(Acts 26:5)*

Paul and Deception:

In *1 Corinthians* Paul clearly implies that the end justifies the means but one may ask is deceit the mark of a prophet or apostle?

*For though I be free from all [men], yet have I made myself servant unto all, that I might gain the more. (1 Corinthians 9:19)*

*And* unto the Jews I became as a Jew, that I might gain the Jews; to them that are under the law, as under the law, that I might gain them that are under the law; *(1 Corinthians 9:20)*

To them that are without law, as without law, *(being not without law to God, but under the law to Christ,)* that I might gain them that are without law. *(1 Corinthians 9:21)*

*To the weak became I as weak, that I might gain the weak:* I am made all things to all [men], *that I might by all means save some. (1 Corinthians 9:22)*

*And this I do for the gospel's sake, that I might be partaker thereof with [you]. (1 Corinthians 9:23)*

**Contrast this modus operandi of Paul *"the apostle"* with his own words in *2 Corinthians*:**

*For such [are] false apostles, deceitful workers, transforming themselves into the apostles of Christ. (2 Corinthians 11:13)*

*And no marvel; for Satan himself is transformed into an angel of light. (2 Corinthians 11:14)*

*For our exhortation [was] not of deceit, nor of uncleanness, nor in guile: (1 Thessalonians 2:3)*

*But have renounced the hidden things of dishonesty, not walking in craftiness, nor handling the word of God deceitfully; but by manifestation of the truth commending ourselves to every man's conscience in the sight of God. (2 Corinthians 4:2)*

Or Jeremiah:

**Cursed [be] he that doeth the work of the LORD deceitfully,** . . . *(Jeremiah 48:10)*

So one must ask does God at any time accept deceit in matters of religion and faith? Is there a high standard of absolute truthfulness or morality that transcends all times and to which all apostles must abide. Did Paul meet this standard?

## Paul's Moment Of Conversion

**We note two differing accounts of Paul's conversion in *Acts 9* and *Acts 22*.**

# ACTS 9

*And Saul, yet breathing out threatenings and slaughter against the disciples of the Lord, went unto the high priest, (Acts 9:1)*
*And desired of him letters to Damascus to the synagogues, that if he found any of this way, whether they were men or women, he might bring them bound unto Jerusalem . (Acts 9:2)*
*And as he journeyed, he came near Damascus:* and suddenly there shined round about him a light from heaven*: (Acts 9:3)*
*And he fell to the earth,* and heard a voice saying unto him, *Saul, Saul, why persecutest thou me? (Acts 9:4)*
*And he said, Who art thou, Lord? And the Lord said, I am Jesus whom thou persecutest: [it is] hard for thee to kick against the pricks. (Acts 9:5)*
*And he trembling and astonished said, Lord, what wilt thou have me to do? And the Lord [said] unto him, Arise, and go into the city, and it shall be told thee what thou must do.*(Acts 9:6)
*And* the men which journeyed with him stood speechless, hearing a voice, but seeing no man. *(Acts 9:7)*
*And Saul arose from the earth; and when his eyes were opened, he saw no man: but they led him by the hand, and brought [him] into Damascus. (Acts 9:8)*
*And he was three days without sight, and neither did eat nor drink. (Acts 9:9)*
*And there was a certain disciple at Damascus, named Ananias; and to him said the Lord in a vision, Ananias. And he said, Behold, I [am here], Lord. (Acts 9:10, KJV)*

# ACTS 22

*Men, brethren, and fathers, hear ye my defence [which I make] now unto you. (Acts 22:1)*

*(And when they heard that he spake in the Hebrew tongue to them, they kept the more silence: and he saith,) (Acts 22:2)*

*I am verily a man [which am] a Jew, born in Tarsus, [a city] in Cilicia, yet brought up in this city at the feet of Gamaliel, [and] taught according to the perfect manner of the law of the fathers, and was zealous toward God, as ye all are this day. (Acts 22:3)*

*And I persecuted this way unto the death, binding and delivering into prisons both men and women. (Acts 22:4)*

*As also the high priest doth bear me witness, and all the estate of the elders: from whom also I received letters unto the brethren, and went to Damascus, to bring them which were there bound unto Jerusalem, for to be punished. (Acts 22:5)*

*And it came to pass, that, as I made my journey, and was come nigh unto Damascus about noon,* **suddenly there shone from heaven a great light round about me.** *(Acts 22:6)*

**And I fell unto the ground, and heard a voice** *saying unto me, Saul, Saul, why persecutest thou me? (Acts 22:7)*

*And I answered,* **Who art thou, Lord? And he said unto me, I am Jesus of Nazareth,** *whom thou persecutest. (Acts 22:8)*

**And they that were with me saw indeed the light, and were afraid; but they heard not the voice of him that spake to me.** *(Acts 22:9)*

*And I said, What shall I do, Lord? And the Lord said unto me, Arise, and go into Damascus; and there it shall be told thee of all things which are appointed for thee to do. (Acts 22:10)*

*And when I could not see for the glory of that light, being led by the hand of them that were with me, I came into Damascus. (Acts 22:11)*

*And one Ananias, a devout man according to the law, having a good report of all the Jews which dwelt [there], (Acts 22:12)*

*Came unto me, and stood, and said unto me, Brother Saul, receive thy sight. And the same hour I looked up upon him. (Acts 22:13)*

*And he said, The God of our fathers hath chosen thee, that thou shouldest know his will, and see that Just One, and shouldest hear the voice of his mouth. (Acts 22:14)*

If we contrast these two versions of Paul's moment of conversion (1) *"And the men which journeyed with him stood speechless, **hearing a voice**, but seeing no man" (Acts 9:7)* with (2) *"And they that were with me **saw indeed the light**, and were afraid; **but they heard not the voice** of him that spake to me" (Acts 22:9)* we are left with two contradictory statements that are difficult to explain. Did his companions hear or not hear the voice?
**In his *"moment of truth"* Paul sees a light:**

*"And as he journeyed, he came near Damascus: and suddenly there shined round about him a light from heaven:" (Acts 9:3)*

However, Paul contradicts his own words:

*"For such [are] false apostles, deceitful workers, transforming themselves into the apostles of Christ (2 Corinthians 11:13) And no marvel; for Satan himself is transformed into an angel of light." (2 Corinthians 11:14)*

Is seeing light a good or a bad thing? Did Paul inadvertently pass judgment upon himself?
After reading and studying the above passages can anyone reasonably trust Paul?

**Jesus on telling the truth:**

*Ye are of [your] father the devil, and the lusts of your father ye will do. He was a murderer from the beginning, and abode not in the truth, because there is no truth in him. When he speaketh a lie, he speaketh of his own: for he is a liar, and the father of it. (John 8:44)*

وَدَّت طَّآئِفَةٌ مِّنَ أَهْلِ ٱلْكِتَٰبِ لَوْ يُضِلُّونَكُمْ وَمَا يُضِلُّونَ إِلَّآ أَنفُسَهُمْ وَمَا يَشْعُرُونَ ۞

*It is the wish of a section of the People of the Book (Jews and Christians) to lead you astray. **But they shall lead astray (Not you), but themselves, and they do not perceive. (Koran 3:69)***

وَمَنْ أَظْلَمُ مِمَّنِ افْتَرَىٰ عَلَى اللَّهِ كَذِبًا أَوْ قَالَ أُوحِيَ إِلَيَّ وَلَمْ يُوحَ

إِلَيْهِ شَيْءٌ وَمَن قَالَ سَأُنزِلُ مِثْلَ مَا أَنزَلَ اللَّهُ وَلَوْ تَرَىٰ إِذِ

الظَّالِمُونَ فِي غَمَرَاتِ الْمَوْتِ وَالْمَلَائِكَةُ بَاسِطُوا أَيْدِيهِمْ أَخْرِجُوا

أَنفُسَكُمُ الْيَوْمَ تُجْزَوْنَ عَذَابَ الْهُونِ بِمَا كُنتُمْ تَقُولُونَ عَلَى اللَّهِ غَيْرَ

الْحَقِّ وَكُنتُمْ عَنْ آيَاتِهِ تَسْتَكْبِرُونَ ۝

*And who can be more unjust than he who invents a lie against God, or says: "I have received inspiration," whereas he is not inspired in anything;* and who says, "I will reveal the like of what God has revealed." And if you could but see when the unjust are in the confusion of death, while the angels are stretching forth their hands (saying): "Yield up your souls! This day you shall be recompensed with the torment of degradation because of what you used to utter against God other than the truth. And you used to scornfully reject His signs" (Koran 6:93)

## RESURRECTION OF JESUS?

Isaiah 52 does not mention the resurrection but is considered by Christian scholars to promote the idea of Jesus dying for our sins. Although there is a hint of this there is no mention of the resurrection or the Trinity. The Old Testament did not develop the concept of original sin early on so we have to ask did God change His modus operandi? The resurrection is not mentioned in the Old Testament and we must ask is it a true historical event? Why was Jesus not resurrected for the whole world to see—including Pontius Pilate and King Herod? Hence, if we can break away with preconceived ideas we can begin to see other possibilities. Furthermore, Isaiah 52:13 has a striking resemblance to the Koranic verse 158 in chapter 4.

## Isaiah 52

*See, my servant will act wisely; **he will be raised and lifted up** and highly exalted. (Isaiah 52:13, Today's New International Version)*

بَل رَّفَعَهُ ٱللَّهُ إِلَيْهِ وَكَانَ ٱللَّهُ عَزِيزًا حَكِيمًا ﴿١٥٨﴾

*Nay,* **God raised him up unto Himself;** *and God was ever Mighty, Wise (Koran 4:158)*

We should note that prophet Muhammad did not have access to all these present day translations of the Bible yet there is a truth that is unfolding from all this confusion. The reader by now should be well versed in some of the inconsistencies of different Biblical translations not to mention internal Biblical logical contradictions such as demonstrated in Paul's vision and his justification of being deceitful. So how can anyone reconcile the present day Biblical scripture with the Koranic version? The Koran supplies the answer:

فَوَيْلٌ لِّلَّذِينَ يَكْتُبُونَ ٱلْكِتَـٰبَ بِأَيْدِيهِمْ ثُمَّ يَقُولُونَ هَـٰذَا مِنْ عِندِ ٱللَّهِ لِيَشْتَرُوا۟ بِهِۦ ثَمَنًا قَلِيلًا فَوَيْلٌ لَّهُم مِّمَّا كَتَبَتْ أَيْدِيهِمْ وَوَيْلٌ لَّهُم مِّمَّا يَكْسِبُونَ ﴿٧٩﴾

***Therefore woe be unto those who write the Scripture with their hands and then say, "This is from God,"*** *that they may purchase a small gain therewith. Woe unto them for that their hands have written, and woe unto them for that they earn thereby. (Koran 2:79)*

Surely there was a sense of remorse after the crucifixion of Jesus. After all even if someone makes certain statements that is no justification for cold-blooded murder. Once a crime is committed there is usually guilt; perhaps this may explain the evolutionary concept of a Jesus who did not die in vain but rather died for our sins. Hence, the idea of a demigod developed to lend credence to the concept of 'forgiveness of our sins'. The self-forgiveness for the collective sin of those who participated directly or indirectly in this awful crime could bring some kind of closure. Hence, humanity could somehow reach some sort of inner peace and in this way seek forgiveness from God.

## Origin Of The Christmas Tree?

*"Hear ye the word which the Lord speaketh unto you, O house of Israel: Thus saith the Lord,* **Learn not the way of the heathen**, *and be not dismayed at the signs of heaven; for the heathen are dismayed at them. For* **the customs of the people are vain: for one cutteth a tree out of the forest, the work of the hands of the workman, with the ax. They deck it with silver and with gold;** *they fasten it with nails and with hammers, that it move not.* **(Bible, Jeremiah 10:1-9, KJV)**

The above Biblical quotation is only meant to illustrate that certain customs and traditions may become incorporated into religions and possibly take on more significance than they deserve replacing the true spirit of God and religious scriptures. Should one cut 'living' trees for no meaningful purpose? Maybe the above verse is meant to raise our awareness to 'customs' that are 'vain' so that we may always examine our 'way of life' in the hope of finding meaning and purpose in all the goals that we strive to achieve.

# Knowledge & Science In The Koran

Presently we will explore signs that the Koran imparted detailed information in the sciences and other realms of knowledge that was well beyond its time. If the knowledge and science in the message is not possibly consistent with a certain period of time then we should take note that this person is not speaking of his own authority but rather on the authority of a Higher Power. To this end we will analyze the knowledge revealed to us in scripture to determine if the message and the messenger are truly genuine. This journey is laborious but a rewarding process as it will lead us to connect with our Creator; a Creator who has given us life and the means of sustenance.

## ALCOHOL

يَتَأَيُّهَا ٱلَّذِينَ ءَامَنُوا لَا تَقْرَبُوا ٱلصَّلَوٰةَ وَأَنتُمْ سُكَرَىٰ حَتَّىٰ تَعْلَمُوا مَا

تَقُولُونَ وَلَا جُنُبًا إِلَّا عَابِرِى سَبِيلٍ حَتَّىٰ تَغْتَسِلُوا وَإِن كُنتُم مَّرْضَىٰ أَوْ

عَلَىٰ سَفَرٍ أَوْ جَآءَ أَحَدٌ مِّنكُم مِّنَ ٱلْغَآئِطِ أَوْ لَٰمَسْتُمُ ٱلنِّسَآءَ فَلَمْ تَجِدُوا

مَآءً فَتَيَمَّمُوا صَعِيدًا طَيِّبًا فَٱمْسَحُوا بِوُجُوهِكُمْ وَأَيْدِيكُمْ إِنَّ ٱللَّهَ كَانَ

عَفُوًّا غَفُورًا ﴿٤٣﴾

*O you who believe! Approach not the prayer when you are in a drunken state until you know the meaning of what you utter . . . . . (Koran 4:43)*

يَسْـَٔلُونَكَ عَنِ ٱلْخَمْرِ وَٱلْمَيْسِرِ ۖ قُلْ فِيهِمَآ إِثْمٌ كَبِيرٌ وَمَنَٰفِعُ لِلنَّاسِ
وَإِثْمُهُمَآ أَكْبَرُ مِن نَّفْعِهِمَا ۗ وَيَسْـَٔلُونَكَ مَاذَا يُنفِقُونَ قُلِ ٱلْعَفْوَ ۗ كَذَٰلِكَ
يُبَيِّنُ ٱللَّهُ لَكُمُ ٱلْأَيَٰتِ لَعَلَّكُمْ تَتَفَكَّرُونَ ﴿٢١٩﴾

*They ask you concerning intoxicants (alcoholic drink) and gambling. Say: "In them is a great sin, and (some) benefit for men, but the sin of them is greater than their benefit."... (Koran 2:219)*

إِنَّمَا يُرِيدُ ٱلشَّيْطَٰنُ أَن يُوقِعَ بَيْنَكُمُ ٱلْعَدَٰوَةَ وَٱلْبَغْضَآءَ فِى ٱلْخَمْرِ
وَٱلْمَيْسِرِ وَيَصُدَّكُمْ عَن ذِكْرِ ٱللَّهِ وَعَنِ ٱلصَّلَوٰةِ ۖ فَهَلْ أَنتُم مُّنتَهُونَ ﴿٩١﴾

**Satan wants only to excite enmity and hatred between you with intoxicants** *and gambling, and hinder you from the remembrance of God and from prayer.* **So, will you not then abstain?** *(Koran 5:91)*

Alcohol may impair judgment leading to arguments and fights between friends. As noted above the Koran states *"Satan wants only to excite enmity and hatred between you with intoxicants"* . . .

The medical adverse effects of alcohol, on the liver, range from inflammation *(alcoholic hepatitis)* to scarring *(liver cirrhosis)*. Also, alcohol may cause esophageal varices that may bleed profusely. Alcohol may cause alcohol withdrawal seizures, and delerium tremens or *D.T.'s*. Alcohol impairs bone marrow resulting in decreased and impaired platelets or white blood cells with accompanying decreased immunity against infection as well as an increased bleeding tendency. Alcohol can affect the brain and heart. The increased likelihood of a fall may result in an intracranial bleed *(subdural hematomas)* while drunk driving also has its obvious consequences. Scientists now know that a little alcohol is beneficial in that it may have a favorable effect on the cholesterol profile; although even a little alcohol can increase the risk of breast cancer in women.

The cost of treating alcoholics and their medical complications as well as lost productivity due to absenteeism is certainly a burden to society. Clearly, the individual and collective societal ill effects of alcohol outweigh its benefits. As noted above the author of the Koran states that alcohol could have favorable human effects but that its unfavorable effects outweigh its usefulness.

# BIG BANG

أَوَلَمْ يَرَ ٱلَّذِينَ كَفَرُوٓاْ أَنَّ ٱلسَّمَٰوَٰتِ وَٱلْأَرْضَ كَانَتَا رَتْقًا فَفَتَقْنَٰهُمَا ۖ وَجَعَلْنَا مِنَ ٱلْمَآءِ كُلَّ شَىْءٍ حَىٍّ ۚ أَفَلَا يُؤْمِنُونَ ﴿٣٠﴾

*Have not those who disbelieve known that **the heavens and the earth were joined together as one united piece, then We parted them?** And We have made from water every living thing. Will they not then believe? (Koran 21:30)*

The three criteria needed to support the big bang theory were (1) expansion of the universe (2) cosmic background radiation (3) and primordial helium such as deuterium. Today these predictions are known facts that support the big bang as being the origin of the universe.

## Expanding Universe

Aleksander Friedmann and Georges Lemaitre were the two prominent scientists who essentially proposed the Big Bang Theory. Albert Einstein initially believed in a static universe and rejected Friedman's and Lemaitre's theory but later revised his own thinking based on Hubble's discoveries.

**Edwin Hubble** made the observation that the universe is continuously expanding. Hubble discovered that distant galaxies are not stationary but are, in fact, moving away from one another. In 1929, he discovered that a galaxy's velocity is proportional to its distance. Galaxies that are twice as far from us move twice as fast. Another consequence is that the **universe is expanding in every direction. This observation means that it has taken every galaxy the same amount of time to move from a common**

**starting position to its current position**. Hubble's observations provided the foundation of the Big Bang theory while the Big Bang provided the foundation of the universe.

The equation generally used to show the **age of the universe** is:
*(distance of a particular galaxy)/(that galaxy's velocity) = (time) or*

*4.6 x 10^26 cm/1 x 10^9 cm/sec = 4.6 x 10^17 sec*

This equation, equaling 4.6 x 10^17 seconds, comes out to be approximately **fifteen billion years**. This calculation is almost exactly the same for every galaxy that can be studied.

## Cosmic Background (CMB) Radiation

The early universe should have been very hot and **cosmic background (CMB) radiation** is the remnant heat leftover from the Big Bang. In 1965 Arno Penzias and Robert Wilson won the Nobel Prize for discovering CMB radiation.

The **radiation** did not originate from one location but instead **came from all directions at once.** The detection, from the farthest reaches of the universe, of the left over radioactivity after the initial explosion further supported the Big Bang. In the Big Bang energy and matter were created; also space is expanding with matter creating space.

NASA's COBE satellite launched November 18, 1989 was able to detect cosmic microwaves emanating from the outer reaches of the universe via the Far Infrared Absolute Spectrophotometer (FIRAS). In 1992, the COBE team published their discovery of fluctuations in this radiation. The cosmic microwave background (CMB) spectrum had a temperature of 2.725 +/-0.002 K. This observation matched the predictions of the hot Big Bang theory extraordinarily well, and indicated that nearly all of the radiant energy of the Universe was released within the first year after the Big Bang *(Big Bang Theory Passes Test, January 7, 1993, Paula Cleggett-Haleim, Headquarters, Washington, D.C. Randee Exler, Goddard Space Flight Center, Greenbelt, Md.).* These microwaves were remarkably uniform which illustrated the homogeneity of the early stages of the universe. However, the satellite also discovered that as the universe began to cool and was still expanding, small fluctuations began to exist due to temperature differences. These fluctuations verified prior calculations of the possible cooling and development of the universe just fractions of a second after its creation. These fluctuations in the universe provided a more detailed description of the first moments after the Big Bang.

Recently, the **Nobel Prize in Physics for 2006** was awarded jointly to **John C. Mather** NASA Goddard Space Flight Center, Greenbelt, MD, USA, and **George F. Smoot** University of California, Berkeley, CA, USA *"for their discovery of the blackbody form and anisotropy of the cosmic microwave background radiation".* On the Noble (Prize) Foundation website we read: *"The COBE results provided increased support for the Big Bang scenario for the origin of the Universe, as this is the only scenario that predicts the kind of cosmic microwave background radiation measured by COBE."*

NASA's *Microwave Anisotropy Probe (MAP),* launched June 30, 2001, is an attempt to map the Big Bang remnant by measuring the temperature of the cosmic background radiation. *(http://map.gsfc.nasa.gov/m_mm.html).*

## Primordial Helium

In 1995 scientists using NASA's Astro-2 observatory, which was operated in the payload bay of the Space Shuttle Endeavour, **detected *primordial helium***, such as deuterium, in the far reaches of the universe. These findings are consistent with an important aspect of the Big Bang theory that a mixture of hydrogen and helium was created at the beginning of the universe. Hydrogen (H2) is the single commonest element in the universe.

Until about 200,000 years after the big bang, the hydrogen in the universe was fully ionized, and opaque. After about one to three minutes had passed since the creation of the universe, **protons and neutrons began to react with each other to form deuterium, an isotope of hydrogen**. Deuterium, or heavy hydrogen, soon collected another neutron to form tritium. **Rapidly following this reaction was the addition of another proton that produced a helium nucleus**. Scientists believe that there was **one helium nucleus for every ten protons** within the first three minutes of the universe. About 200,000 years after the big bang, when the temperature decreased to about 3000 Kelvin, excess protons were able to capture an electron to create neutral hydrogen (H2), a colorless, transparent gas. The **universe today is observed to contain one helium atom for every ten or eleven atoms of hydrogen.**

## DEFINITIONS
**Deuterium** = proton + neutron.

**Helium nucleus** = two protons and two neutrons.

**Helium gas** = two protons, two neutrons and two electrons.

**Hydrogen nucleus** = a proton.

**Hydrogen atom** = proton + electron.

**Hydrogen gas (H2)** = two hydrogen atoms.

## SMOKEY HEAVENS

ثُـــمَّ ٱسْتَوَىٰٓ إِلَـــى ٱلسَّـــمَآءِ وَهِـــىَ دُخَـــانٌ فَقَـــالَ لَهَـــا
وَلِلْأَرْضِ ٱئْتِيَا طَوْعًا أَوْ كَرْهًا قَالَتَآ أَتَيْنَا طَآئِعِينَ ⑪

*Then He rose over towards the **heaven when it was smoke**, and said to it and to the earth: "Come both of you willingly or unwillingly." They both said: "We come, willingly." (Koran 41:11)*

Immediately after the Big Bang when the universe was in its infancy there was a state of smoke. The gaseous state of smoke is an accurate description.

Today we know that the Milky Way Galaxy is filled with *clouds of gas and dust*. These clouds appear as black regions or as glowing nebula when illuminated by stars. The *interstellar medium*, mainly filled with hydrogen gas, incorporates microscopic *dust grains. Interstellar dust grains* collect along with interstellar hydrogen gas to form *Interstellar dust clouds* The *dust or tiny grains are the size of 'smoke' particles.* Interstellar dust grains are composed of clumps of atoms and molecules that are microscopic measuring 10 ^–5 making them comparable in size to smoke or soot. The gas fills most of the volume of the cloud but the dust is what makes them opaque. Dust has played an important role in star formation throughout much of cosmic history.

Interstellar dust **mostly originates from the atmospheres of very old stars.** The interstellar dust grains are made of silicon monoxide (SiO) grains or graphite "carbon" grains. *Interstellar dust grains* are microscopic measuring approximately 0.1 micron making them the *size of 'smoke'* particles. The dust in these galaxies converts nearly 100% of the starlight into infrared radiation. The cooling effect of dust in some clouds assists in their collapse to form new generations of stars and planetary systems. Hence, one may conclude that interstellar dust grains are like *'smoke'* particles and were part of the early evolutionary process of star formation.

## DEFINITIONS

**Hydrogen atom**—one proton and one electron.

**Hydrogen gas**—is composed of two hydrogen atoms.

**Interstellar medium**—is the space between stars. Approximately 99% of ISM is gas (hydrogen and helium) and the remaining 1% is interstellar dust.

**Interstellar dust**—occurs by condensation in regions around evolved stars. Composed of silicon monoxide (SiO) if the star contains more oxygen than carbon or graphite when the star contains more carbon than oxygen.

Smoke particles—90% of wood smoke particles are smaller than 0.1 micron. The major component of wood smoke is carbon monoxide (CO).

## EXPANDING UNIVERSE

وَٱلسَّمَآءَ بَنَيْنَٰهَا بِأَيْيْدٍ وَإِنَّا لَمُوسِعُونَ ﴿٤٧﴾

*With power did We construct the heaven. Verily, We are **expanding** the vastness of **space** thereof. (Koran 51:47)*

Thanks to Edwin Hubble we now know that the universe is expanding. A direct consequence of the big bang is the continuing creation and expansion of space.

## BIG CRUNCH

يَوْمَ نَطْوِى ٱلسَّمَآءَ كَطَيِّ ٱلسِّجِلِّ لِلْكُتُبِ كَمَا بَدَأْنَآ أَوَّلَ خَلْقٍ نُّعِيدُهُۥ

وَعْدًا عَلَيْنَآ إِنَّا كُنَّا فَٰعِلِينَ ﴿١٠٤﴾

*And the Day when We shall roll up the heavens like a scroll rolled up for books, as We began the first creation, We shall repeat it, a promise binding upon Us. Truly, We shall do it. (Koran 21:104)*

يَوْمَ تُبَدَّلُ ٱلْأَرْضُ غَيْرَ ٱلْأَرْضِ وَٱلسَّمَٰوَٰتُ وَبَرَزُواْ لِلَّهِ ٱلْوَٰحِدِ ٱلْقَهَّارِ

﴿٤٨﴾

*On the Day when the earth will be changed to another earth and so will be the heavens, and they (all creatures) will appear before God, the One, The Irresistible. (Koran 14:48)*

According to modern cosmology there is a theory that the density of matter in the universe will create gravitational forces that will eventually cause the universe to stop expanding. The gravitational pull of matter in the universe will then slow the expansion and gravity will cause the universe to collapse upon itself ending in what cosmologists have termed the *Big Crunch*. The *Big Crunch* will be the reverse of the *Big Bang*. The above two verses suggest that following the *Big Crunch* a **second** *Big Bang* will occur.

# BURNING SEA

وَٱلْبَحْرِ ٱلْمَسْجُورِ ۝

*And by the kindled sea (set on fire). (Koran 52:6)*

What would you think if you we were living in the seventh century A.D. and you heard someone talking about a sea set on fire? Now we know that there volcanoes under the sea.

# WE SENT DOWN THE IRON

لَقَدْ أَرْسَلْنَا رُسُلَنَا بِٱلْبَيِّنَتِ وَأَنزَلْنَا مَعَهُمُ ٱلْكِتَبَ وَٱلْمِيزَانَ لِيَقُومَ ٱلنَّاسُ بِٱلْقِسْطِ وَأَنزَلْنَا ٱلْحَدِيدَ فِيهِ بَأْسٌ شَدِيدٌ وَمَنَفِعُ لِلنَّاسِ وَلِيَعْلَمَ ٱللَّهُ مَن يَنصُرُهُ وَرُسُلَهُ بِٱلْغَيْبِ إِنَّ ٱللَّهَ قَوِيٌّ عَزِيزٌ ۝

*We verily sent Our messengers with clear proofs and sent down with them the Book and the Balance, that mankind may observe justice; and We sent down Iron, wherein is mighty power and many benefits for mankind, that God may know him who helpeth Him and His messengers, though unseen. Lo! God is Strong, Almighty (Koran 57:25)*

This Koranic verse implies that iron was *"sent down"* to the earth. Elements on Earth such as oxygen, calcium, iron, and gold came long ago from exploding stars (*quote found in fifth paragraph of article: http://hubblesite.org/ newscenter/archive/releases/2004/23/image/a*). In 1999 astrophysicist *Gunther*

*Korschinek*, from the *Technical University of Munich*, discovered Iron-60 enrichment in deep-sea rock of the *South Pacific Ocean* that is thought to be 2.8 million years old. This form of iron is so rare that it is thought to most likely be a direct result of a supernova.

Supernovae are massive exploding giant stars. When the explosion occurs, the resulting illumination can be as bright as an entire galaxy. Supernovae are the main source of all the elements heavier than oxygen. These elements are produced by fusion (for iron fifty-six, 56Fe, and lighter elements), and by nucleosynthesis during the supernova explosion for elements heavier than iron. Iron is the most abundant element by mass of our entire planet, making up 35% of the mass of the earth as a whole.

There are type Ia and type 2 supernovas. During the explosion of a type Ia supernova, the most prominently synthesized heavy elements are iron-group elements. During the formation of a type 2 supernova (core collapse is thought to be powered by gravitational forces) the resultant iron core subsequently expands. Type 2 supernovas are explosions that release radio energy, X-rays, cosmic rays as well as sending into interstellar space many of the heavier elements, such as iron, that are found in the Earth's solar system.

The earth in comparison to its neighbor the moon has significantly higher iron content and the secret to this is explained during the time of their creation. The moon may have formed by fission (moon spun off the earth). However, calculation of the total angular momentum and energy required would not have resulted in the present earth-moon system. Presently the moon moves 3.8 cm per year away from the earth. Also, the moon and earth did not form at the same time (co-creation) as the moon has a lower iron content and is therefore less dense than the earth. Another old theory was that the moon may have formed somewhere else in the solar system where there was little iron, and then was captured into the earth's orbit. However, this theory was also discarded as lunar rocks and the earth have the same isotope composition. The earth's iron core and creation of the moon is presently best explained by the *Giant Impact Theory* proposed by Bill Hartman in 1974. This theory via computer simulation proposed that a planet or impactor the size of mars collided with the earth. The iron core of the impactor fused with the earth (inner clump) while the outer clump resulted in the moon. This theory is supported by the fact that moon has exactly the same oxygen isotope (oxygen 16 levels) composition as the earth, whereas meteorites from other parts of the solar system have different oxygen isotope compositions. Hence, the earth's iron content is the result of an extraneous impact and this supports the Koranic view. The Koran did not state *"We gave you iron"* which would be the natural and expected statement but curiously and precisely stated *"We sent down iron"*.

## CHEST TIGHTNESS AT HIGH ALTITUDE

فَمَن يُرِدِ ٱللَّهُ أَن يَهْدِيَهُ يَشْرَحْ صَدْرَهُ لِلْإِسْلَـٰمِ وَمَن يُرِدْ أَن يُضِلَّهُ يَجْعَلْ صَدْرَهُ ضَيِّقًا حَرَجًا كَأَنَّمَا يَصَّعَّدُ فِى ٱلسَّمَآءِ كَذَٰلِكَ يَجْعَلُ ٱللَّهُ ٱلرِّجْسَ عَلَى ٱلَّذِينَ لَا يُؤْمِنُونَ ۝

*And whomsoever God wills to guide, He opens his breast to Islam, and whomsoever He wills to send astray, He makes his chest **closed and constricted**, as if he is climbing up to the sky. Thus God puts the wrath on those who believe not (Koran 6:125)*

Clinical studies have shown that at an altitude of 14,000 feet, 0.5 percent of adults and 8 percent of children under age 16 will suffer from pulmonary edema. Males and females are equally affected. In *high altitude pulmonary edema (HAPE)*, the lungs become waterlogged, thus increasing hypoxic symptoms to potentially critical levels, leading to respiratory failure. A very rapid resting heartbeat *(tachycardia)*, very rapid breathing rate *(tachypnea)*, difficulty breathing *(dyspnea)* and blue skin *(cyanosis)* are early indications of HAPE. Altitude illness rarely occurs at elevations below 2500 m (8000 ft). *High Altitude Pulmonary Edema (HAPE)* symptoms include **Chest tightness**, fullness, or congestion.

# CLOUDS, HAIL AND LIGHTNING

أَلَمْ تَرَ أَنَّ اللَّهَ يُزْجِى سَحَابًا ثُمَّ يُؤَلِّفُ بَيْنَهُ ثُمَّ يَجْعَلُهُ رُكَامًا فَتَرَى
الْوَدْقَ يَخْرُجُ مِنْ خِلَلِهِ وَيُنَزِّلُ مِنَ السَّمَاءِ مِن جِبَالٍ فِيهَا مِنْ بَرَدٍ
فَيُصِيبُ بِهِ مَن يَشَاءُ وَيَصْرِفُهُ عَن مَّن يَشَاءُ يَكَادُ سَنَا بَرْقِهِ يَذْهَبُ
بِالْأَبْصَرِ ﴿٤٣﴾

*Have you not seen how God makes the clouds move gently,* then joins
them together, ***then makes them into a stack,*** *and then you see the rain come
out of it? And* **He sends down hail** *from mountains (clouds) in the sky, and
He strikes with it whomever He wills, and turns it from whoever He wills.
The vivid flash of its lightning nearly blinds the sight.* (Koran 24:43)

This verse first states that clouds are first *joined together* or **stacked.**
This *stacking* forms what meteorologists call *cumulonimbus* clouds. The
second part of this verse suggests that *hail* is the cause of *lightning.*

When warmer less dense air is underneath cooler denser air the
atmosphere is unstable. Therefore an updraft (strong current of rising air)
of warm air brings about stability. Clouds form when moist air is cooled
so much that the water vapor in it begins to condense into tiny liquid
drops or ice particles. The sun warms moist air near the earth's surface.
As the air becomes warmer it starts to rise. Then as it raises it cools and
condenses forming cumulus clouds. Most thunderstorms are associated
with towering clouds known as cumulonimbus. Not all cumulonimbus
clouds bring thunderstorms, heavy showers or hail.

Water droplets inside a storm cloud are sent toward the top of the
cloud by strong upward winds where they turn to ice. Some pieces of ice
grow larger forming hail while others remain very small. As the pieces
of hail get larger they fall down thru the cloud colliding with smaller ice
particles that are still being forced upwards. This collision transfers some
electrons to the hail.

The **electrons give the hail a negative charge** while the small ice
particles that have lost electrons gain a positive charge. The upward forces
of the warm wind or updrafts push the lighter positive ice particles upward,
giving the top of the cloud a positive charge, while the heavier hail collects
in the lower part of the cloud, giving it a negative charge. These forces

prevent attraction between the upper positively charged small ice particles and the lower negatively charged hale particles.

Negative charges collecting at the base of the cloud repel the electrons near the ground's surface. This leaves the ground surface with a positive charge. Attraction between the lower, negatively charged, cloud and the positive atoms on the ground grows stronger until the **electrons shoot down a pathway from the cloud causing a flash of lightning**. The light from the flash starts at the ground and moves upwards. The *National Oceanic & Atmospheric Administration (NOAA)*, U.S. Department of Commerce website provides a useful site which explains how lightening forms *(http://www.noaa.gov/questions/question_041702.html)*.

## Meteorological Definitions

**Thunder**—sound waves caused by the intense heating and expansion of air along the lightning path. Lightning causes thunderstorms. Thunderstorms are often accompanied by hail.

**Hail**—Hail forms when strong currents of rising air, known as updrafts, carry water droplets above the freezing level in thunderstorms and the water freezes into ice. The updrafts carrying droplets of supercooled water hit the balls of ice and freeze instantly, making the hailstones grow.

**Hail's negative charge**—is due to the accepted hypothesis involving collisions between hail pellets and ice crystals. Growth of hail pellets is due to the collision with supercooled cloud droplets or ice crystals. The hail pellets, in the lower regions of the cloud, normally acquire a negative charge and the smaller ice crystals, in the upper regions of the cloud, acquire a positive charge. Within the thunderstorm clouds **the hail's negative charges, electrons, concentrate at the base of the cloud**. Since like charges repel, some of the negative charges on the ground are pushed down away from the surface, leaving a net positive charge on the surface. Opposite charges attract, so the positive and negative charges are pulled toward each other. This first invisible stroke is called a stepped leader. As soon as the negative and positive parts of the stepped leader connect there is a conductive path from the cloud to the ground and the negative charges rush down it causing the visible stroke.

**Cumulonimbus cloud**—has powerful updrafts capable of carrying water drops well above the freezing altitude, where they become supercooled and eventually form ice particles.

**Severe thunderstorm**—has high winds, lightning, large hail or tornadoes.

## CREATED ALL THE PAIRS

سُبْحَنَ ٱلَّذِى خَلَقَ ٱلْأَزْوَٰجَ كُلَّهَا مِمَّا تُنۢبِتُ ٱلْأَرْضُ وَمِنْ أَنفُسِهِمْ وَمِمَّا لَا يَعْلَمُونَ ۝

*Glory be to Him, Who has **created all the pairs of that which the earth produces, as well as of their own (human) kind, and of that which they know not,** (Koran 36.36)*

At the level of human reproduction, we have male and female sexual pairing. In the human body there is internal and external symmetry or pairing. To exemplify, internally there are two cerebral hemispheres, optic tracts, acoustic nerves, thyroid glands, lungs, adrenal glands, kidneys, and ovaries while externally there are two eyes, ears, breasts, hands and feet.

سُبْحَنَ ٱلَّذِى خَلَقَ ٱلْأَزْوَٰجَ كُلَّهَا مِمَّا تُنۢبِتُ ٱلْأَرْضُ وَمِنْ أَنفُسِهِمْ وَمِمَّا لَا يَعْلَمُونَ ۝

*And **of everything We have created pairs,** that you may be mindful, (Koran 51:49)*

Everywhere around us we find the phenomenon of pairing whether we look at DNA sequence, electric charge in atoms, or the reproduction of life forms. In nature, the joining of two different entities results in coupling or pairing. Also, division, mitosis, and fission result in splitting causing duplication or pairing. In essence, creation abounds with the phenomenon of pairs.

One might wish to argue that creation is only limited to living organisms but the following quotation should suffice in negating that assertion:

وَمِن كُلِّ شَيْءٍ خَلَقْنَا زَوْجَيْنِ لَعَلَّكُمْ تَذَكَّرُونَ ۝

*Verily! In the **creation of the heavens and the earth**, and in the alternation of night and day, there are indeed signs for men of understanding. (Koran 3:190)*

## DNA

DNA is the genetic material of chromosomes that we inherit from our parents. DNA essentially determines the characteristics of all living organisms. The nucleotide bases adenine, thymine, guanine and cytosine are the building blocks of DNA. Four small molecules, adenine(A), cytosine(C), guanine(G), and thymine(T), form either AT or GC pairs.

## RNA

Messenger RNA (mRNA) is single-stranded and of positive polarity. Its sequence of nucleotides is called "sense" because it results in a gene product (protein). However, RNA can form duplexes just as DNA does. All that is needed is a second strand of RNA whose sequence of bases is complementary to the first strand. For example:

5′ C A U G 3′ mRNA
3′ G U A C 5′ Antisense RNA

The second strand is called the antisense strand or anti-mRNA because its sequence of nucleotides is the complement of message sense. Anti-mRNA has negative polarity. Thus, we have RNA of **dual** polarity.

Single-stranded genomes may be of positive (i.e. mRNA) or negative (i.e. anti-mRNA) polarity. Positive-stranded RNA is essentially equivalent to mRNA and can often be immediately translated into proteins. Negative-stranded RNA must first be converted into positive RNA (mRNA) before it can be translated into proteins. Similarly, there is sense strand DNA and antisense strand DNA.

## Pairing in Reproduction

An ordinary **human cell contains two of each type of chromosome** and for that reason is called diploid. The members of each pair are known as homologous chromosomes. All the chromosomes typical of the species are present in pairs. **Cell division** occurs by a process called **mitosis** where we get a **pair of identical cells**.

**Sexual reproduction** is where a **pair of** specialized reproductive or sex **cells fuse**. In animals, sexual reproduction is accomplished through the union or pairing of gametes to form a zygote. The diploid phase (**two** complete sets of chromosomes) of the animal life cycle is the dominant phase, while the gametes are the only haploid elements.

Sexual reproduction can also be seen **in plant life.** Flowers are the means by which plants recruit bees to pollinate other plants. Flowers contain both male and female gametes. Pollen attaches itself to these hairs while the bee is foraging around the flower for nectar. When a bee lands, on a plant, pollen attach to hair-like structures at the base of their legs. As the bee flies away to another flower the pollen, male gamete, trapped at the base of its legs, might fall or get caught on another plant's female gametes thus sexual reproduction occurs.

Plant reproduction is sexual or asexual. **Asexual plant reproduction** uses existing plant parts to grow a new **genetically identical plant**. **Gametophyte generation** begins with a spore produced by meiosis. The spore is haploid, and all the cells derived from it by mitosis are also haploid. In due course, this multicellular structure produces gametes by mitosis. Then **sexual reproduction** produces the diploid **sporophyte generation**. Haploid gametes fuse to form the zygote and grow into sporophyte generation. The alternate phase of the plant life cycle is the sporophyte, the diploid plant form, with each cell containing **two** complete sets of chromosomes. The sporophyte develops from the union of two gametes, and in turn, the sporophyte forms spores that develop into gametophytes. The alternation between haploid gametophyte and diploid sporophyte phases, known as alternation of generations, occurs in all multicellular plants. **Sporophyte generation** starts with a zygote whose cells contain the diploid number of chromosomes. Eventually certain cells will undergo meiosis, forming spores and starting a new gametophyte generation. The **Spore** is a **haploid cell** formed following meiosis, which then undergoes mitosis and gives rise to a haploid individual, such as the gametophyte in green algae or plants. In fungi, a haploid spore gives rise to a new mycelium.

The gametophyte is dominant in very primitive plants, fungi and some algae. As plants advanced in evolutionary development, the sporophyte became the increasingly dominant plant form and the gametophyte form becomes correspondingly reduced. However, with alternation of generations the gametophyte may become dominant.

Some **yeast**, which are a type of fungus, **reproduce** through **binary fission**. Other yeasts reproduce by **budding**. A parent yeast cell forms a growth, or bud, on its surface. As this bud gets bigger, the parent cell's nucleus **divides into two by mitosis.** Other fungi reproduce through **spore formation**. Fungi can produce spores either without sex or when **two fungal cells fuse** and share DNA. Some species can do both sexual and asexual reproduction.

**Algae** reproduce without sex by mitosis. Some species can reproduce sexually. **Protozoa** reproduce by binary fission, budding or by schizogony which is multiple fission.

**Bacteria and viruses** reproduce by **fission**. Bacteria multiply by **splitting into two** cells. Bacteria have the necessary genetic DNA material or chromosomal information needed for replication. Bacteria have ribosomes to copy DNA for reproduction.

Viruses only have core DNA or RNA and must invade plant cells, animal cells or bacteria to reproduce. Bacteriophages are DNA viruses that use bacteria for replication. Viral replication occurs by lytic or lysogenic pathways. In the **lytic pathway** phage **DNA is duplicated** and the host cell dies rapidly, releasing virus particles. In the **lysogenic pathway,** the **viral DNA is duplicated**, along with the bacterial chromosome, when the bacterium divides. In the lysogenic pathway, the host cell for replicating the viral genes is not killed rapidly and the viral infection enters a latent period.

# DEFINITIONS

**DNA (deoxyribonucleic acid)**—is the molecule that encodes genetic information. DNA is the substance of inheritance, which directs the growth, organization, development, and function of cells. DNA is a double stranded molecule held together by weak bonds between base pairs of nucleotides. Adenine (A) always combines with thymine (T) while guanine (G) always combines with cytosine (C) giving a paired combination.

**Fertilization/syngamy**—syngamy is a fusion of gametes.

**Fission**—is an asexual reproductive process whereby a unicellular organism divides into two or more independently maturing daughter cells.

**Gamete types**—(1) isogamy (equal gametes). Although the gametes appear identical, there are subtle genetic or physiological differences known as mating types; typical of algae. (2) anisogamy (unequal gametes). Both gametes are motile, but one is distinctly larger than the other; also typical of some algae. (3) Oogamy one gamete is large and non-motile (the egg) while the much-smaller gamete is motile (sperm). This phenomenon is present in algae that are more advanced and all higher land plants.

**Meiosis**—the parent cell divides to produce daughter cells that differ in their genetic content from each other and from their parent cell. Gametes (sperm and egg) occur through meiosis. Just before meiosis, each chromosome replicates to form two identical copies in the form of strands called chromatids joined together at a point called the centromere. At the beginning of the second meiotic sequence, called the equational division, each cell nucleus contains one chromosome from each homologous pair and each chromosome is of two identical strands (except where crossing over has occurred).

**Mitosis**—is a process whereby the resultant identical daughter cells (a pair of cells) contain the same genetic information as the parent cell. The two new nuclei each contain a complete copy of the parental chromosomes. Cells reproduce by mitosis. Mitosis occurs in growth and repair after injury. This process is used for asexual reproduction, to produce identical pairs.

**Sexual reproduction**— uses gametes and spores to produce a genetically different plant. Sexual reproduction depends on the specialized form of cell division called meiosis to produce cells that can recombine to shuffle the organism's genes. Meiosis is a reduction division where a single diploid cell turns into four haploid cells. Meiosis begins by separating homologous pairs of chromosomes. The second meiotic division happens much like mitosis. The net result of meiosis is four haploid cells where the chromosome number is halved.

## Electrons, protons and positrons

In the stable atom there is pairing of electrons and protons. The atomic number is the number of positive charges, protons, in the nucleus of an atom. In a neutral atom this is also the number of orbital electrons that float around the atom.

**Positrons** are positively charged electrons. We utilize the pairing of positrons and electrons in the nuclear medicine field. Positron emission tomography utilizes annihilation reactions between electrons and positrons. A special camera detects the resultant dual 511 KeV energy; which in the field of nuclear medicine is utilized to obtain useful physiological images.

When a neutron within a radioactive nucleus transforms into a proton it also emits an electron by a process called beta decay. Hence, the **proton and electron pair** is produced. Protons have a **positive charge** while electrons have a **negative charge**.

## Neutrinos and antineutrinos

According to the Standard Model, twelve particles are the base of matter, six quarks and six leptons. Apart from the neutrino, all the particles, leptons and quarks, have been experimentally proven by particles accelerators and detectors (or bubble chambers). **For each charged lepton** (electron, muon, tau) **is associated a neutral lepton or neutrino**. The same rule applies for the **quarks**, which are **grouped by pairs**.

Within the standard model, the neutrino has a zero mass, a zero charge and a spin 1/2. Neutrinos are electrically neutral and do not carry an electric charge. Neutrinos seem to have a spin always oriented in the direction opposite to their velocity (left helicity). The anti-neutrino is always of right helicity (spin in the same direction as the velocity).

# EARTH LIKE AN EGG

وَٱلۡأَرۡضَ بَعۡدَ ذَٰلِكَ دَحَىٰهَآ ۝

*and the Earth, after that, He made it like an egg* (Koran 79:30)

An oval or ovoid (Latin origin: ovum or egg) is any *curve* resembling an *egg* or an *ellipse*. The earth is a type of ellipse called an oblate spheroid (disk shaped) where the 'x' and 'y' axis radii are equal. Visualization of the horizon may be explained by a flat surface that ends just like the edge of a table or by an earth that is round. Visualization of a lunar eclipse, when the moon passes through the earth's shadow, is a more convincing explanation for the earth being round.

The voyages of Christopher Columbus (1451–1506) to the new world suggested that the earth is round. Sir Isaac Newton (1642–1727) by discovering and measuring the force of gravity suggested that the earth was round as the weight of an object anywhere on the surface of the earth was roughly constant.

The above verse suggests the creation of an *oval but not perfectly round shaped earth*. Certainly this contradicts the concept of a flat earth as was commonly believed. The *earth's three layers, crust, mantle and core*, are similar to the *egg's eggshell, egg white and egg yolk*. The overall average thickness of the *crust* (beneath the oceans) is 5 km. Beneath the continents the *crust* averages 30 km while under large mountain ranges, such as the Alps, Himalayas or the Sierra Nevada, the *crust* is up to 100 km. Below the *crust* is the 2,900 km thick stony *mantle* while Earth's metallic *core* (iron-nickel alloy) is 3,450 km thick.

As the thickness of the *core* exceeds the *mantle* and the *mantle* thickness exceeds the *crust* so does the *egg yolk* thickness or diameter exceed the thickness of the *egg white* and the *egg white* thickness exceeds that of the *eggshell*. Just as the *eggshell* is the most brittle part of the egg the earth's *crust* is very thin, rigid and prone to earthquakes. One can think of nothing better in nature that is as readily available as the egg to best explain this concept. *The likeness of the earth to the egg is both external and internal.*

## DEVELOPMENT OF BONE & MUSCLE

ثُـــمَّ خَلَقْنَـا ٱلنُّطْفَـــةَ عَلَقَــةً فَخَلَقْنَـا ٱلْعَلَقَــةَ مُضْغَــةً فَخَلَقْنَـا

ٱلْمُضْغَةَ عِظَـٰمًا فَكَسَوْنَا ٱلْعِظَـٰمَ لَحْمًا ثُمَّ أَنشَأْنَـٰهُ خَلْقًا ءَاخَرَ ۚ

فَتَبَارَكَ ٱللَّـهُ أَحْسَـنُ ٱلْخَـٰلِقِينَ ﴿١٤﴾

*Then We made the sperm into a cling; then of that cling We made a chewed lump; **then we made** out of that lump **bones and clothed the bones with muscle**; then we developed out of it another creature. So blessed be God, the best to create! (Koran 23:14)*

The last paragraph of the *'Skeletal Muscle'* section on page 371 of the book entitled *'The Developing Human, Clinically Oriented Embryology'* (*Fifth Edition, Moore and Persaud, Chapter 16, The Muscular System*) describes the formation of limb muscles stating, *"The musculature of the limbs develops **in situ** from the mesenchyme surrounding the developing bones. This mesenchyme is derived from the somatic layer of lateral mesoderm. **There is no apparent migration of myotonic mesoderm into the human limb buds.**"* On page 371 the authors also quote *O'Rahilly and Gardner 1975*, *"It is now generally well maintained that somites do not contribute to the limb buds of human embryos."* They go on further noting that *"the somite origin of limb musculature in the avian limb is well established."* Hence, human embryological discoveries support:

1.) Development of bones before muscle. Limb buds develop from mesoderm.

2.) Subsequent clothing of bone by muscles. Skeletal muscle develops from somatic layer of lateral mesoderm in situ.

## DEFINITIONS

Mesoderm—the middle layer of the 3 germ cell layers of the embryo (between the ectoderm and the endoderm) develops into cartilage, bone, and muscle.

Somite = paraxial mesoderm $\longrightarrow$ dermatomyotome $\longrightarrow$ myotome $\longrightarrow$ skeletal muscle.

## EMBRYOLOGICAL ORIGIN OF SEMINAL FLUID

فَلْيَنظُرِ ٱلْإِنسَـٰنُ مِمَّ خُلِقَ ۝

خُلِقَ مِن مَّآءٍ دَافِقٍ ۝

يَخْرُجُ مِنۢ بَيْنِ ٱلصُّلْبِ وَٱلتَّرَآئِبِ ۝

*Now let man but think from what he is created! He is created from water gushing forth, proceeding from **between the backbone and the ribs**. (Koran 86:5-7)*

## FIG. 1111
### (By permission)

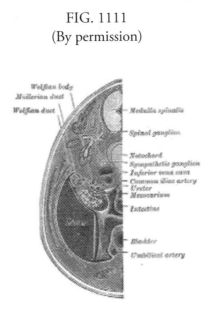

*Transverse section of human embryo eight and a half to nine weeks old (From model by Keibel). Henry Gray (1825–1861). Anatomy of the Human Body. 1918.*

The location of the *mullerian duct*, future female reproductive organ, and *wollfian duct*, future male reproductive organ is well illustrated in fig. 1111. During development of the embryo both the *mullerian* and *wollfian ducts* are located between the backbone and the ribs. The reproductive fluid or semen is released from the male reproductive organ or testes. Hence during fetal development the origin of seminal fluid is from a region between the backbone and the ribs. One has to ask how is it possible that a mortal human being could have used such precise language, many years ago, to describe the embryological origin of seminal fluid.

# EMBRYOLOGY OF FETAL DEVELOPMENT

وَلَقَدۡ خَلَقۡنَا ٱلۡإِنسَٰنَ مِن سُلَٰلَةٖ مِّن طِينٖ ۝

*And indeed We created man out of an extract (sulala) of clay (water and earth).*

ثُمَّ جَعَلۡنَٰهُ نُطۡفَةٗ فِى قَرَارٖ مَّكِينٖ ۝

*Thereafter We made him as a "NUTFA" (drop) in a safe lodging (womb of the woman).*

ثُمَّ خَلَقۡنَا ٱلنُّطۡفَةَ عَلَقَةٗ فَخَلَقۡنَا ٱلۡعَلَقَةَ مُضۡغَةٗ فَخَلَقۡنَا
ٱلۡمُضۡغَةَ عِظَٰمٗا فَكَسَوۡنَا ٱلۡعِظَٰمَ لَحۡمٗا ثُمَّ أَنشَأۡنَٰهُ خَلۡقًا ءَاخَرَۚ
فَتَبَارَكَ ٱللَّهُ أَحۡسَنُ ٱلۡخَٰلِقِينَ ۝

*Then We made the "NUTFA" into a "ALAQA" (cling or leach like) then We made the cling into a "MODGHA" (chewed lump of flesh), then We made out of that chewed lump of flesh bones, then We clothed the bones with flesh, and then We brought it forth as another creation. So blessed be, God the Best of creators (Koran 23:12-14)*

We did create man from a *"sulala"* made of clay *(Koran 23:12)* grammatically means from *"the genealogy"* of clay. We now know that all the atoms found in humans are found in the earth.

This sequence of fetal development agrees with present day embryology. An embryology book by *Dr. Keith Moore* called *The Developing Human* discusses these verses. The *"nutfa"* (little drop) is the seminal fluid. This is followed by the stage of *"alaqa"* (in Arabic the leech is called *alaqa* and the verb *alaqa* means to stick or to attach to), which is a precise description of the blastocyst as it attaches to the endometrium or inner linning of the uterus. This resemblance of the human embryo to a leech is an appropriate description of the human embryo when it clings to the endometrium of the uterus. The fetus resembles a *"modgha"* or chewed food. The molar teeth markings create an indentation or *"modgha"* (please see the following illustrated diagrams).

*1.* *"NUTFA"* in Arabic means a **'little drop'** and is the seminal fluid.

*2.* *"ALAQA"* in Arabic the leech is called **alaqa.**

The verb **ALAQA** means to **'cling, stick or attach to'**
IMPLANTATION: The blastocyst similarly clings or attaches to the
   endometrium

*3.* *"MODGHA"* means **'chewed food'** in Arabic.

Molar teeth markings create an indentation.
The fetus resembles a *"MODGHA"* or chewed food.

FIG. 20

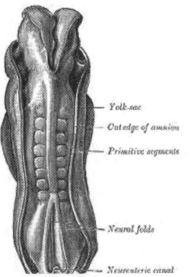

Yolk-sac
Cut edge of amnion
Primitive segments

Neural folds
Neurenteric canal

Dorsum of human embryo, **2.11 mm.** in length.
(After Eternod). Henry Gray (1825–1861).
Anatomy of the Human Body. 1918.

(With permission http://www.bartleby.com/107/i20)

FIG. 59

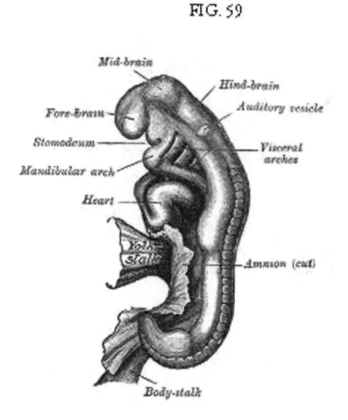

Human embryo: between eighteen and twenty-one days old.
(His.) Henry Gray (1825–1861).
Anatomy of the Human Body. 1918.

(With permission http://www.bartleby.com/107/illus59.html)

## FIG. 60

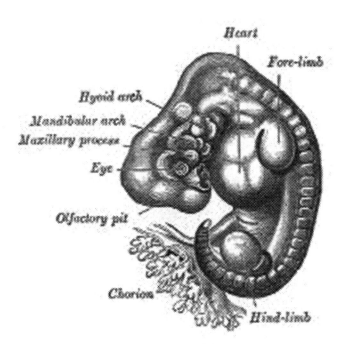

Human embryo: twenty-seven to thirty days old.
(His.) Henry Gray (1825–1861).
Anatomy of the Human Body. 1918.

(With permission http://www.bartleby.com/107/i60)

At an embryonic age of 28 days old (4 weeks) the embryo measures 8 mm (1/4 inch) in length. (http://en.wikipedia.org/wiki/Prenatal_development)

The naked eye could not see such a fetal imprints or the details of minute millimeter sized embryos as powerful lenses were not invented till the seventeenth century A.D. During the time of Koranic revelation microscopes were not yet invented. The fine details of minute millimeter sized embryos cannot be seen with the unaided eye. **Microscopes were not yet invented in the 7th century**. Zaccharias Jansse, Dutch, in 1590 worked with spectacles and could magnify 20-30 times. Anton van Leeuwenhoek (1632-1723), from Holland, developed a microscope that magnified 200 times. **Powerful lenses were not invented till the 17th century.** The above illustration reveals the "curved" chain of beads appearance. Human dental imprints or "modgha" on a piece of gum would result in a similar pattern.

## THREE VEILS OF DARKNESS

خَلَقَكُم مِّن نَّفْسٍ وَاحِدَةٍ ثُمَّ جَعَلَ مِنْهَا زَوْجَهَا وَأَنزَلَ لَكُم مِّنَ ٱلْأَنْعَٰمِ ثَمَٰنِيَةَ أَزْوَٰجٍ يَخْلُقُكُمْ فِى بُطُونِ أُمَّهَٰتِكُمْ خَلْقًا مِّنۢ بَعْدِ خَلْقٍ فِى ظُلُمَٰتٍ ثَلَٰثٍ ذَٰلِكُمُ ٱللَّهُ رَبُّكُمْ لَهُ ٱلْمُلْكُ لَآ إِلَٰهَ إِلَّا هُوَ فَأَنَّىٰ تُصْرَفُونَ

He created you (all) from a single person (Adam); then made from him his wife (Eve). And He has sent down for you of cattle eight pairs (of the sheep, two, male and female; of the goats, two, male and female; of the oxen, two, male and female; and of the camels, two, male and female). **He creates you in the wombs of your mothers** in stages, one after another, **in three veils of darkness,** such is God your Lord. His is the kingdom, there is no God but He. How then are you turned away? (Koran 39:6)*

The **"three veils of darkness"** are now thought to refer to the (1) amnion, (2) chorion and (3) uterus.

## FINGERPRINTS

أَيَحْسَبُ ٱلْإِنسَٰنُ أَلَّن نَّجْمَعَ عِظَامَهُ ٢

*Does man think that We shall not assemble his bones?*

بَلَىٰ قَـٰدِرِينَ عَلَىٰٓ أَن نُّسَوِّىَ بَنَانَهُۥ ٤

*Yes, We are Able to put together in **perfect order** the tips of his fingers. (Koran 75:3-4)*

The fingertips are unique as they positively identify a person as no two individuals have the same fingerprints. Why did the author of this verse which is over 1300 years old choose to affirm that not only would our Creator resurrect our bones but would also reconstruct our fingertips in perfect order? Could not the author have just said he put our body or bones together and left it at that? The precision of the language should leave the reader wondering what is so special about the fingertips? Why was not the author more general and just say that "We would assemble his fingers, fingernails, hair or skin."

## IRAM

أَلَمْ تَرَ كَيْفَ فَعَلَ رَبُّكَ بِعَادٍ ٦

*Did you not see how your Lord dealt with Ad (people)?*

إِرَمَ ذَاتِ ٱلْعِمَادِ ٧

**Iram that had very tall like lofty pillars,**

ٱلَّتِى لَمْ يُخْلَقْ مِثْلُهَا فِى ٱلْبِلَٰدِ ٨

*The like of which were not created in the land? (Koran 89:6-8)*

The *Koran* refers to a city called **Iram** the existence of which was not mentioned in any historical documents till the ancient city of *Ebla* was discovered (*National Geographic, December 1978*).

120

The *Ebla tablets* mention Sodom and Gomorrah, as well as **Iram**; an obscure city that is referred to in *sura 89* of the Koran (**National Geographic**, *December 1978, page 736*). An archaeological article in **Time magazine** suggests that a city called *Ubar* with *pillars reaching a height of 9 meters or 30 feet* probably represents *Iram (Time, February 17, 1992, page 69)*.

The city of Iram, thought to have existed from 2800 BC till 300 AD, was rediscovered in 1992. With the help of NASA's Challenger space shuttle *Ubar* was found underneath the desert sands of Oman.

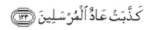

*Ad (people)* **belied the Messengers**.

إِذْ قَالَ لَهُمْ أَخُوهُمْ هُودٌ أَلَا تَتَّقُونَ ﴿١٢٤﴾

*When their brother Hud said to them: "Will you not fear God and obey Him?*

إِنِّى لَكُمْ رَسُولٌ أَمِينٌ ﴿١٢٥﴾

*Verily! I am a trustworthy Messenger to you.*

فَاتَّقُوا اللَّهَ وَأَطِيعُونِ ﴿١٢٦﴾

*So fear God, keep your duty to Him, and obey me.*

وَمَآ أَسْئَلُكُمْ عَلَيْهِ مِنْ أَجْرٍ إِنْ أَجْرِىَ إِلَّا عَلَىٰ رَبِّ الْعَٰلَمِينَ ﴿١٢٧﴾

*No reward do I ask of you for it, my reward is only from the Lord of the worlds. (Koran 26:123-127)*

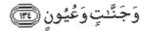

*He has aided you with cattle and children. (Koran 26:133)*

*And gardens and springs. (Koran 26:134)*

During the archaeological excavations remains of cattle and evidence of an agricultural existence were discovered. Also frankincense was discovered which **would support the presence of gardens.**

*And as for **Ad, they were destroyed by a furious violent wind;***

***Which God imposed on them for seven nights and eight days in succession**, so that you could see men lying overthrown (destroyed), as if they were hollow trunks of date-palms. (Koran 69:6-7)*

Archaeologists have determined that the octagonal pillar structure was built around a *water reservoir in a limestone cavern (**springs**, Koran 26:134)* that collapsed, plunging much of the city into a gaping hole. The Koran states that a **natural disaster,** and not war, **destroyed the people of Iram.** Could the weight of the tremendous sandstorm mentioned in the Koran have also caused the limestone cavern to collapse?

# LYING

أَرَءَيْتَ إِن كَذَّبَ وَتَوَلَّىٰ ﴿١٣﴾

*See if he denies and turns away?*

أَلَمْ يَعْلَم بِأَنَّ ٱللَّهَ يَرَىٰ ﴿١٤﴾

*Knows he not that God does see (what he does)?*

كَلَّا لَبِن لَّمْ يَنتَهِ لَنَسْفَعًا بِٱلنَّاصِيَةِ ﴿١٥﴾

*Nay! If he ceases not, We will catch him by the forelock,*

نَاصِيَةٍ كَٰذِبَةٍ خَاطِئَةٍ ﴿١٦﴾

*A lying, sinful forelock! (Koran 96:13-16)*

The *"frontal"* brain region is responsible for planning, motivation, and formulation of thought processes such as lying. How did the author of the Koran, over 1300 years ago, know that the frontal brain region is responsible for lying? A paper published by the Department of Psychology at the University of Southern California *(The British Journal of Psychiatry, 2005,187:320-325)* revealed that liars had a 22 percent increase in prefrontal white matter and a 14.2 percent decrease in prefrontal gray matter when compared with the normal group.

# MEMORIZATION

وَلَقَدْ يَسَّرْنَا ٱلْقُرْءَانَ لِلذِّكْرِ فَهَلْ مِن مُّدَّكِرٍ ۝

*And We have indeed **made the Koran easy to remember**, then is there any that will remember (or receive admonition)? (Koran 54:17)*

Many Muslims can recite the entire Koranic text cover to cover. Some children accomplish this feat by their early teens. The Arabic text of the Koran is approximately 600 pages. Could any human author write a 200 page book in any language or style and then be able to recite his own book cover to cover?

# MOSES AND PHARAOH

Moses fled when he was forty years old *(Acts 7:23)*, after killing the Egyptian who had struck a fellow Hebrew, and dwelt in Midian for forty years *(Acts 7:30)* prior to leading the Hebrews out of Egypt. Subsequently Moses wandered in the wilderness for forty years before dying at the age of 120 years *(Deuteronomy 34:7)*.

# ACTS

*And when he was cast out, Pharaoh's daughter took him up, and nourished him for her own son. (Acts 7:21)*
*And Moses was learned in all the wisdom of the Egyptians, and was mighty in words and in deeds. (Acts 7:22)*
*And when he was full forty years old, it came into his heart to visit his brethren the children of Israel (Acts 7:23, KJV)*

*Then fled Moses at this saying, and was a stranger in the land of Midian, where he begat two sons. (Acts 7:29)*

*And* when forty years were expired, *there appeared to him in the wilderness of mount Sina an angel of the Lord in a flame of fire in a bush.* (Acts 7:30, KJV)

## DEUTERONOMY

*And **Moses [was] an hundred and twenty years old when he died**: his eye was not dim, nor his natural force abated. (Deuteronomy 34:7, KJV)*

The cities of Pithom and Ramses *(Exodus 1:11)* were built by the children of Israel during the reign of *Ramses II* (one of the references to this topic may be found in *Davis Dictionary of the Bible, p. 209 and 681, 1973, 4th edition, ISBN0-87836-001-8)*. Pithom has been excavated with some bricks being made with straws and some without straws (see *Davis Dictionary of the Bible, p.646, 1973, 4th edition, ISBN0-87836-001-8)*. This discovery fits the Biblical account as quoted below in Exodus 5. Pithom is found in the region of present-day Tel Al-Maskuta not far from Ismailia a city at the Suez Canal. Ramses (Pi-Ramses "House of Ramses") has been identified as Tel Al-Daba'a near the modern village of Khatana-Qantir on the Nile Delta. Ramses rebuilt the old Hyksos capital city of Avaris in the Nile Delta and called it Pi-Ramses.

## EXODUS I

*Now there arose up a new king over Egypt, which knew not Joseph.* (Exodus 1:8)

*Therefore they did set over them taskmasters to afflict them with their burdens. And they built for Pharaoh treasure cities, Pithom and Raamses. (Exodus 1:11)*

*And they made their lives bitter with hard bondage, in morter, and in brick, and in all manner of service in the field: all their service, wherein they made them serve, [was] with rigour. (Exodus 1:14)*

*And Pharaoh charged all his people, saying, Every son that is born ye shall cast into the river, and every daughter ye shall save alive (Exodus 1:22, KJV)*

## EXODUS 2

*And the daughter of Pharaoh came down to wash [herself] at the river; and her maidens walked along by the river's side; and when she saw the ark among the flags, she sent her maid to fetch it. (Exodus 2:5)*
*And when she had opened [it], she saw the child: and, behold, the babe wept. And she had compassion on him, and said, This [is one] of the Hebrews' children (Exodus 2:6)*

*And the child grew, and she brought him unto Pharaoh's daughter, and he became her son. And she called his name Moses: and she said, Because I drew him out of the water. (Exodus 2:10)*
*And it came to pass in those days, when Moses was grown, that he went out unto his brethren, and looked on their burdens: and he spied an Egyptian smiting an Hebrew, one of his brethren. (Exodus 2:11)*
*And he looked this way and that way, and when he saw that [there was] no man, he slew the Egyptian, and hid him in the sand. (Exodus 2:12)*

*Now when Pharaoh heard this thing, he sought to slay Moses. But Moses fled from the face of Pharaoh, and dwelt in the land of Midian: and he sat down by a well. (Exodus 2:15, KJV)*

## EXODUS 5

*And afterward **Moses and Aaron went in, and told Pharaoh**, Thus saith the LORD God of Israel, **Let my people go**, that they may hold a feast unto me in the wilderness. (Exodus 5:1)*
*And Pharaoh said, Who [is] the LORD, that I should obey his voice to let Israel go? I know not the LORD, neither will I let Israel go. (Exodus 5:2)*

*And Pharaoh said, Behold, the people of the land now [are] many, and ye make them rest from their burdens. (Exodus 5:5)*

*And* Pharaoh commanded *the same day the taskmasters of the people, and their officers, saying, (Exodus 5:6)*
*Ye shall no more give the people straw to make brick, as heretofore: let them go and gather straw for themselves. (Exodus 5:7)*

*And the taskmasters hasted [them], saying, Fulfil your works, [your] daily tasks, as when there was straw. (Exodus 5:13)*
*And the officers of the children of Israel, which Pharaoh's taskmasters had set over them, were beaten, [and] demanded, Wherefore have ye not fulfilled your task in making brick both yesterday and to day, as heretofore? (Exodus 5:14)*
*Then the officers of the children of Israel came and cried unto Pharaoh, saying, Wherefore dealest thou thus with thy servants? (Exodus 5:15)*
*There is no straw given unto thy servants, and they say to us, Make brick: and, behold, thy servants [are] beaten; but the fault [is] in thine own people. (Exodus 5:16)*
*But he said, Ye [are] idle, [ye are] idle: therefore ye say, Let us go [and] do sacrifice to the LORD. (Exodus 5:17)*
*Go therefore now, [and] work; for there shall no straw be given you, yet shall ye deliver the tale of bricks. (Exodus 5:18)*
*And the officers of the children of Israel did see [that] they [were] in evil [case], after it was said, Ye shall not minish [ought] from your bricks of your daily task. (Exodus 5:19)*
*And they met Moses and Aaron, who stood in the way, as they came forth from Pharaoh: (Exodus 5:20)*
*And they said unto them, The LORD look upon you, and judge; because ye have made our savour to be abhorred in the eyes of Pharaoh, and in the eyes of his servants, to put a sword in their hand to slay us. (Exodus 5:21)*

*For since I came to Pharaoh to speak in thy name, he hath done evil to this people; neither hast thou delivered thy people at all. (Exodus 5:23, KJV)*

*Then the LORD said unto Moses, Now shalt thou see what I will do to Pharaoh: for with a strong hand shall he let them go, and with a strong hand shall he drive them out of his land. (Exodus 6:1, KJV).*

# EXODUS 12

*That ye shall say, It [is] the sacrifice of the LORD'S passover, who passed over the houses of the children of Israel in Egypt, when he smote the Egyptians, and delivered our houses. And the people bowed the head and worshipped. (Exodus 12:27)*

*And it came to pass, that at midnight* the LORD smote *all the firstborn in the land of Egypt, from* the firstborn of Pharaoh *that sat on his throne unto the firstborn of the captive that [was] in the dungeon; and all the firstborn of cattle. (Exodus 12:29)*
*And Pharaoh rose up in the night, he, and all his servants, and all the Egyptians; and there was a great cry in Egypt; for [there was] not a house where [there was] not one dead. (Exodus 12:30)*
And he called for Moses and Aaron by night, and said, Rise up, [and] get you forth from among my people, *both ye and the children of Israel; and go, serve the LORD, as ye have said. (Exodus 12:31)*

*And the children of Israel journeyed from Rameses to Succoth, about six hundred thousand on foot [that were] men, beside children. (Exodus 12:37)*

# EXODUS 14

*And I will harden Pharaoh's heart, that he shall follow after them; and I will be honoured upon Pharaoh, and upon all his host; that the Egyptians may know that I [am] the LORD. And they did so. (Exodus 14:4)*
*And it was told the king of Egypt that the people fled: and the heart of Pharaoh and of his servants was turned against the people, and they said, Why have we done this, that we have let Israel go from serving us? (Exodus 14:5)*
*And* he made ready his chariot, *and took his people with him: (Exodus 14:6)*
*And he took six hundred chosen chariots, and all the chariots of Egypt, and captains over every one of them. (Exodus 14:7)*

*And the Egyptians shall know that I [am] the LORD, when I have gotten me honour upon Pharaoh, upon his chariots, and upon his horsemen. (Exodus 14:18)*

*Thus the LORD saved Israel that day out of the hand of the Egyptians; and Israel saw the Egyptians dead upon the seashore. (Exodus 14:30, KJV)*

## EXODUS 15

*For the horse of Pharaoh went in with his chariots and with his horsemen into the sea, and the LORD brought again the waters of the sea upon them; but the children of Israel went on dry [land] in the midst of the sea (Exodus 15:19, KJV)*

## PSALM 136

*O give thanks to the Lord of lords: for his mercy [endureth] for ever. (Psalms 136:3)*
*To him who alone doeth great wonders: for his mercy [endureth] for ever. (Psalms 136:4)*
*To him that by wisdom made the heavens: for his mercy [endureth] for ever. (Psalms 136:5)*
*To him that stretched out the earth above the waters: for his mercy [endureth] for ever. (Psalms 136:6)*
*To him that made great lights: for his mercy [endureth] for ever: (Psalms 136:7)*
*The sun to rule by day: for his mercy [endureth] for ever: (Psalms 136:8)*
*The moon and stars to rule by night: for his mercy [endureth] for ever. (Psalms 136:9)*
*To him that smote Egypt in their firstborn: for his mercy [endureth] for ever: (Psalms 136:10)*
*And brought out Israel from among them: for his mercy [endureth] for ever: (Psalms 136:11)*
*With a strong hand, and with a stretched out arm: for his mercy [endureth] for ever. (Psalms 136:12)*
*To him which divided the Red sea into parts: for his mercy [endureth] for ever: (Psalms 136:13)*
*And made Israel to pass through the midst of it: for his mercy [endureth] for ever: (Psalms 136:14)*

**But overthrew Pharaoh and his host in the Red sea:** *for his mercy [endureth] for ever. (Psalms 136:15, KJV)*

There is a debate amongst historians as to whether the Pharoah of the oppression and the exodus is one and the same Pharoah or two separate Pharoahs.

*For since I came to Pharaoh to speak in thy name, he hath done evil to this people; neither hast thou delivered thy people at all. (Exodus 5:23)*
*Then the LORD said unto Moses, Now shalt thou see what I will do to Pharaoh: for with a strong hand shall he let them go, and with a strong hand shall he drive them out of his land. (Exodus 6:1).*

From the above Biblical quotation (sequential sentences) it would seem logical to conclude that the Pharoah of the oppression is the same as the Pharoah of the Exodus.

*Now therefore, behold, the cry of the children of Israel is come unto me: and I have also seen the oppression wherewith the Egyptians oppress them. (Exodus 3:9)*
*Come now therefore, and I will send thee unto Pharaoh, that thou mayest bring forth my people the children of Israel out of Egypt. (Exodus 3:10)*

Whichever of these conclusions the reader may reach it should become certain that the Pharaoh of the oppression is *Ramses II (**1279–1212 BC**)*. Historically he is called *Ramses the Great* for he presided over the wealthiest reign of ancient Egyptian civilization and commissioned the greatest number of buildings and monuments of any Pharaoh. At Luxor, The Ramesseum, a mortuary temple, contains the remains of a sixty foot 1,000 ton granite statue of the *Ramses II*. The mummy of *Ramses the Great*, discovered in Luxor in 1881, can be seen in the present day Egyptian capital of Cairo. The mummy of *Ramses the Great* is a *"sign" (Koran 10:92)* that may be seen at the Cairo Museum. The reign of *Ramses the II* was the longest of any Pharoah spanning almost 67 years. By *"hardening" (Exodus 14:4)* Pharaoh's heart God brought about his destruction and an eventual end to ancient Egypt's wealth *(Koran 10:88)*. Historically ancient Egypt's wealth declined after the reigns of *Ramses II* and his son *Merneptah*. *Ramses II* died in his early nineties while according to the Bible the Exodus occurred when Moses was eighty years old. *Merneptah*, the thirteenth son of *Ramses* took the throne. According to the Bible *Ramses's* first born died in the plague *(Exodus 12:29)*. *Ramses II's* family mausoleum, considered the largest tomb in Egypt was discovered in 1995. There about 50 of his 52 sons were buried. *Ramses II* had as many as 100 children.

قَالَ أَلَمْ نُرَبِّكَ فِينَا وَلِيدًا وَلَبِثْتَ فِينَا مِنْ عُمُرِكَ سِنِينَ ۝

*(Pharaoh) said (to Moses): "Did we not bring you up among us as a child? And you did dwell many years of your life with us. (Koran 26:18*

وَتِلْكَ نِعْمَةٌ تَمُنُّهَا عَلَيَّ أَنْ عَبَّدتَّ بَنِي إِسْرَآئِيلَ ۝

*"And this is the past favor with which you reproach me, that you have enslaved the Children of Israel."(Koran 26:22*

وَأَوْحَيْنَا إِلَىٰ مُوسَىٰ وَأَخِيهِ أَن تَبَوَّءَا لِقَوْمِكُمَا بِمِصْرَ بُيُوتًا وَٱجْعَلُوا بُيُوتَكُمْ قِبْلَةً وَأَقِيمُوا ٱلصَّلَوٰةَ وَبَشِّرِ ٱلْمُؤْمِنِينَ ۝

*And We inspired Moses and his brother (saying): "Take dwellings for your people in Egypt, and make your dwellings as places for your worship, and perform prayers, and give glad tidings to the believers."(Koran 10:87)*

وَقَالَ مُوسَىٰ رَبَّنَا إِنَّكَ ءَاتَيْتَ فِرْعَوْنَ وَمَلَأَهُ زِينَةً وَأَمْوَٰلًا فِى ٱلْحَيَوٰةِ ٱلدُّنْيَا رَبَّنَا لِيُضِلُّوا عَن سَبِيلِكَ رَبَّنَا ٱطْمِسْ عَلَىٰ أَمْوَٰلِهِمْ وَٱشْدُدْ عَلَىٰ قُلُوبِهِمْ فَلَا يُؤْمِنُوا حَتَّىٰ يَرَوُا ٱلْعَذَابَ ٱلْأَلِيمَ ۝

*And Moses said: "Our Lord! You have indeed bestowed on Pharaoh and his chiefs splendour and wealth in the life of this world, our Lord! That they may lead men astray from Your Path. Our Lord!* **Destroy their wealth, and harden their hearts, so that they will not believe until they see the painful torment.***"(Koran 10:88)*

131

قَالَ قَدْ أُجِيبَت دَّعْوَتُكُمَا فَٱسْتَقِيمَا وَلَا تَتَّبِعَآنِّ سَبِيلَ ٱلَّذِينَ لَا يَعْلَمُونَ

۸۹

*God said: "Accepted is Your prayer (O Moses and Aaron) So stand ye straight, And follow not the path of those who know not..(Koran 10:89)*

◆ وَجَـٰوَزْنَا بِبَنِىٓ إِسْرَٰٓءِيلَ ٱلْبَحْرَ فَأَتْبَعَهُمْ فِرْعَوْنُ وَجُنُودُهُۥ بَغْيًا

وَعَدْوًا حَتَّىٰٓ إِذَآ أَدْرَكَهُ ٱلْغَرَقُ قَالَ ءَامَنتُ أَنَّهُۥ لَآ إِلَٰهَ إِلَّا ٱلَّذِىٓ ءَامَنَتْ

بِهِۦ بَنُوٓا۟ إِسْرَٰٓءِيلَ وَأَنَا۠ مِنَ ٱلْمُسْلِمِينَ ۹۰

*And We took the Children of Israel across the sea, and **Pharaoh with his army followed them in oppression and enmity, till when drowning overtook him,** he said: "I believe that there is no God but the One in Whom the Children of Israel believe, and I am one of the Muslims (those who submit to God's Will)."(Koran 10:90)*

ءَآلْـَٰٔنَ وَقَدْ عَصَيْتَ قَبْلُ وَكُنتَ مِنَ ٱلْمُفْسِدِينَ ۹۱

*Now (you believe) while you refused to believe before and you were one of the corruptors. (Koran 10:91)*

فَٱلْيَوْمَ نُنَجِّيكَ بِبَدَنِكَ لِتَكُونَ لِمَنْ خَلْفَكَ ءَايَةً وَإِنَّ كَثِيرًا

مِّنَ ٱلنَّاسِ عَنْ ءَايَٰتِنَا لَغَٰفِلُونَ ۹۲

*So this day **We shall deliver your** (dead) **body** (out from the sea) **that you may be a sign to those who come after you!** And verily, many among mankind are heedless of Our signs. (Koran 10:92)*

The Koranic verse *"So this day **We shall deliver your** (dead) **body** (out from the sea) that you may be a sign to those who come after you"(Koran 10:92)*

is a revelation made many years before the discovery of the mummified remains of Pharoah.

Merenptah, Ramses II's son, ruled nine years. Merenptah is the only Pharoah whose name is mentioned in association with Israel. On a stele found near his funerary temple the text reads, after referring to a victorious campaign against the Libyans, "Israel has been destroyed". This stele discovered by Petrie in 1896, can be seen in the Cairo Museum, and is considered the oldest known archaeological evidence for the existence of Israel outside of the Old Testament. Could it be that Merenptah was somehow trying to vindicate his father's demise by concocting an imaginary victory? Who would have known that the Hebrews might not have also drowned in the Red Sea especially since they did not return to challenge the Egyptians? Could Merenptah, by so claiming, also have tried to bolster his own reign since all Pharaohs were supposed to be invincible gods? What better time to make such a claim, early on during his reign, when his ego was boosted by a victory against the Libyans. This claim would also support the fact that during Mernptah's reign the Exodus had transpired and the Hebrews had already left Egypt. After all history shows that his father, Ramses II, who was almost defeated, greatly exaggerated his own victory against the Hittites at Kadesh, Syria.

## JEWISH PROPHECY

وَلَقَدْ ءَاتَيْنَا بَنِىٓ إِسْرَٰٓءِيلَ ٱلْكِتَٰبَ وَٱلْحُكْمَ وَٱلنُّبُوَّةَ وَرَزَقْنَٰهُم مِّنَ ٱلطَّيِّبَٰتِ وَفَضَّلْنَٰهُمْ عَلَى ٱلْعَٰلَمِينَ ﴿١٦﴾

*And **surely We gave to the children of Israel the Book and the wisdom and the prophethood,** and We provided them with goodly things, **and We favored them above the nations.** (Koran 45:16)*

وَلَقَدۡ أَخَذَ ٱللَّهُ مِيثَـٰقَ بَنِىٓ إِسۡرَٰٓءِيلَ وَبَعَثۡنَا مِنۡهُمُ ٱثۡنَىۡ عَشَرَ نَقِيبًا ◆

وَقَالَ ٱللَّهُ إِنِّى مَعَكُمۡ لَئِنۡ أَقَمۡتُمُ ٱلصَّلَوٰةَ وَءَاتَيۡتُمُ ٱلزَّكَوٰةَ وَءَامَنتُم

بِرُسُلِى وَعَزَّرۡتُمُوهُمۡ وَأَقۡرَضۡتُمُ ٱللَّهَ قَرۡضًا حَسَنًا لَّأُكَفِّرَنَّ عَنكُمۡ

سَيِّـَٔاتِكُمۡ وَلَأُدۡخِلَنَّكُمۡ جَنَّـٰتٍ تَجۡرِى مِن تَحۡتِهَا ٱلۡأَنۡهَـٰرُ فَمَن كَفَرَ

بَعۡدَ ذَٰلِكَ مِنكُمۡ فَقَدۡ ضَلَّ سَوَآءَ ٱلسَّبِيلِ ﴿١٢﴾

*And **God made a covenant with the children of Israel**, and We raised up among them twelve chieftains; and **God said: Surely I am with you**; if you keep up prayer and pay the poor-rate and believe in My apostles and assist them and offer to God a goodly gift, I will most certainly cover your evil deeds, and I will most certainly cause you to enter into gardens beneath which rivers flow, but whoever disbelieves from among you after that, he indeed shall lose the right way. (Koran 5:12)*

The Koran confirms the covenant with the people of Israel as a chosen people as noted above but as we shall see this covenant is conditional as confirmed in both the Bible and the Koran. The expulsion of the Jewish people from the land of Israel is known as the diaspora.

## King Nebuchadnezzar

*Zedekiah [was] one and twenty years old when he began to reign, and **reigned eleven years in Jerusalem.** (2 Chronicles 36:11)*
*And he did [that which was] evil in the sight of the LORD his God, [and] humbled not himself before Jeremiah the prophet [speaking] from the mouth of the LORD.(2 Chronicles 36:12)*
*And he also rebelled against king Nebuchadnezzar, who had made him swear by God: but he stiffened his neck, and hardened his heart from turning unto the LORD God of Israel. (2 Chronicles 36:13)*
*Moreover all the chief of the priests, and the people, transgressed very much after all the abominations of the heathen; and polluted the house of the LORD which he had hallowed in Jerusalem. (2 Chronicles 36:14)*

*And the LORD God of their fathers sent to them by his messengers, rising up betimes, and sending; because he had compassion on his people, and on his dwelling place: (2 Chronicles 36:15)*

*But they mocked the messengers of God, and despised his words, and misused his prophets, until the wrath of the LORD arose against his people, till [there was] no remedy. (2 Chronicles 36:16)*

*Therefore he brought upon them the king of the Chaldees, who slew their young men with the sword in the house of their sanctuary, and had no compassion upon young man or maiden, old man, or him that stooped for age: he gave [them] all into his hand. 2 (Chronicles 36:17)*

Leviticus is the third of the five books of the Law (Pentateuch or Torah). In the passages below, we note that God threatened his people should they break his covenant. Was this fateful prophecy fulfilled during the reign of King Nebuchadnezzar?

*And the LORD spake unto Moses, saying, (Leviticus 12:1)*

*Ye shall not steal, neither deal falsely, neither lie one to another (Leviticus 19:11)*

*And the man that committeth adultery with another man's wife, even he that committeth adultery with his neighbour's wife, the adulterer and the adulteress shall surely be put to death. (Leviticus 20:10)*

*And he that killeth any man shall surely be put to death. (Leviticus 24:17)*

*And **if ye shall despise my statutes, or if your soul abhor my judgments, so that ye will not do all my commandments, but that ye break my covenant:** (Leviticus 26:15)*

*I also will do this unto you; I will even appoint over you terror, consumption, and the burning ague, that shall consume the eyes, and cause sorrow of heart: and ye shall sow your seed in vain, for your enemies shall eat it. (Leviticus 26:16)*

*These are the commandments, which the LORD commanded Moses for the children of Israel in mount Sinai. (Leviticus 27:34)*

The Biblical verse *"That then the LORD thy God will turn thy captivity, and have compassion upon thee, and **will return and gather thee from all the nations,** whither the LORD thy God hath scattered thee"(Deuteronomy 30:3)* appears to have been fulfilled by the creation of the modern Jewish state of Israel. The only other prominent and truly sovereign Jewish state is that during the reign of King Solomon. King Solomon, born in circa1030 B.C., was the last king of the united twelve tribes of Israel. The northern kingdom of Israel, Samaria, fell in 721 B.C. to the Assyrians while the fall of the southern kingdom of Israel, Judah, fell in 586 B.C to King Nebuchadnezzar (630 to 562 B.C.) of the Babylonians (Babylon is capital of the Chaldees) resulting in what is commonly known as the diaspora.

## DEUTERONOMY 30

And ***it shall come to pass, when all these things are come upon thee, the blessing and the curse, which I have set before thee***, *and thou shalt call [them] to mind among all the nations, whither the LORD thy God hath driven thee, (Deuteronomy 30:1)*

*And shalt return unto the LORD thy God, and shalt obey his voice according to all that I command thee this day, thou and thy children, with all thine heart, and with all thy soul; (Deuteronomy 30:2)*

*That then the LORD thy God will turn thy captivity, and have compassion upon thee, and will return and gather thee from all the nations, whither the LORD thy God hath scattered thee. (Deuteronomy 30:3)*

*If [any] of thine be driven out unto the outmost [parts] of heaven, from thence will the LORD thy God gather thee, and from thence will he fetch thee: (Deuteronomy 30:4)*

*And the LORD thy God will bring thee into the land which thy fathers possessed, and thou shalt possess it; and he will do thee good, and multiply thee above thy fathers. (Deuteronomy 30:5, KJV)*

*See, I have set before thee this day life and good, and death and evil; (Deuteronomy 30:15)*

*In that I command thee this day to love the LORD thy God, to walk in his ways, and to keep his commandments and his statutes and his judgments, that thou mayest live and multiply: and the LORD thy God shall bless thee in the land whither thou goest to possess it. (Deuteronomy 30:16)*

*But if thine heart turn away, so that thou wilt not hear, but shalt be drawn away, and worship other gods, and serve them; (Deuteronomy 30:17)*
*I denounce unto you this day, that ye shall surely perish, [and that] ye shall not prolong [your] days upon the land, whither thou passest over Jordan to go to possess it. (Deuteronomy 30:18)*
*I call heaven and earth to record this day against you, [that] I have set before you life and death, blessing and cursing: therefore choose life, that both thou and thy seed may live: (Deuteronomy 30:19)*
*That thou mayest love the LORD thy God, [and] that thou mayest obey his voice, and that thou mayest cleave unto him: for he [is] thy life, and the length of thy days: that thou mayest dwell in the land which the LORD sware unto thy fathers, to Abraham, to Isaac, and to Jacob, to give them. (Deuteronomy 30:20, KJV)*

Interestingly the Bible uses the term *"multiply thee"* to describe the Jewish peoples relatively increased numbers or population (*And the LORD thy God will bring thee into the land which thy fathers possessed, and thou shalt possess it; and he will do thee good, and **multiply thee** above thy fathers—Deuteronomy 30:5*). The Koran also foretells that after the diaspora the Jews would return to Israel in great numbers and would be bestowed with wealth. Hence, these prophecies foretell of the 'final days' after the diaspora with the creation of the present Jewish nation in 1948.

وَقُلْنَا مِنۢ بَعْدِهِۦ لِبَنِىٓ إِسْرَٰٓءِيلَ ٱسْكُنُوا۟ ٱلْأَرْضَ فَإِذَا جَآءَ وَعْدُ ٱلْءَاخِرَةِ جِئْنَا بِكُمْ لَفِيفًا ۝

*And We said to the Children of Israel after him: **"Dwell in the land, then, when the final and the last promise comes near We shall bring you altogether** as mixed crowd (gathered out of various nations). (Koran 17:104)*

ثُمَّ رَدَدْنَا لَكُمُ ٱلْكَرَّةَ عَلَيْهِمْ وَأَمْدَدْنَـٰكُم بِأَمْوَٰلٍ وَبَنِينَ وَجَعَلْنَـٰكُمْ

أَكْثَرَ نَفِيرًا ﴿٦﴾

*Then We gave you once again, a return of victory over them. And We helped you with wealth and children and made you more numerous in manpower. (Koran 17:6)*

إِنْ أَحْسَنتُمْ أَحْسَنتُمْ لِأَنفُسِكُمْ وَإِنْ أَسَأْتُمْ فَلَهَا فَإِذَا جَآءَ وَعْدُ ٱلْأَخِرَةِ

لِيَسُۥُٔواْ وُجُوهَكُمْ وَلِيَدْخُلُواْ ٱلْمَسْجِدَ كَمَا دَخَلُوهُ أَوَّلَ مَرَّةٍ وَلِيُتَبِّرُواْ

مَا عَلَوْاْ تَتْبِيرًا ﴿٧﴾

*If you do good, you do good for yourselves, and if you do evil (you do it) against yourselves. Then, when the final and the last promise comes near, your faces will become sorrowful and they will enter the mosque (of Jerusalem) as they had entered it before, and destroy with utter destruction all that fell in their hands. (Koran 17:7)*

## MOUNTAINS AS PEGS AND EARTH STABILIZERS

أَلَمْ نَجْعَلِ ٱلْأَرْضَ مِهَـٰدًا ﴿٦﴾

Have We not made the earth as a wide expanse, (Koran 78:6)

وَٱلْجِبَالَ أَوْتَادًا ﴿٧﴾

and the mountains as pegs? (Koran 78:7)

وَأَلْقَىٰ فِى ٱلْأَرْضِ رَوَاسِىَ أَن تَمِيدَ بِكُمْ وَأَنْهَـٰرًا وَسُبُلًا لَّعَلَّكُمْ تَهْتَدُونَ

*And He has affixed into the earth mountains standing firm, lest it should shake with you, and rivers and roads, that you may guide yourselves. (Koran 16:15)*

وَٱلْجِبَالَ أَرْسَـٰهَا

*And the mountains He has fixed firmly (Koran 79:32)*

These verses reveal two discoveries that were unknown at the time of revelation. The first is that mountains have **pegs** (Koran 78:7) or downward extensions into the earth. The second is that continental mass stabilization is achieved through the roots of mountains.

Continental crust averages about 35 km thick but under some mountain chains, crustal thickness is approximately twice that thickness. As with icebergs at sea far more of any mountain extends below the surface than is visible above the ground. In the same way, tall mountains usually have roots or **pegs** extending deeper into the earth than low mountains made up of the same rock type. In both cases, far more mass lies hidden from view than can be seen at the surface. Mountains must have roots deep enough to support their own above ground weight. *Mountains have deep **roots***, as determined through seismological and gravity studies. As erosion lowers mountains, isostasy raises them up again. These processes operate until the mountain belt reaches *"normal"* crustal thickness again. Mountain *"pegs"* in the 7th century AD was a phenomenon waiting to be discovered.

Continents can be divided into two subdivisions, active belts of mountain making, and **inactive regions of old, stable rock**. Tectonic activity is *the breaking and bending of the earth's crust by forces below the earth's surface*. Belts of mountain-making only account for a small portion of the continental crust, as most crust consists of inactive regions. These inactive regions can be subdivided into two categories: **continental shields** and **mountain roots. Continental shields** are *low-lying continental surfaces beneath which lie igneous and metamorphic rocks in a complex arrangement.* Exposed shields include very old sedimentary and metamorphic rocks, greater than 570 million years in age, and consist largely of low hills and plateaus. They have many thousands of meters of rock eroded. The Canadian Shield is an example of an exposed shield, and covers much of northern North America. **Mountain roots** are *remains of older eroded mountain belts that lie within the continental shields.*

*Manhattan Island* stands on one of the most **stable** parts of the North American crust, ancient metamorphic rock, as indicated by the geologic names Byram Gneiss, Inwood Marble and Manhattan Schist. These are the **roots of long-extinct mountains.** This solid and stable bedrock makes Manhattan Island an unlikely site for a devastating earthquake. Hence, one may conclude that *old mountain roots are stabilizing forces or pegs that help prevent earthquakes or shaking of the earth.*

### Geological Definitions

Stable Cratons—relatively flat, tectonically stable interiors of the continents. Divided into shield and platform areas.

Shields—is composed of very old, basement rocks that metamorphosed during tectonic activity billions of years ago. These mountain belts of the Precambrian are now stable showing no signs of recent tectonic activity. These large mountains subsequently eroded to a relatively flat surface.

Canadian shield or Precambrian shield—continental crust made up of blocks of high-grade metamorphic rocks that are roughly the same age.

Precambrian Era—longest period of Earth's history is called the Precambrian Eon. Most of the continents have a large exposed area of hard, crystalline Precambrian rock. The Canadian Shield is such an area.

Isostasy and Crustal Uplift—the concept of the Earth's crust in gravitational balance or equilibrium is called isostasy. Low-density crust floats on a denser mantle that flows. The floating of Earth's crust atop the mantle is termed isostasy. The heat that drives plate tectonics causes the mountains to form. The concept of isostasy explains the elevation difference between oceans and continents. Oceanic crust is thinner and denser than continental crust causing it to float lower on the mantle. Continental crust is thicker and less dense, which makes it more buoyant, allowing it to float higher on the mantle.

Plate tectonics or continental drift—the concept that lighter rocks of the continental masses are not fixed in place but rather float.

## NERVE ENDINGS

إِنَّ ٱلَّذِينَ كَفَرُوا۟ بِـَٔايَـٰتِنَا سَوْفَ نُصْلِيهِمْ نَارًا كُلَّمَا نَضِجَتْ جُلُودُهُم

بَدَّلْنَـٰهُمْ جُلُودًا غَيْرَهَا لِيَذُوقُوا۟ ٱلْعَذَابَ إِنَّ ٱللَّهَ كَانَ عَزِيزًا حَكِيمًا ﴿٥٦﴾

*Surely! Those who disbelieved in Our signs, We shall burn them in Fire. As often as their skins are roasted through,* **We shall change them for other skins** *that they may taste the punishment. Truly, God is Ever Most Powerful, All Wise. (Koran 4:56)*

This verse suggests that the author was knowledgeable of where sensory nerve fibers ended. How was the author so sure that sensory nerve fibers did not end in adipose tissue, muscle or even bone? For a society living in desert tents, the lack of mistakes and precision of language should leave one pondering how could one man know so much about so many things?

# ORBITAL MOTION

لَا ٱلشَّمْسُ يَنۢبَغِى لَهَآ أَن تُدۡرِكَ ٱلۡقَمَرَ وَلَا ٱلَّيۡلُ سَابِقُ ٱلنَّهَارِ وَكُلٌّ فِى فَلَكٍ يَسۡبَحُونَ ۝

*It is not for the sun to overtake the moon, nor does the night outstrip the day.*
***Everything floats in an orbit.*** *(Koran 36:40)*

The ***sun circles the Milky Way at a speed of about 486,000 miles per hour.*** The sun and planets each rotate on their axes. The ***Earth orbits the sun at about 67,000 miles an hour.*** The orbit of the Moon around the Earth is completed in approximately 27.3 days. Hence, the sun and the moon each follow their respective orbits in a predetermined course. The earth rotates about its axis once each day (approximately every 24 hours), while revolving around the sun, giving us night and day.

# OZONE LAYER

وَجَعَلۡنَا ٱلسَّمَآءَ سَقۡفًا مَّحۡفُوظًا وَهُمۡ عَنۡ ءَايَٰتِهَا مُعۡرِضُونَ ۝

*And We have made the sky a protective roof. Yet they turn away from the signs that these things point to. (Koran 21:32)*

The ozone layer offers protection or safety from harmful radiation. The above verse states that the sky is a protective roof. The verse continues to say how could anyone object to the significance of these words given their implied meaning (i.e. given these secrets of creation how could anyone reject the divine authorship of this sign). How could a mortal human accidentally mention a fact that would remain undiscovered for many centuries? What would have led anyone to have the insight and certainty that the sky offers protection? If anything, the sky sends thunderstorms, hail and lightening.

# PLANETARY MOTION

خَلَقَ ٱلسَّمَـٰوَٰتِ وَٱلْأَرْضَ بِٱلْحَقِّ يُكَوِّرُ ٱلَّيْلَ عَلَى ٱلنَّهَارِ وَيُكَوِّرُ ٱلنَّهَارَ
عَلَى ٱلَّيْلِ وَسَخَّرَ ٱلشَّمْسَ وَٱلْقَمَرَ كُلٌّ يَجْرِى لِأَجَلٍ مُّسَمًّى أَلَا هُوَ ٱلْعَزِيزُ
ٱلْغَفَّـٰرُ ۝

*He has created the heavens and the earth with truth. **He coils the night onto the day and coils the day onto the night.** And He has subjected the sun and the moon, each running (on a fixed course) for an appointed term. Verily, He is the All Mighty, the Oft-Forgiving. (Koran 39:5)*

وَهُوَ ٱلَّذِى خَلَقَ ٱلَّيْلَ وَٱلنَّهَارَ وَٱلشَّمْسَ وَٱلْقَمَرَ كُلٌّ فِى فَلَكٍ يَسْبَحُونَ
۝

*And He it is Who has created the night and the day, and **the sun and the moon, each in an orbit floating.** (Koran 21:33)*

وَتَرَى ٱلْجِبَالَ تَحْسَبُهَا جَامِدَةً وَهِىَ تَمُرُّ مَرَّ ٱلسَّحَابِ صُنْعَ ٱللَّهِ ٱلَّذِى
أَتْقَنَ كُلَّ شَىْءٍ إِنَّهُ خَبِيرٌ بِمَا تَفْعَلُونَ ۝

***"When you look at the mountains, you think that they are standing still, but they are moving like the clouds.*** *Such is the manufacture of God, who perfected everything. He is fully Cognizant of everything you do."* (Koran 27:88)

Coiling the night into day and day into night suggests that a rotational type motion is responsible for light and darkness. The word coil refers to a circular or rotational type motion. The author also knew that the moon and sun **each** has its own orbital motion.

143

The whole solar system and stars visible on a clear dark night orbit the center of our home galaxy, a spiral disk of some 200 billion stars called the Milky Way. It takes the sun 226 million years to circle its home galaxy. The **sun circles the Milky Way** at a speed of about 486,000 miles per hour. The sun and planets each rotate on their axes. The Earth rotates on its axis at about 1,100 miles an hour and orbits the sun at about 67,000 miles an hour. A fundamental fact of the universe is that everything is moving.

Finally without giving away the unknown scientific fact of the time we are told that the mountains (earth) are also moving. How could anyone at that time have known that just as the clouds are visibly moving the seemingly stationary mountains are also moving? As we now know the rotational motion of the earth is the obvious reason that the mountains are essentially moving. It seems that the author of this verse wanted mankind to discover this fact at a later date and time.

Claudius **Ptolemy**, an astronomer who lived in Alexandria (87–150 A.D), believed that the earth was *"motionless"* and situated at the center of the universe while the sun and moon were planets that revolved around the earth. This concept was similar to Aristotle's concept from the fourth century B.C.

**Nicholas Copernicus**'s *"On the Revolutions of the Celestial Orbs"*, published posthumously in 1543, gave weight to the theory, without definite proof, that the sun was at the center of the universe, with the earth a planet revolving around the sun. He also suggested that the earth's rotation around its axis explained the daily visibility of the sun, moon and stars. **Galileo** (1564–1642) using his telescope was instrumental in proving these theories of planetary motion. **Sir Isaac Newton** (1642–1727) by discovering and measuring the force of gravity surmised that the greater mass of the sun supported a heliocentric theory with the smaller planets revolving around the sun.

## POSITION OF THE STARS

$$﴾ فَلَا أُقْسِمُ بِمَوَاقِعِ النُّجُومِ ٧٥ ﴿$$

*So I swear by the position of the stars. (Koran 56:75)*

$$وَإِنَّهُ لَقَسَمٌ لَّوْ تَعْلَمُونَ عَظِيمٌ ٧٦﴿$$

*And verily, that is indeed a great oath, if you but know. (Koran 56:76)*

Scientifically we now know that the position of stars in space is always changing. When we look at a star its position has actually moved and it is no longer in the same position that we think we are seeing it in. The emphasis in these verses is on a great oath that is made on the *"position"* of the stars as. How did the author of this verse know that the position of the stars is such an unusually great phenomenon? In the seventh century A.D. with only the unaided eye one would have thought that the position of the stars is fixed.

## QUEEN OF SHEBA

*And when **the queen of Sheba heard of the fame of Solomon concerning the name of the LORD**, she came to prove him with hard questions. (1Kings10:1)*

*And she came to Jerusalem with a very great train, with camels that bare spices, and very much gold, and precious stones: and when she was come to Solomon, she communed with him of all that was in her heart. (1Kings10:2)*

***And Solomon told her all her questions: there was not any thing hid from the king, which he told her not. (1Kings10:3)***

*And when the queen of Sheba had seen all Solomon's wisdom, and the house that he had built, (1Kings10:4)*

*And the meat of his table, and the sitting of his servants, and the attendance of his ministers, and their apparel, and his cupbearers, and his ascent by which he went up unto the house of the LORD; **there was no more spirit in her**. (1Kings10:5)*

*And she said to the king, It was a true report that I heard in mine own land of thy acts and of thy wisdom. (1 Kings 10:6)*

The statement *"there was not any thing hid from the king, which he told her not"* suggests that there were secrets that only the *Queen of Sheba* was aware of and that because King Solomon revealed these secrets to her she become convinced of his message and believed in the Lord. Since *"there was no more spirit in her"* she could not contest or deny his message. Similarly, the Koran relates a specific incident that left the Queen of Sheba in a state of awe where she had no recourse but to accept Solomon's message.

فَمَكَثَ غَيْرَ بَعِيدٍ فَقَالَ أَحَطتُ بِمَا لَمْ تُحِطْ بِهِۦ وَجِئْتُكَ مِن سَبَإٍ بِنَبَإٍ يَقِينٍ ۝

*And he tarried not long, then said: I comprehend that which you do not comprehend and I have brought to you a **sure information from Sheba**. (Koran 27:22)*

إِنِّى وَجَدتُّ ٱمْرَأَةً تَمْلِكُهُمْ وَأُوتِيَتْ مِن كُلِّ شَىْءٍ وَلَهَا عَرْشٌ عَظِيمٌ ۝

*Surely I found a woman ruling over them, and she has been given abundance and **she has a mighty throne**: (Koran 27:23)*

إِنَّهُۥ مِن سُلَيْمَٰنَ وَإِنَّهُۥ بِسْمِ ٱللَّهِ ٱلرَّحْمَٰنِ ٱلرَّحِيمِ ۝

*Surely it is from Solomon, and surely it is in the name of God, the Beneficent, the Merciful; (Koran 27:30)*

أَلَّا تَعْلُوا عَلَيَّ وَأْتُونِي مُسْلِمِينَ ﴿٣١﴾

*Saying: exalt not yourselves against me and come to me in submission.*
*(Koran 27:31)*

قَالَ يَٰٓأَيُّهَا ٱلْمَلَؤُا۟ أَيُّكُمْ يَأْتِينِى بِعَرْشِهَا قَبْلَ أَن
يَأْتُونِى مُسْلِمِينَ ﴿٣٨﴾

He (**Solomon**) *said: O chiefs! which of you can* **bring to me her throne
before they come** *to me in submission? (Koran 27:38)*

قَالَ نَكِّرُوا۟ لَهَا عَرْشَهَا نَنظُرْ أَتَهْتَدِىٓ أَمْ تَكُونُ مِنَ ٱلَّذِينَ لَا يَهْتَدُونَ ﴿٤١﴾

He (**Solomon**) *said:* **Alter her** *throne for her, we will see whether she follows
the right way or is of those who do not go aright. (Koran 27:41)*

فَلَمَّا جَآءَتْ قِيلَ أَهَٰكَذَا عَرْشُكِ قَالَتْ كَأَنَّهُۥ هُوَ وَأُوتِينَا ٱلْعِلْمَ مِن قَبْلِهَا
وَكُنَّا مُسْلِمِينَ ﴿٤٢﴾

**So when she came, it was said: Is your throne like this? She said: It is as
it were the same,** *and we were given the knowledge before it,* **and we were
submissive.** *(Koran 27:42)*

قِيلَ لَهَا ٱدْخُلِى ٱلصَّرْحَ فَلَمَّا رَأَتْهُ حَسِبَتْهُ لُجَّةً وَكَشَفَتْ عَن سَاقَيْهَا قَالَ إِنَّهُۥ صَرْحٌ مُّمَرَّدٌ مِّن قَوَارِيرَ قَالَتْ رَبِّ إِنِّى ظَلَمْتُ نَفْسِى وَأَسْلَمْتُ مَعَ سُلَيْمَٰنَ لِلَّهِ رَبِّ ٱلْعَٰلَمِينَ ﴿٤٤﴾

*It was said to her: Enter the palace; but when she saw it she deemed it to be a great expanse of water, and bared her legs. He said: Surely it is a palace made smooth with glass. She said: **My Lord! surely I have been unjust to myself, and I submit with Solomon to God, the Lord of the worlds.** (Koran 27:44)*

# RELATIVITY

ٱللَّهُ ٱلَّذِى خَلَقَ ٱلسَّمَٰوَٰتِ وَٱلْأَرْضَ وَمَا بَيْنَهُمَا فِى سِتَّةِ أَيَّامٍ ثُمَّ ٱسْتَوَىٰ عَلَى ٱلْعَرْشِ مَا لَكُم مِّن دُونِهِۦ مِن وَلِىٍّ وَلَا شَفِيعٍ أَفَلَا تَتَذَكَّرُونَ ﴿٤﴾

*God is the one Who created the heavens and the earth, and all that is between them in six Days. Then He rose over the Throne. You (mankind) have none, besides Him, as a protector or an intercessor. Will you not then remember? (Koran 32:4)*

يُدَبِّرُ ٱلْأَمْرَ مِنَ ٱلسَّمَاءِ إِلَى ٱلْأَرْضِ ثُمَّ يَعْرُجُ إِلَيْهِ فِى يَوْمٍ كَانَ مِقْدَارُهُۥٓ أَلْفَ سَنَةٍ مِّمَّا تَعُدُّونَ ﴿٥﴾

*He directs the whole affair from heaven to earth. Then it (affair) will again ascend to Him on **a day whose length is a thousand years by the way you measure.** (Koran 32:5)*

تَعْرُجُ ٱلْمَلَـٰئِكَةُ وَٱلرُّوحُ إِلَيْهِ فِى يَوْمٍ كَانَ مِقْدَارُهُۥ خَمْسِينَ أَلْفَ سَنَةٍ

⊛

*The angels and the Spirit ascend to Him in **a Day the measure whereof is fifty thousand years** (Koran 70:4)*

Albert Einstein proposed the theory of relativity whereby space and time are relative. Time changes according to the speed of a moving object relative to the frame of reference of an observer.

## ROSE COLORED PAINTING

فَإِذَا ٱنشَقَّتِ ٱلسَّمَآءُ فَكَانَتْ وَرْدَةً كَٱلدِّهَانِ ۝

*When the sky disintegrates, and turns rose colored like paint (Koran 55:37)*

فَبِأَىِّ ءَالَآءِ رَبِّكُمَا تُكَذِّبَانِ ۝

*Which of your Lord's marvels can you deny? (Koran 55:38)*

A dying (disintegrating) star as can now be seen thru the Hubble telescope gives off colorful gas that may appear like a *rose colored* painting. How could a non-divine author of the Koran have known that the *Cat's Eye Nebula* with its rose colored petals would one day be discovered?

### NGC 6543(Cat's Eye Nebula)

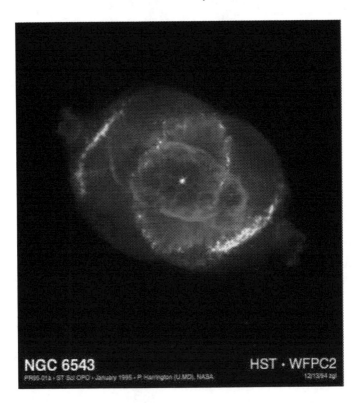

The color picture may be seen on the www at: *http://antwrp.gsfc.nasa.gov/apod/ap991031.html*

Picture of the *NGC 6543(Cat's Eye Nebula) nebula, a 'dying star'*, as taken by the NASA *Hubble Space Telescope*. The red color is hydrogen gas and the green color is nitrogen gas.

# ROMAN VICTORY

غُلِبَــــتِ ٱلــــرُّومُ ۝

*The Romans have been defeated.*

فِىٓ أَدۡنَى ٱلۡأَرۡضِ وَهُم مِّنۢ بَعۡدِ غَلَبِهِمۡ سَيَغۡلِبُونَ ۝

*In the lowest land, and they, after their defeat, will be victorious,*

فِى بِضۡعِ سِنِينَۗ لِلَّهِ ٱلۡأَمۡرُ مِن قَبۡلُ وَمِنۢ بَعۡدُۚ وَيَوۡمَئِذٍ يَفۡرَحُ ٱلۡمُؤۡمِنُونَ ۝

*Within three to nine years. The decision of the matter is with God, **before and after,** and on that Day, the believers will rejoice, (Koran 30:2-4)*

The above revelation occurred, at Mecca, sometime after the Eastern Roman Byzantine Empire was defeated at the hands of the Sassanids (Persians). The Sassanids captured Syria then Jerusalem in **614 AD** followed by Egypt. The Christian inhabitants of Jerusalem were massacred at the hand of the Sassanids who were pagans of the Zoroastrian faith. The Sassanids, in 614 AD, defeated the Romans according to verse 30:2 in the ***"lowest land".*** History confirms that the Sassanids wreaked havoc on the Christian monasteries along the Jordan River in the vicinity of Jericho and Jerusalem. The altitude of the Dead Sea shoreline is approximately 1,300 feet (400 meters) below sea level. The Jordan River empties into the Dead Sea. The Dead Sea is 50 miles long and 11 miles wide. The **lowest point on earth** is located at the **shore of the Dead Sea,** on the Israel-Jordan border. Jerusalem is approximately 12 miles west of the Dead Sea and 22 miles west of Jericho. Jericho is 10 miles north of the Dead Sea. Jericho besides being the oldest town on earth is the lowest town on earth as it lies 820 feet (260 meters) below sea level.

When several years passed with no visible Roman victory, the pagans of Mecca began taunting the Muslims, as fulfillment of the prophecy was not in sight. Prophet Muhammad and his companions left Mecca for Medina in 622 AD. By the **year 623 AD**, Heraclius, the Christian Byzantine Roman Emperor, fought and defeated the pagan (Zoroastrian) Persian King Chosroe II in a series of battles. The Romans were finally victorious on December 12, **627 AD** at the final and decisive battle of Nineveh (located on the eastern shore of the river Tigris—modern day Iraq). The Romans retook Jerusalem by **629 AD**. Earlier in the year of 627 AD, *before* the final and decisive Roman victory in December 12, 627 AD, the Muslims won the Battle of the Trench against the Meccans at Medina. Also *afterwards* the Muslims marched on and captured Mecca in 630 AD. Muhammad the prophet of Islam died in the year 632 AD. In 636 AD Muslim Arabs captured Jerusalem.

## SEVEN SKIES

هُوَ ٱلَّذِى خَلَقَ لَكُم مَّا فِى ٱلْأَرْضِ جَمِيعًا ثُمَّ ٱسْتَوَىٰ إِلَى ٱلسَّمَآءِ فَسَوَّىٰهُنَّ سَبْعَ سَمَٰوَٰتٍ ۚ وَهُوَ بِكُلِّ شَىْءٍ عَلِيمٌ ۝

*He Who created for you all that is on earth. Then He rose over towards the sky and made them seven skies and He is the All-Knower of everything. (Koran 2:29)*

ٱلَّذِى خَلَقَ سَبْعَ سَمَٰوَٰتٍ طِبَاقًا ۖ مَّا تَرَىٰ فِى خَلْقِ ٱلرَّحْمَٰنِ مِن تَفَٰوُتٍ ۖ فَٱرْجِعِ ٱلْبَصَرَ هَلْ تَرَىٰ مِن فُطُورٍ ۝

*Who has created the **seven skies one above another**, you can see no fault in the creations of the Most Beneficent. Then look again: "Can you see any rifts?"(Koran 67:3)*

Defined by temperature variations the earth's atmosphere contains seven different layers: (1) troposphere (2) tropopause (3) stratosphere (4) stratopause (5) mesosphere (6) mesopause and (7) thermosphere.

(1) The troposphere exists from the surface of the earth to approximately 11 kilometers. This layer contains about 75% of the total mass of the atmosphere. It is also the layer where the majority of our weather occurs. Maximum air temperature in the troposphere occurs near the earth's surface. Temperature decreases with altitude so that at the top of the troposphere the temperature is—55 degrees Celsius.

(2) The tropopause, extending from 11 to 20 kilometers, is an isothermal layer where temperature remains constant over a distance of 9 kilometers.

(3) The stratosphere extends from 20 to 48 kilometers above the earth's surface. In the stratosphere temperature increases with altitude because ozone gas found in this layer absorbs ultraviolet sunlight creating heat energy. Ozone (O3) is primarily found in the atmosphere between the altitudes of 20 to 30 kilometers. Jets fly in the stratosphere where there are no violent storms.

(4) The stratopause is an isothermal layer.

(5) In the mesosphere, the atmosphere reaches its coldest temperatures (about-90 degrees Celsius) at a height of approximately 80 kilometers.

(6) The mesopause is an isothermal layer.

(7) The thermosphere, extending from altitudes of 90 to 100 kilometers, is the hottest layer in the atmosphere as oxygen molecules absorb solar radiation. Temperatures reach up to1200 degrees celsius or 2200 fahrenheit.

The thermosphere causes ionospheres and therefore the ionosphere is part of the thermosphere. Ions form because of very high temperatures in the thermosphere. *"Thermo"* relates to heat or high temperatures.

The exosphere is an ill-defined region where molecules, ions or gases escape into outer space. Exo meaning *"outside of our atmosphere"* is where hydrogen, helium and atomic oxygen are found while in the earth's immediate atmosphere there is a predominance of nitrogen and oxygen gas. The exosphere merges with interplanetary space. The exosphere is beyond the thermosphere and theoretically extends to 100,000 km; this is where the sun's gravitational field exceeds the earth's gravitational field. Hence, it would be reasonable to surmise that the exosphere, a transitional zone that extends into outer space, is in essence not a part of the earth's atmosphere.

## SKIES WITH A PURPOSE

ثُـــمَّ أَسْــتَوَىٰ إِلَـــى ٱلسَّـــمَآءِ وَهِـــىَ دُخَـــانٌ فَقَـــالَ لَهَـــا وَلِلْأَرْضِ ٱئْتِيَا طَوْعًا أَوْ كَرْهًا قَالَتَآ أَتَيْنَا طَآئِعِينَ ﴿١١﴾

*Then He rose over towards the sky when it was smoke, and said to it and to the earth: "Come both of you willingly or unwillingly." They both said: "We come, willingly." (Koran 41:11)*

فَقَضَىٰهُنَّ سَبْعَ سَمَٰوَاتٍ فِى يَوْمَيْنِ وَأَوْحَىٰ فِى كُلِّ سَمَآءٍ أَمْرَهَا وَزَيَّنَّا ٱلسَّمَآءَ ٱلدُّنْيَا بِمَصَٰبِيحَ وَحِفْظًا ذَٰلِكَ تَقْدِيرُ ٱلْعَزِيزِ ٱلْعَلِيمِ ﴿١٢﴾

*Then He completed and finished seven skies in two Days and **He made in each sky its affair** ... (Koran 41:12)*

**"He made in each sky its affair"** implies a different function for each of the seven skies. Rainfall, being essential for sustaining life, is contained in, and originates from, the troposphere. In this layer 99% of water vapor is contained. The **ozone layer,** found in the stratosphere, protects life from harmful ultraviolet radiation. The ionosphere, found in the thermosphere, also protects from harmful radiation. Most meteoroids as they pass through the atmosphere are vaporized due to intense heat generated from friction.

# SOLAR AND LUNAR YEARS

وَلَبِثُوا۟ فِى كَهْفِهِمْ ثَلَٰثَ مِا۟ئَةٍ سِنِينَ وَٱزْدَادُوا۟ تِسْعًا ﴿٢٥﴾

*And they stayed in their Cave three hundred (solar) years, and increased by nine (for lunar years). (Koran 18:25)*

قُلِ ٱللَّهُ أَعْلَمُ بِمَا لَبِثُوا۟ لَهُۥ غَيْبُ ٱلسَّمَٰوَٰتِ وَٱلْأَرْضِ أَبْصِرْ بِهِۦ وَأَسْمِعْ مَا لَهُم مِّن دُونِهِۦ مِن وَلِىٍّ وَلَا يُشْرِكُ فِى حُكْمِهِۦٓ أَحَدًا ﴿٢٦﴾

*Say: "God knows best how long they stayed. With Him is (the knowledge of) the unseen of the heavens and the earth. How clearly He sees, and hears (everything)! They have no Helper, other than Him, and He makes none to share in His Decision and His Rule." (Koran 18:26)*

In the above verse, we come to conclude that three hundred solar years are practically equivalent to three hundred and nine lunar years (300 x 365.24 days/solar year = 109,572 days while 309 x 354.37 days/lunar year = 109,500 days).

The above verse implies a connection between the lunar and solar calendars. The Chinese, Hebrew and Indian peoples incorporate both these calendars resulting in a solar/lunar calendar. The solar calendar is useful for determining the seasons while for a Muslim the lunar calendar gives the variability that may make for a shorter fasting day in the winter months or a longer fasting day in the summer not to mention the possibility of a pilgrimage during a cooler or hotter season during an average lifetime.

Also planting during a full moon when the moon is closest to the earth may increase crop yields. This is due to the moon's gravitational tides and increased rainfall promoting successful germination. Hence, God in his infinite wisdom may have been giving mankind a hint that there are uses for both the solar and lunar calendars *(Koran 18:25)*.

إِنَّ عِدَّةَ ٱلشُّهُورِ عِندَ ٱللَّهِ ٱثْنَا عَشَرَ شَهْرًا فِى كِتَـٰبِ ٱللَّهِ يَوْمَ خَلَقَ ٱلسَّمَـٰوَٰتِ وَٱلْأَرْضَ مِنْهَآ أَرْبَعَةٌ حُرُمٌ ذَٰلِكَ ٱلدِّينُ ٱلْقَيِّمُ فَلَا تَظْلِمُوا۟ فِيهِنَّ أَنفُسَكُمْ وَقَـٰتِلُوا۟ ٱلْمُشْرِكِينَ كَآفَّةً كَمَا يُقَـٰتِلُونَكُمْ كَآفَّةً وَٱعْلَمُوٓا۟ أَنَّ ٱللَّهَ مَعَ ٱلْمُتَّقِينَ ۞

*Verily, the number of months with God is twelve months* (in a year), so *was it ordained by God on the Day when He created the heavens and the earth; of them four are Sacred, (i.e. the 1st, the 7th, the 11th and the 12th months of the Islamic calendar). That is the right religion, so wrong not yourselves therein, and fight against the polytheists as they fight against you collectively. But know that God is with those who are pious (Koran 9:36)*

The above verse refers to sacred months when war by Muslims should not be declared or fought so that they may rest. Also, the variability of the seasons in the lunar calendar may allow one to plan for a war in different types of weather. Imagine if the favorable climate for a war always fell on the sacred months when wars should not be declared. For example although Hitler had no religious constraints he may have fared better in his Russian campaign if he had paid heed to the seasons. One wonders if Hitler read history as Napoleon fell to a similar fate while fighting the Russians during a long and cold winter.

Verily, the number of months with God is twelve months (Koran 9:36).

**The word *'months'* is found twelve times in the Koran** *and this can be verified using a search engine (http://quod.lib.umich.edu/k/koran/simple. html). The word months referred to in Koran 9:37 is not actual text but rather explanatory and is placed in brackets.*

**Again verify for yourself:**

*http://www.2muslims.com/cgi-bin/hadith/quran/quran.cgi*

Just enter the word **months** and scroll to the bottom and you will get 12.

This observation appears to take on more significance in view of the fact the Koran stating that God *"keeps a count of all things"(Koran 72:28)*?

*. . . and He keepeth count of all things (Koran 72:28).*

## SPACE TRAVEL

يَٰمَعْشَرَ ٱلْجِنِّ وَٱلْإِنسِ إِنِ ٱسْتَطَعْتُمْ أَن تَنفُذُواْ مِنْ أَقْطَارِ ٱلسَّمَٰوَٰتِ وَٱلْأَرْضِ فَٱنفُذُواْ لَا تَنفُذُونَ إِلَّا بِسُلْطَٰنٍ ۝

*O assembly of Jinns and humans, if you can penetrate the regions of the heavens and the earth, then penetrate them. You will not penetrate them save with a power. (Koran 55:33)*

During ancient times, one may have thought that it might be possible to fly with a pair of wings. But how could anyone be certain that a source of energy could be harnessed not only to fly airplanes but also to travel into outer space (and go to the moon)?

## THE NIGHT COILS OVER THE DAY

خَلَقَ ٱلسَّمَٰوَٰتِ وَٱلْأَرْضَ بِٱلْحَقِّ يُكَوِّرُ ٱلَّيْلَ عَلَى ٱلنَّهَارِ وَيُكَوِّرُ ٱلنَّهَارَ عَلَى ٱلَّيْلِ وَسَخَّرَ ٱلشَّمْسَ وَٱلْقَمَرَ كُلٌّ يَجْرِى لِأَجَلٍ مُّسَمًّى أَلَا هُوَ ٱلْعَزِيزُ ٱلْغَفَّٰرُ ۝

*He created the heavens and the earth in true (proportions): He makes the* **Night coil** *(yokawer)* **over the Day, and the Day coil over the Night***: He has subjected the sun and the moon (to His law): Each one follows a course for a time appointed. Is He not the Exalted in Might—The forgiver? (Koran 39:5)*

**Word: Yokawer means a coiling or rotatory type motion.**

**Root: kawer Root Def: coiled, gathered like a turban, rounded, rotated, rolled.**

The above verse implies that the night coils over the day, and the day coils over the night. Such an explicit description and understanding of this phenomenon requires knowledge of the rotatory motion of the earth. Whether the sun revolves around the earth or vice versa the day/ night phenomenon can only be explained if we accept that the earth rotates on its axis—unless one were to postulate that the sun revolves around the earth in 24 hours. French physicist Leon Foucault in 1851 proved the Earth's rotation using a pendulum that hung from the domed ceiling of the Pantheon in Paris. The pendulum would swing in the same direction to the right never retracing the same path. To state that the night coils on the day or vice versa not only requires that the earth rotate on its axis but also implies that the earth's shape is most likely round or oval. The Arabic word "ball" pronounced "kora" is also derived from the same root noted above. Hence, a "round about motion" is responsible for the alterations of "night and day" and this is emphasized in the Koranic verse above by also applying this terminology to the alterations of "day and night".

In contrast, by quoting the Old Testament "*The sun* also ariseth, and the sun goeth down, and *hasteth to his place where he arose*" (Ecclesiastes 1:5, King James Version) we are left with the distinct impression that this verse supports the geocentric views of Aristotle where the earth was at the center of our known universe. This is one of the reasons the Catholic Church condemned Galileo in 1616 for suggesting that the earth moved and that the sun, instead of the earth, was at the center of the universe. Also, in this heliocentric view, Galileo wrongly assumed that the sun did not move. As we now know, the sun rotates on its axis and follows an orbit. The earth revolves around the sun in 365 days. How did the author of the Koran avoid this Biblical error and yet with such precision of language describe this natural phenomenon?

# UNDERWATER CURRENTS

أَوْ كَظُلُمَٰتٍ فِى بَحْرٍ لُّجِّىٍّ يَغْشَىٰهُ مَوْجٌ مِّن فَوْقِهِۦ
مَوْجٌ مِّن فَوْقِهِۦ سَحَابٌ ظُلُمَٰتٌۢ بَعْضُهَا فَوْقَ بَعْضٍ إِذَآ أَخْرَجَ يَدَهُۥ
لَمْ يَكَدْ يَرَىٰهَا وَمَن لَّمْ يَجْعَلِ ٱللَّهُ لَهُۥ نُورًا فَمَا لَهُۥ مِن نُّورٍ ۝

*Or as like the darkness in a vast deep sea, covers it **a wave above which
is a wave, above which is layer upon layer of clouded darkness**, if a
man stretches out his hand, he can hardly see it. And for whom God has not
appointed light, for him there is no light. (Koran 24:40)*

Underwater currents called deep-sea currents explain the principle of *"a
wave above a wave"*. The increased density of water at greater sea depths
contributes to the formation of underwater currents.

*"Layer upon layer of darkness"* refers to the gradual separation of the
light spectrum within the sea, one color at a time, until complete darkness
is finally achieved. All seven wavelengths of the light spectrum are gradually
and individually absorbed until at great depths of water we have complete
darkness. The reason the ocean appears blue is that the blue wavelength is
reflected back from deeper waters while the six other wavelengths of the
light spectrum are absorbed at the closer surface waters. This phenomenon
explains the *"layer upon layer of darkness"*. The darkness in the sea is likened
to the inability to see when flying thru 'clouds' or driving thru fog.

The above Koranic verse notes that deep-sea currents are a phenomenon
*"above which"* we find the phenomenon of layers of light. At depths of 200
meters, there is no sunlight penetration. Bottom ocean currents can be
detected at even greater depths of 3000 to 3600 meters.

# WATER BARRIERS

### Water Barrier Between Salt And Fresh Water Bodies:

$$وَهُوَ ٱلَّذِى مَرَجَ ٱلْبَحْرَيْنِ هَـٰذَا عَذْبٌ فُرَاتٌ وَهَـٰذَا مِلْحٌ أُجَاجٌ وَجَعَلَ بَيْنَهُمَا بَرْزَخًا وَحِجْرًا مَّحْجُورًا ۝$$

*And He Who has let free the two kinds of water, one palatable and sweet, and the other salty and bitter, and He has set between them **a barrier and a forbidding partition.*** *(Koran 25:53)*

An estuary is where fresh river water meets the sea. Fresh river water and salt water have different densities that resist mixing. In highly stratified estuaries or salt wedge estuaries, characteristic of deep/high volume rivers, strong vertical haloclines are formed. The salt wedge estuary is named after its salinity structure. The saline water intrudes from the sea as a wedge below the river water. Low-density river water slides over the top of the dense seawater. These salinity variations result in the formation of haloclines. The deep water has an almost uniform salinity. There is a net outflow in the surface layer and inflow in the deeper water. In this situation a very strong halocline exists between the two layers. The **halocline forms a partition that helps maintain the significantly distinct properties of the fresh and salt-water bodies.**

Water Barrier Between Two Salt Water Bodies:

$$مَرَجَ ٱلْبَحْرَيْنِ يَلْتَقِيَانِ ۝$$

$$بَيْنَهُمَا بَرْزَخٌ لَّا يَبْغِيَانِ ۝$$

*He has set free the two seas meeting together. Between them is **a barrier,** which they do not transgress.* *(Koran 55:19-20).*

With two seas such as the Mediterranean Sea or Atlantic Ocean, the salinity of the Mediterranean Sea is higher due to greater evaporation.

There too a barrier is caused by the difference in the densities of these water bodies. In the study of oceanography, these transition zones, called pycnoclines, form invisible **barriers** that do not allow much movement between different water zones.

**Oceanology Definitions**

**Haloclines**—salinity variations or abrupt salinity changes with depths. Such a barrier has formed between the Mediterranean Sea and Atlantic Ocean, at the strait of Gibraltar, even though other forces such as tides or currents are present; this particular halocline forms at a depth of 1000 meters.

**Thermoclines**—abrupt temperature changes with depth.

**Pycnoclines**—density layering or abrupt density changes at certain depths. Pycnoclines may form because of haloclines, thermoclines or both.

**Salinity**—e.g. 35 gm salt per one 1000 gm of water is expressed as 35.00. Salinity in the sea is 35.00 while in the river is <0.500.

# THE NUMBER NINETEEN

لَوَّاحَةٌ لِّلْبَشَرِ ﴿٢٩﴾

*A sign for mankind*

عَلَيْهَا تِسْعَةَ عَشَرَ ﴿٣٠﴾

*Over it is nineteen*

وَمَا جَعَلْنَآ أَصْحَبَ ٱلنَّارِ إِلَّا مَلَتَبِكَةً وَمَا جَعَلْنَا عِدَّتَهُمْ إِلَّا فِتْنَةً لِّلَّذِينَ

كَفَرُواْ لِيَسْتَيْقِنَ ٱلَّذِينَ أُوتُواْ ٱلْكِتَبَ وَيَزْدَادَ ٱلَّذِينَ ءَامَنُوٓاْ إِيمَنَا وَلَا

يَرْتَابَ ٱلَّذِينَ أُوتُواْ ٱلْكِتَبَ وَٱلْمُؤْمِنُونَ وَلِيَقُولَ ٱلَّذِينَ فِى قُلُوبِهِم

مَّرَضٌ وَٱلْكَفِرُونَ مَاذَآ أَرَادَ ٱللَّهُ بِهَذَا مَثَلًا كَذَلِكَ يُضِلُّ ٱللَّهُ مَن يَشَآءُ

وَيَهْدِى مَن يَشَآءُ وَمَا يَعْلَمُ جُنُودَ رَبِّكَ إِلَّا هُوَ وَمَا هِىَ إِلَّا ذِكْرَىٰ لِلْبَشَرِ

﴿٣١﴾

*And We have set none but angels as guardians of the Fire, and We have fixed
their number (19) only as a trial for the disbelievers, in order that the people
of the Scripture (Jews and Christians) may arrive at a certainty (that this
Koran is the truth and the believers may increase in Faith) and that no doubts
may be left for the people of the Scripture and the believers, and that those in
whose hearts is a disease (of hypocrisy) and the disbelievers may say: "What
God intends by this (curious) example?" Thus God leads astray whom He wills
and guides whom He wills. And none can know the hosts of your Lord but He.
And this is nothing else than a reminder to mankind.*

كَلَّا وَٱلْقَمَرِ ﴿٣٢﴾

*Nay, and by the moon,*

وَٱلَّيْلِ إِذْ أَدْبَرَ ﴿٣٣﴾

*And by the night when it withdraws,*

وَٱلصُّبْحِ إِذَآ أَسْفَرَ ﴿٣٤﴾

*And by the dawn when it brightens,*

$$\text{إِنَّهَا لَإِحْدَى الْكُبَرِ} \ ⑮$$

*One of the great miracles,*

$$\text{نَذِيرًا لِّلْبَشَرِ} \ ⑯$$

*A warning to mankind, (Koran 74:29-36)*

In the above Koranic verses, the number nineteen is described *as a sign, a reminder, a great miracle* and *a warning to mankind*. The Koranic phenomenon of the number nineteen was referenced, and commented on, in the **Scientific American** journal (*Scientific American, September 1980, page 22, article by Martin Gardner*).

*"One of the great miracles" (Koran 74:35)* = 7+4+3+5=**19**.

$$\text{وَيَقُولُونَ لَوْلَا أُنزِلَ عَلَيْهِ ءَايَةٌ مِّن رَّبِّهِۦ فَقُلْ إِنَّمَا الْغَيْبُ لِلَّهِ}$$
$$\text{فَانتَظِرُوا إِنِّى مَعَكُم مِّنَ الْمُنتَظِرِينَ} \ ⑳$$

*And they say: "How is it that not a sign is sent down on him from his Lord?" Say: "The unseen belongs to God Alone, so wait you, verily I am with you among those who wait. (Koran 10:20)*

$$\text{لِيَعْلَمَ أَن قَدْ أَبْلَغُوا رِسَالَاتِ رَبِّهِمْ وَأَحَاطَ بِمَا لَدَيْهِمْ وَأَحْصَىٰ كُلَّ}$$
$$\text{شَيْءٍ عَدَدًا} \ ㉘$$

*He (God) protects them (the Messengers)], till He sees that they have conveyed the Messages of their Lord. And He surrounds all that which is with them, and **He keeps count of all things** (Koran 72:28).*

*"He keeps count of all things"* (72:28) = 7+2+ 2+8=19.

163

# THE MOON

كَلَّا وَٱلْقَمَرِ ٣٢

*Nay, and by the moon, (74:32)*

ٱقْتَرَبَتِ ٱلسَّاعَةُ وَٱنشَقَّ ٱلْقَمَرُ ١

*The Hour has drawn near, and **the moon has been cleft asunder**
(Koran 54:1)*

Relating to the number nineteen there is an affirmation *"nay by the
moon"(Koran 74:32).* The Apollo 11 Facts (http://www.nasm.si.edu/
apollo/AS11/a11facts.htm) reveal that the lunar module departed the
moon at the 54th minute and 1st second or sura number 54 and verse 1
[LM Departed Moon: **July 21, 1969** 17:**54:01** UT (1:**54:01** p.m. EDT)/
Koran 54:1]. This information comes from NASA and the National Air
and the Smithsonian Space Museum. The Apollo 11 lunar module was
the first mission to bring back lunar rocks. The first verse of the *Koranic*
chapter entitled *"The Moon"* states metaphorically *"the hour has drawn
near and **the moon has been cleft asunder"**(Koran 54:1).*

If we add the sura number (54), the verse number (1), the day (21),
the month (7) and the year (1969) the result is a number divisible by
nineteen (54 + 1 + 21 + 7 + 1969 = 2052 *or 19 x 108*).

***"HE KEEPS COUNT OF ALL THINGS"***
*(72:28) = 7+2+ 2+8=**19**.*

بِسْمِ ٱللَّهِ ٱلرَّحْمَٰنِ ٱلرَّحِيمِ ١

*In the Name of God, the Most Beneficent, the Most Merciful. (Koran 1:1)*

**The first verse** *(1:1)* of the Koran **consists of 19 Arabic letters.**

إِنَّهُۥ مِن سُلَيْمَـٰنَ وَإِنَّهُۥ بِسْمِ ٱللَّهِ ٱلرَّحْمَـٰنِ ٱلرَّحِيمِ ۝

*"Verily! It is from Solomon, and verily! It (reads): In the Name of God, the Most Beneficent, the Most Merciful; (Koran 27:30)*

**The first verse** *(1:1)* **occurs in the Quran 114 times** *(19X6)* despite its absence from the beginning of Sura 9 it is found in Sura 27 (see above).

ٱقْرَأْ بِٱسْمِ رَبِّكَ ٱلَّذِى خَلَقَ ۝

*Read! In the Name of your Lord, Who has created (all that exists),*

خَلَقَ ٱلْإِنسَـٰنَ مِنْ عَلَقٍ ۝

*Has created man from a cling (that which clings to the uterus)*

ٱقْرَأْ وَرَبُّكَ ٱلْأَكْرَمُ ۝

*Read! And your Lord is the Most Generous,*

ٱلَّذِى عَلَّمَ بِٱلْقَلَمِ ۝

*Who has taught (the writing) by the pen Read!*

عَلَّمَ ٱلْإِنسَـٰنَ مَا لَمْ يَعْلَمْ ۝

*Has taught man that which he knew not. (Koran 96:1-5)*

**The *"first"* revealed verses of the Koran** (96:1-5) **consist of 19 words and 76 letters** *(19 X 4).*

Hence: **The Koran has 114 chapters or suras** *(19 X 6).*

Hence, we begin to see that the number nineteen is a common phenomenon whereby many things seem to be divisible by the number nineteen.

# THE QURANIC (KORANIC) INITIAL "Qaf " ( ‎ق or ‎ﻕ )

There are only two chapters or *suras (42 and 50)* in the entire Koran *(Quran)* that are initialed with the letter *"Qaf"*. The texts of the two "Qaf" initialed suras each contain *57 Qaf (3x 19)*.

حـــــمّ ① 

*Ha Meem.(42:1)*

عـــــسـق ② 

*Ain Seen **Qaf**. (42:2)*

ق وَٱلۡقُرۡءَانِ ٱلۡمَجِيدِ ① 

***Qaf** and the Glorious Quran.(50:1)*

Sura 50 is entitled *"Qaf,"* prefixed with *"Qaf,"* and the first verse reads, *"Qaf and the Glorious Quran."* This indicates that *"Q"* stands for *"Quran,"* and **the sum of the Qafs in the two Qaf initialed suras** (57+57 =114) **represents the Quran's 114 suras** *(19x6)*. The Quran is described in Sura *"Qaf"* as Glorious (ٱلۡمَجِيد), and the Arabic word *"Glorious"* has a gematrical value of *57(19x3)*: *Meem (40) + Jeem (3) + Yeh (10) + Dal (4) = 57(3x19)*.

Sura **42** consists of **53** verses, and **42 + 53** = *95* = *19x5*.
Sura **50** consists of **45** verses, and **50 + 45** = *95* = *19x5*.

**This observation would suggest that both the length** (number of verses in a sura) **and sequence** (sura number/order) **of Quranic chapters**

**were predetermined to fit this number nineteen phenomenon.** Hence, this would be consistent with the Koranic claim that God is to preserve and protect the Koran in its original form.

## GEMATRICAL VALUES

The number system as we know it today evolved with time. Prior to this, alphabets were used as numerals. The Roman numeral system (I, V, X, C, etc.) is an example of such a system (**I = 1, V = 5, X = 10, L = 50, C = 100, D = 500, and M = 1,000**). The number assigned to each letter is its *"Gematrical Value."* The numerical values of the Arabic alphabet also known as *"Abjad"* are shown below.

|  |  |  |  |  |  |  |  |  | ى<br>*Alef*<br>1 |
|---|---|---|---|---|---|---|---|---|---|
| ى<br>*Yeh*<br>10 | ط<br>*Tah*<br>9 | ح<br>*Ha*<br>8 | ز<br>*Zein*<br>7 | و<br>*Waw*<br>6 | ه<br>*Heh*<br>5 | د<br>*Dal*<br>4 | ج<br>*Jeem*<br>3 | ب<br>*Beh*<br>2 | |
| ق<br>*Qaf*<br>100 | ص<br>*Sad*<br>90 | ف<br>*Fe*<br>80 | ع<br>*Ain*<br>70 | س<br>*Seen*<br>60 | ن<br>*Noon*<br>50 | م<br>*Meem*<br>40 | ل<br>*Laam*<br>30 | ك<br>*Kaf*<br>20 | |
| غ<br>*Ghayn*<br>1000 | ظ<br>*Za*<br>900 | ض<br>*Dad*<br>800 | ذ<br>*Zhal*<br>700 | خ<br>*Kha*<br>600 | ث<br>*The*<br>500 | ت<br>*Te*<br>400 | ش<br>*Sheen*<br>300 | ر<br>*Ra*<br>200 | |

لَّقَدْ كَفَرَ ٱلَّذِينَ قَالُوٓاْ إِنَّ ٱللَّهَ ثَالِثُ ثَلَـٰثَةٍ وَمَا مِنْ إِلَـٰهٍ إِلَّآ إِلَـٰهٌ وَٰحِدٌ وَإِن لَّمْ يَنتَهُواْ عَمَّا يَقُولُونَ لَيَمَسَّنَّ ٱلَّذِينَ كَفَرُواْ مِنْهُمْ عَذَابٌ أَلِيمٌ ٧٣

*Surely, disbelievers are those who said: "God is the third of the three (in a Trinity)." But there is no god but* **One God***. And if they cease not from what they say, verily, a painful torment will befall the disbelievers among them. (Koran 5:73)*

The gematrical value of the Arabic word *"one"* (اوحد) is 19. Could it be that the number nineteen was intentionally chosen to reaffirm that there is only One God?

# THE SEVEN PAIRS

وَلَقَدْ ءَاتَيْنَـٰكَ سَبْعًا مِّنَ ٱلْمَثَانِى وَٱلْقُرْءَانَ ٱلْعَظِيمَ ۝

*"We have given you the **seven pairs** and the Great Koran" (15:87)*

Fourteen different lettered initials precede 29 suras or chapters of the Koran. In total there are 30 Koranic initials but only 14 are different. Fourteen letters of the Arabic alphabet participate in these initials. Hence, **seven pairs of different initials** participate in this phenomenon. These seven pairs of unique initials have no actual literary meaning and although they are found in the Koran, they are in the linguistic sense extraneous to it. This would explain the precision of the word *"and"* in sura 15 and verse 87 *"the seven pairs **and** the Great Koran"*. Dividing the number fourteen, by two, gives us the seven pairs. Could this be a hint whereby a process of division ties in the number nineteen to the Koranic initials? Is there a special Koranic phenomenon divisible by the number nineteen? Could it be that the number nineteen is part of a sign, miracle or pattern found in the readable Koranic text?

الٓمٓ ۝

*Alef Laam Meem (2:1)*

الٓمٓ ۝

*Alef Laam Meem (3:1)*

الٓمٓصٓ ۝

*Alef Laam Meem Saad (7:1)*

الٓرۚ تِلْكَ ءَايَـٰتُ ٱلْكِتَـٰبِ ٱلْحَكِيمِ ۝

*Alef Laam Ra. These are the Verses of the Book (the Koran) of Wisdom (10:1)*

الٓرۚ كِتَـٰبٌ أُحْكِمَتْ ءَايَـٰتُهُۥ ثُمَّ فُصِّلَتْ مِن لَّدُنْ حَكِيمٍ خَبِيرٍ ۝

*Alef Laam Ra. (This is) a Book, the Verses whereof are perfected, and then explained in detail from One (God), Who is All-Wise and Well-Acquainted (with all things). (11:1)*

الٓرۚ تِلْكَ ءَايَـٰتُ ٱلْكِتَـٰبِ ٱلْمُبِينِ ۝

*Alef Laam Ra. These are the Verses of the Manifest Book (12:1)*

الٓمٓرۚ تِلْكَ ءَايَـٰتُ ٱلْكِتَـٰبِ وَٱلَّذِىٓ أُنزِلَ إِلَيْكَ مِن رَّبِّكَ ٱلْحَقُّ وَلَـٰكِنَّ أَكْثَرَ ٱلنَّاسِ لَا يُؤْمِنُونَ ۝

**Alef Laam Meem Ra** *These are the Verses of the Book (the Koran), and that which has been revealed unto you from your Lord is the truth, but most men believe not. (13:1)*

الٓرۚ كِتَـٰبٌ أَنزَلْنَـٰهُ إِلَيْكَ لِتُخْرِجَ ٱلنَّاسَ مِنَ ٱلظُّلُمَـٰتِ إِلَى ٱلنُّورِ بِإِذْنِ رَبِّهِمْ إِلَىٰ صِرَٰطِ ٱلْعَزِيزِ ٱلْحَمِيدِ ۝

*Alef Laam Ra. (This is) a Book which We have revealed unto you (O Muhammad) in order that you might lead mankind out of darkness into light by their Lord's Permission to the Path of the All-Mighty, the Owner of all Praise. (14:1)*

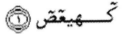

*Alef Laam Ra. These are the Verses of the Book, and of a Koran that makes things clear. (15:1)*

كهيعص ①

**Kaf Heh Yeh Ain Saad** *(19:1)*

طه ①

**Tah Heh** *(20:1)*

طسم ①

**Tah Seen Meem** *(26:1)*

**Tah Seen.** *These are the Verses of the Koran, and a Book that makes things clear; (27:1)*

طسم ①

*Tah Seen Meem (28:1)*

الٓمٓ ①

*Alef Laam Meem (29:1)*

الٓمٓ ۝

*Alef Laam Meem (30:1)*

الٓمٓ ۝

*Alef Laam Meem (31:1)*

الٓمٓ ۝

*Alef Laam Meem (32:1)*

يٓسٓ ۝

**Yeh Seen** *(36:1)*

صٓ وَٱلۡقُرۡءَانِ ذِى ٱلذِّكۡرِ ۝

**Saad.** *By the Koran full of reminding. (38:1)*

حمٓ ۝

**Ha Meem** *(40:1)*

حمٓ ۝

*Ha Meem (41:1)*

حمٓ ۝

*Ha Meem (42:1)*

عٓسٓقٓ ۝

**Ain Seen Qaf** *(42:2)*

حـــمّ ①

*Ha Meem (43:1)*

حـــمّ ①

*Ha Meem (44:1)*

حـــمّ ①

*Ha Meem (45:1)*

حـــمّ ①

*Ha Meem (46:1)*

قٓ وَٱلۡقُرۡءَانِ ٱلۡمَجِيدِ ①

**Qaf.** *By the Glorious Koran. (Koran 50:1)*

نٓ وَٱلۡقَلَمِ وَمَا يَسۡطُرُونَ ①

**Noon.** *By the pen and what the (angels) write (in the Records of men). (Koran 68:1)*

The 30 Koranic initials are found in 29 suras. Only 14 of these 30 Koranic initials are unique or different *(English initials* **bolded***).*

| *No* | Sura No | *Sura Title* | *Koranic Initials* |
|------|---------|--------------|--------------------|
| *1* | *2* | *The Heifer* | **Alef Laam Meem** |
| *2* | *3* | *The Amramites* | *Alef Laam Meem* |
| *3* | *7* | *The Purgatory* | **Alef Laam Meem Saad** |
| *4* | *10* | *Jonah* | **Alef Laam Ra** |
| *5* | *11* | *Hud* | *Alef Laam Ra* |
| *6* | *12* | *Joseph* | *Alef Laam Ra* |
| *7* | *13* | *Thunder* | **Alef Laam Meem Ra** |
| *8* | *14* | *Abraham* | *Alef Laam Ra* |
| *9* | *15* | *Al-Hijr Valley* | *Alef Laam Ra* |
| *10* | *19* | *Mary* | **Kaf Heh Yeh Ain Saad** |
| *11* | *20* | *TahHeh* | **Tah Heh** |
| *12* | *26* | *The Poets* | **Tah Seen Meem** |
| *13* | *27* | *The Ant* | **Tah Seen** |
| *14* | *28* | *History* | *Tah Seen Meem* |
| *15* | *29* | *The Spider* | *Alef Laam Meem* |
| *16* | *30* | *The Romans* | *Alef Laam Meem* |
| *17* | *31* | *Luqmaan* | *Alef Laam Meem* |
| *18* | *32* | *Prostration* | *Alef Laam Meem* |
| *19* | *36* | *YehSeen* | **Yeh Seen** |
| *20* | *38* | *Saad* | **Saad** |
| *21* | *40* | *Forgiver* | **Ha Meem** |
| *22* | *41* | *Elucidated* | *Ha Meem* |
| *23* | *42* | *Consultation* | *Ha Meem /* **Ain Seen Qaf** |
| *24* | *43* | *Ornaments* | *Ha Meem* |
| *25* | *44* | *Smoke* | *Ha Meem* |
| *26* | *45* | *Kneeling* | *Ha Meem* |
| *27* | *46* | *The Dunes* | *Ha Meem* |
| *28* | *50* | *Q* | **Qaf** |
| *29* | *68* | *The Pen* | **Noon** |

# KORANIC INITIALS

وَلَقَدۡ ءَاتَيۡنَـٰكَ سَبۡعٗا مِّنَ ٱلۡمَثَانِي وَٱلۡقُرۡءَانَ ٱلۡعَظِيمَ ۝

*We have given you **the seven pairs** and the Great Koran (15:87)*

The Koran has 29 chapters (or suras) that are prefixed with unusual *"Koranic initials"* that have no obvious literary meaning. Each set of *"Koranic initials"* consists of one to five Arabic letters. Fourteen unique *"Koranic initials"* participate in this unusual phenomenon. Hence, **seven pairs** of *"Koranic initials"* participate in this phenomenon *(7 x 2 = 14)*. The above Koranic verse implies that God gave us *"the seven pairs"* and the Great Koran.

Fourteen Arabic letters (half of the Arabic alphabet) participate in the formation of the 14 different sets of *"Koranic initials"* that prefix 29 chapters (suras) of the Koran. If we add the gematrical value of each one of these 14 letters (693) plus the number 29 (the 29 chapters prefixed with the 14 different *"Koranic initials"*) we get a number divisible by 19 (693 + 29 = 722 = *19 x 38*). Also if we add the total gematrical value of these 14 initials (693) plus the sum of the chapter "number" where the initial "first" occurs (295) we get a total of 988 *(693 + 295 = 19 x 52)*. The subsequent table summarizes these findings whereby the number *"19"* phenomenon participates in the formation of the *"seven pairs"* computations.

| The 14 Letters of the "Koranic Initials" | | |
|---|---|---|
| Letter | Gematrical Value | Chapter # where letter 1st occurs |
| Alef  ﺍ | 1 | 2 |
| Laam  ﻝ | 30 | 2 |
| Meem ﻡ or ﻤ | 40 | 2 |
| Saad  ﺹ | 90 | 7 |
| Ra  ﺭ | 200 | 10 |
| Kaf  ﻙ | 20 | 19 |
| Heh  ﻩ or ﻪ | 5 | 19 |
| Yeh  ﻱ | 10 | 19 |
| Ain  ﻉ or ﻊ | 70 | 19 |
| Tah  ﻁ | 9 | 20 |
| Seen  ﺱ or ﺲ | 60 | 26 |
| Ha  ﺣ | 8 | 40 |
| Qaf  ﻕ | 100 | 42 |
| Noon  ﻥ | 50 | 68 |
| Totals | 693 | 295 |
| 693 + 29 (chapters) = 722 = 19 x 38 | | |
| also 693 + 295 = 988 = 19 x 52 | | |

This observation would again seem to reaffirm that **the sequence (sura number/order) of Koranic chapters was predetermined to simultaneously fit both the "Seven Pairs" and "the letter Qaf enigma".** Otherwise, this "number nineteen" phenomenon could not be fulfilled and would simply fall apart. The *"first"* Qaf must occur in sura 42 for (a) the 19x 5=95 phenomenon to occur and (b) also have the identical 95 value in the two Qaf suras (see *"The Quranic Initial Qaf"* section).

Sura **42** consists of **53** verses, and **42 + 53** = *95* = *19x5*.
Sura **50** consists of **45** verses, and **50 + 45** = *95* = *19x5*.

Also sura number 42 could not have had a different value or we may not have fulfilled the 295 value which is essential for the sum of the first suras (see the *"Seven Pairs"* section).

*"He (God) keeps count of all things" (Koran 72:28)*

# Epilogue

In this final section, we will touch on the true meaning of scripture and the relevance of this message to our spiritual existence. The message eternal in the continuum of scripture will be clarified. Scripture lays the foundation for our relationship with one another as well as our relationship with God. We will better understand our relationship with each other when we understand what God expects of us. The journey that a writer or reader undertakes when studying religion should not be about which religion claims superiority or which religion has more to offer but rather why should I believe. One should ask how could I and why should I believe? We should ponder on what God really wants us to believe in, rather than what our forefathers and we would like to believe in. Only when we search for God with all our mind, heart and soul will we come closer to understanding our true purpose and hopefully live a better and richer life.

## NEW EARTH AND HEAVENS

*The afterlife in the book of Isaiah is associated with the creation of a "new" heaven and earth (Isaiah 66:22). Similarly, the Koran mentions recreation (Koran 21:104) and a "new" earth and heaven (Koran 14:48). This new heaven and earth (paradise), created at the time of resurrection, will somehow be similar to the world we know.*

*For **as the new heavens and the new earth, which I will make**, shall remain before me, **saith the LORD**, so shall your seed and your name remain. (Isaiah 66:22)*

*And it shall come to pass, that from one new moon to another, and from one sabbath to another, shall all flesh come to worship before me, saith the LORD (Isaiah 66:23)*
*And they shall go forth, and **look upon the carcases of the men that have transgressed against me: for their worm shall not die, neither shall their fire be quenched**; and they shall be an abhorring unto all flesh. **(Isaiah 66:24)***

يَوْمَ تُبَدَّلُ ٱلْأَرْضُ غَيْرَ ٱلْأَرْضِ وَٱلسَّمَٰوَٰتُ وَبَرَزُوا۟ لِلَّهِ ٱلْوَٰحِدِ ٱلْقَهَّارِ ۝

*On the Day when **the earth will be changed to another earth and so will be the heavens,** and they (all creatures) will appear before God, the One, The Irresistible. (Koran 14:48)*

يَوْمَ نَطْوِى ٱلسَّمَآءَ كَطَيِّ ٱلسِّجِلِّ لِلْكُتُبِ كَمَا بَدَأْنَآ أَوَّلَ خَلْقٍ نُّعِيدُهُۥ وَعْدًا عَلَيْنَآ إِنَّا كُنَّا فَٰعِلِينَ ۝

*And the Day when We shall roll up the heavens like a scroll rolled up for books, as We began the first creation, We shall repeat it, a promise binding upon Us. Truly, We shall do it. (Koran 21:104)*

# HEREAFTER

## INTRODUCTION

In the Old Testament, Book of Job, we are informed that humans will see God in the afterlife after being resurrected in the flesh *(Job19: 26),* and that hell will be for the wicked *(Psalm 9:17).* At the time of death, prior to resurrection, the spirit shall return to God *(Ecclesiastes Qoh.12 [7]).* To fear God and keep his commandments is the whole duty of man *(Ecclesiastes Qoh.12 [13]).* We are told that there will be reward and punishment *(Isaiah*

*26:19-21*), and that hell will be eternal for those who *"transgress"* against God *(Isaiah 66:24)*. The Book of Daniel also informs us that at the time of resurrection some humans will experience everlasting life, while others may experience everlasting abhorrence *(Daniel 12:2)*.

In the New Testament we are advised that we will meet the prophets in *"The Kingdom of Heaven" (Matthew 8:11)* **that is also known as** *"The Kingdom of God" (Luke 13:28)*. **Again in the New Testament we are advised that humans will have eternal life (for the righteous) or everlasting punishment** *(Matthew 25:46)*. The New Testament also makes a clear reference to the presence of hell *(Matthew 10:2)*.

## OLD TESTAMENT

## AFTERLIFE (BOOK OF JOB)

*And though after my skin worms destroy this body, yet in my flesh shall I see God (Job 19:26)*

## HELL (PSALMS OF DAVID)

**The wicked shall be turned into hell,** *and all the nations that forget God. (Psalm 9:17)*

*Let death seize upon them, and let them go down quick into hell: for wickedness is in their dwellings, and among them. (Psalm 55:15)*

## SEPARATION OF BODY AND SOUL (ECCLESIASTES)

The opening first sentence of the book of Ecclesiastes suggests that the following are the words of King Solomon: *The words of the Preacher, the son of David, king in Jerusalem. (Ecclesiastes Qoh.1:1)*

*Then shall the dust return to the earth as it was: and* the spirit shall return unto God who gave it. *(Ecclesiastes Qoh.12:7)*

## DUTY OF MAN AND JUDGMENT DAY (ECCLESIASTES)

*Let us hear the conclusion of the whole matter:* **Fear God, and keep his commandments: for this is the whole duty of man.** *(Ecclesiastes Qoh.12:13)*
**For God shall bring every work into judgment**, *with every secret thing, whether it be good, or whether it be evil. (Ecclesiastes Qoh.12:14)*

## REWARD AND PUNISHMENT (ISAIAH)

*Thy dead men shall live, together with my dead body shall they arise. Awake and sing, ye that dwell in dust: for thy dew is as the dew of herbs, and the earth shall cast out the dead. (Isaiah 26:19)*
*Come, my people, enter thou into thy chambers, and shut thy doors about thee: hide thyself as it were for a little moment, until the indignation be overpast. (Isaiah 26:20)*
*For, behold, the LORD cometh out of his place to punish the inhabitants of the earth for their iniquity: the earth also shall disclose her blood, and shall no more cover her slain. (Isaiah 26:21)*

## ETERNAL HELL IN THE OLD TESTAMENT

*And they shall go forth, and look upon the carcases of* **the men that have transgressed against me**: *for their worm* **shall not die, neither shall their fire be quenched**; *and they shall be an abhorring unto all flesh. (Isaiah 66:24)*

## HELL (BOOK OF DANIEL)

*And many of them that sleep in the dust of the earth shall awake, some to everlasting life, and some to reproaches and everlasting abhorrence. (Daniel 12:2)*

## NEW TESTAMENT GOSPELS

*And I say unto you, That many shall come from the east and west, and shall sit down with Abraham, and Isaac, and Jacob, in the kingdom of heaven. (Matthew 8:11)*

## BODY AND SOUL IN HELL (MATTHEW)

*And fear not them which kill the body, but are not able to kill the soul: but rather fear him which is able to destroy both soul and body in hell. (Matthew 10:28)*

## ETERNAL AFTERLIFE (NEW TESTAMENT)

***And these shall go away into everlasting punishment: but the righteous into life eternal.*** *(Matthew 25:46)*

*There shall be weeping and gnashing of teeth, when ye shall see Abraham, and Isaac, and Jacob, and all the prophets, in the kingdom of God, and you yourselves thrust out. (Luke 13:28)*

## THE KORAN

The Koran states that the dwellers of hell are those who profit off others (Koran 6:128), the hypocrites (Koran 9:68), those who mock the messengers (Koran 18:106), disbelieve and reject God's communications (Koran 57:19), those who are too proud to serve God (Koran 40:60), the ungrateful and rebellious (Koran 50:24), those who forge lies against God (Koran 29:68), the transgressors (Koran 32:20), and those who believe that God created the world in vain (Koran 38:27). Also the Koran states that those who disbelieve and act unjustly God will guide to eternal hell (Koran 4:168-169). However, for **those who repent,** believe, and perform righteous deeds, **God will change the evil of such persons into good** (Koran 25:70).

وَيَوْمَ يَحْشُرُهُمْ جَمِيعًا يَـٰمَعْشَرَ ٱلْجِنِّ قَدِ ٱسْتَكْثَرْتُم مِّنَ ٱلْإِنسِ وَقَالَ أَوْلِيَآؤُهُم مِّنَ ٱلْإِنسِ رَبَّنَا ٱسْتَمْتَعَ بَعْضُنَا بِبَعْضٍ وَبَلَغْنَآ أَجَلَنَا ٱلَّذِىٓ أَجَّلْتَ لَنَا قَالَ ٱلنَّارُ مَثْوَىٰكُمْ خَـٰلِدِينَ فِيهَآ إِلَّا مَا شَآءَ ٱللَّهُ إِنَّ رَبَّكَ حَكِيمٌ عَلِيمٌ ﴿١٢٨﴾

*One day will He gather them all together, (and say): "O ye assembly of Jinns! Much (toll) did ye take of men." And their friends from among the men shall say:" Our Lord! some of us profited by others and we have reached our appointed term which Thou didst appoint for us." He will say: " The fire is your abode, to abide in it, except as God is willet"; surely your Lord is Wise, Knowing. (Koran 6:128)*

وَعَدَ ٱللَّهُ ٱلْمُنَـٰفِقِينَ وَٱلْمُنَـٰفِقَـٰتِ وَٱلْكُفَّارَ نَارَ جَهَنَّمَ خَـٰلِدِينَ فِيهَا هِىَ حَسْبُهُمْ وَلَعَنَهُمُ ٱللَّهُ وَلَهُمْ عَذَابٌ مُّقِيمٌ ﴿٦٨﴾

*God has promised the hypocritical men and the hypocritical women and the unbelievers the fire of hell to abide therein; Sufficient is it for them; and God has cursed them and they shall have lasting punishment. (Koran 9:68)*

ذَٰلِكَ جَزَآؤُهُمْ جَهَنَّمُ بِمَا كَفَرُوا۟ وَٱتَّخَذُوٓا۟ ءَايَـٰتِى وَرُسُلِى هُزُوًا ﴿١٠٦﴾

*That is their reward, Hell, because they disbelieved and, and held My Signs and My apostles in mockery. (Koran 18:106)*

وَٱلَّذِينَ ءَامَنُوا بِٱللَّهِ وَرُسُلِهِ أُولَٰئِكَ هُمُ ٱلصِّدِّيقُونَّ وَٱلشُّهَدَآءُ عِندَ رَبِّهِمْ لَهُمْ أَجْرُهُمْ وَنُورُهُمْ وَٱلَّذِينَ كَفَرُوا وَكَذَّبُوا بِـَٔايَٰتِنَآ أُولَٰئِكَ أَصْحَٰبُ ٱلْجَحِيمِ ﴿١٩﴾

*And (as for) those who believe in God and His apostles, these it is that are the truthful and the faithful ones in the sight of their Lord: they shall have their reward and their light, and (as for) those who disbelieve and reject Our Signs, these are the inmates of the hell. (Koran 57:19)*

إِنَّ ٱلَّذِينَ كَذَّبُوا بِـَٔايَٰتِنَا وَٱسْتَكْبَرُوا عَنْهَا لَا تُفَتَّحُ لَهُمْ أَبْوَٰبُ ٱلسَّمَآءِ وَلَا يَدْخُلُونَ ٱلْجَنَّةَ حَتَّىٰ يَلِجَ ٱلْجَمَلُ فِى سَمِّ ٱلْخِيَاطِ وَكَذَٰلِكَ نَجْزِى ٱلْمُجْرِمِينَ ﴿٤٠﴾

*Surely (as for) those who reject Our communications and turn away from them haughtily, the doors of heaven shall not be opened for them, nor shall they enter the garden until the camel pass through the eye of the needle; and thus do We reward the guilty. (Koran 7:40)*

وَقَالَ رَبُّكُمُ ٱدْعُونِىٓ أَسْتَجِبْ لَكُمْ إِنَّ ٱلَّذِينَ يَسْتَكْبِرُونَ عَنْ عِبَادَتِى سَيَدْخُلُونَ جَهَنَّمَ دَاخِرِينَ ﴿٦٠﴾

*And your Lord says: Call upon Me, I will answer you; surely those who are too proud for My service shall soon enter hell abased. (Koran 40:60)*

أَلْقِيَا فِى جَهَنَّمَ كُلَّ كَفَّارٍ عَنِيدٍ ﴿٢٤﴾

*Do cast into hell every ungrateful, rebellious one, (Koran 50:24)*

وَمَنْ أَظْلَمُ مِمَّنِ افْتَرَىٰ عَلَى اللَّهِ كَذِبًا أَوْ كَذَّبَ بِالْحَقِّ لَمَّا جَاءَهُ أَلَيْسَ فِى جَهَنَّمَ مَثْوًى لِّلْكَـٰفِرِينَ ﴿٦٨﴾

*And who is more unjust than one who forges a lie against God, or gives the lie to the truth when it has come to him? Will not in hell be the abode of the unbelievers? (Koran 29:68)*

وَأَمَّا الَّذِينَ فَسَقُوا فَمَأْوَىٰهُمُ النَّارُ كُلَّمَا أَرَادُوا أَن يَخْرُجُوا مِنْهَا أُعِيدُوا فِيهَا وَقِيلَ لَهُمْ ذُوقُوا عَذَابَ النَّارِ الَّذِى كُنتُم بِهِ تُكَذِّبُونَ ﴿٢٠﴾

*And as for those who transgress, their abode is the fire; whenever they desire to go forth from it they shall be brought back into it, and it will be said to them: Taste the penalty of the fire which you called a lie. (Koran 32:20)*

وَمَا خَلَقْنَا السَّمَاءَ وَالْأَرْضَ وَمَا بَيْنَهُمَا بَـٰطِلًا ذَٰلِكَ ظَنُّ الَّذِينَ كَفَرُوا فَوَيْلٌ لِّلَّذِينَ كَفَرُوا مِنَ النَّارِ ﴿٢٧﴾

*And **We did not create the heaven and the earth and what is between them in vain;** that is the opinion of those who disbelieve then woe to those who disbelieve on account of the fire. (Koran 38:27)*

يَوْمَ يُحْمَىٰ عَلَيْهَا فِى نَارِ جَهَنَّمَ فَتُكْوَىٰ بِهَا جِبَاهُهُمْ وَجُنُوبُهُمْ وَظُهُورُهُمْ هَـٰذَا مَا كَنَزْتُمْ لِأَنفُسِكُمْ فَذُوقُوا مَا كُنتُمْ تَكْنِزُونَ ﴿٣٥﴾

*On the day when it shall be heated in the fire of hell, then their foreheads and their sides and their backs shall be branded with it; this is what you hoarded up for yourselves, therefore taste what you hoarded. (Koran 9:35)*

$$\text{إِنَّ ٱلَّذِينَ كَفَرُوا وَظَلَمُوا لَمْ يَكُنِ ٱللَّهُ لِيَغْفِرَ لَهُمْ}$$
$$\text{وَلَا لِيَهْدِيَهُمْ طَرِيقًا} \; \textcircled{١٦٨}$$

*Surely (as for) those who disbelieve and act unjustly God will not forgive them*
*nor guide them to a path—(Koran 4:168)*

$$\textcircled{١٦٩} \; \text{إِلَّا طَرِيقَ جَهَنَّمَ خَالِدِينَ فِيهَا أَبَدًا وَكَانَ ذَٰلِكَ عَلَى ٱللَّهِ يَسِيرًا}$$

*Except the path of Hell, to dwell therein forever. And this for God is easy.*
*(Koran 4:169)*

$$\text{إِلَّا مَن تَابَ وَءَامَنَ وَعَمِلَ عَمَلًا صَالِحًا فَأُو۟لَٰٓئِكَ يُبَدِّلُ}$$
$$\text{ٱللَّهُ سَيِّـَٔاتِهِمْ حَسَنَٰتٍ وَكَانَ ٱللَّهُ غَفُورًا رَّحِيمًا} \; \textcircled{٧٠}$$

**Unless he repents, believes, and works righteous deeds,** *for* **God will**
**change the evil of such persons into good,** *and God is Oft-Forgiving, Most*
*Merciful, (Koran 25:70)*

## PARADISE

According to the Koran the dwellers of paradise will live in "*palaces and*
*gardens beneath which rivers flow*" *(Koran 25:10)*, where things are "*similar*"
to what we knew in this world *(Koran 2:25 and Koran 47.15)*, and people
'*will have what they please*' *(Koran 16:31)*. The characteristics of the people
who enter heaven are those who "*fear God*" *(Koran 9:109)*, are "*truthful*"
*(Koran 5:119)*, "*believe and do good*" *(Koran 4:122)* and "*not too proud to*
*serve God*" *(Koran 21:19)*; these people are promised paradise, or gardens
beneath which rivers flow, wherein they will abide forever.

تَبَارَكَ ٱلَّذِى إِن شَآءَ جَعَلَ لَكَ خَيْرًا مِّن ذَٰلِكَ جَنَّٰتٍ تَجْرِى مِن تَحْتِهَا ٱلْأَنْهَٰرُ وَيَجْعَل لَّكَ قُصُورًا ⑩

*Blessed is He Who, if He please, will give you what is better than this, gardens beneath which rivers flow, and He will give you palaces. (Koran 25:10)*

وَبَشِّرِ ٱلَّذِينَ ءَامَنُوا۟ وَعَمِلُوا۟ ٱلصَّٰلِحَٰتِ أَنَّ لَهُمْ جَنَّٰتٍ تَجْرِى مِن تَحْتِهَا ٱلْأَنْهَٰرُ كُلَّمَا رُزِقُوا۟ مِنْهَا مِن ثَمَرَةٍ رِّزْقًا قَالُوا۟ هَٰذَا ٱلَّذِى رُزِقْنَا مِن قَبْلُ وَأُتُوا۟ بِهِۦ مُتَشَٰبِهًا وَلَهُمْ فِيهَآ أَزْوَٰجٌ مُّطَهَّرَةٌ وَهُمْ فِيهَا خَٰلِدُونَ ㉕

*And convey good news to those who believe and do good deeds, that they shall have gardens, beneath rivers flow. Every time they are fed with fruits therefrom, they say: "Why, this is what we were fed with before," for **they are given things in similitude**; and they have therein companions pure (and holy); and they abide therein (for ever). (Koran 2:25)*

مَّثَلُ ٱلْجَنَّةِ ٱلَّتِى وُعِدَ ٱلْمُتَّقُونَ فِيهَآ أَنْهَٰرٌ مِّن مَّآءٍ غَيْرِ ءَاسِنٍ وَأَنْهَٰرٌ مِّن لَّبَنٍ لَّمْ يَتَغَيَّرْ طَعْمُهُ وَأَنْهَٰرٌ مِّنْ خَمْرٍ لَّذَّةٍ لِّلشَّٰرِبِينَ وَأَنْهَٰرٌ مِّنْ عَسَلٍ مُّصَفًّى وَلَهُمْ فِيهَا مِن كُلِّ ٱلثَّمَرَٰتِ وَمَغْفِرَةٌ مِّن رَّبِّهِمْ كَمَنْ هُوَ خَٰلِدٌ فِى ٱلنَّارِ وَسُقُوا۟ مَآءً حَمِيمًا فَقَطَّعَ أَمْعَآءَهُمْ ⑮

*(Here is) **a Parable** of the Garden which the righteous are promised: in it are rivers of water incorruptible; rivers of milk of which the taste never changes; rivers of wine, a joy to those who drink; and rivers of honey pure and clear. In it there are for them all kinds of fruits; and Grace from their Lord. (Can those in such Bliss) be compared to such as shall dwell forever in the Fire, and be given, to drink, boiling water, so that it cuts up their bowels? (Koran 47.15)*

$$ جَنَّٰتُ عَدْنٍ يَدْخُلُونَهَا تَجْرِى مِنْ تَحْتِهَا ٱلْأَنْهَٰرُ لَهُمْ فِيهَا مَا يَشَآءُونَ $$

$$ كَذَٰلِكَ يَجْزِى ٱللَّهُ ٱلْمُتَّقِينَ ﴿٣١﴾ $$

*The gardens of eternity, they shall enter them, rivers flowing beneath them; they shall have in them what they please. Thus does God reward those who guard (against evil), (Koran 16:31)*

$$ أَفَمَنْ أَسَّسَ بُنْيَٰنَهُۥ عَلَىٰ تَقْوَىٰ مِنَ ٱللَّهِ وَرِضْوَٰنٍ خَيْرٌ أَم مَّنْ أَسَّسَ $$

$$ بُنْيَٰنَهُۥ عَلَىٰ شَفَا جُرُفٍ هَارٍ فَٱنْهَارَ بِهِۦ فِى نَارِ جَهَنَّمَ وَٱللَّهُ لَا يَهْدِى $$

$$ ٱلْقَوْمَ ٱلظَّٰلِمِينَ ﴿١٠٩﴾ $$

*Is he, therefore, better who lays his foundation on fear of God and (His) good pleasure, or he who lays his foundation on the edge of a cracking hollowed bank, so it broke down with him into the fire of hell; and God does not guide the unjust people. (Koran 9:109)*

$$ وَٱلَّذِينَ ءَامَنُوا۟ وَعَمِلُوا۟ ٱلصَّٰلِحَٰتِ سَنُدْخِلُهُمْ جَنَّٰتٍ تَجْرِى مِن $$

$$ تَحْتِهَا ٱلْأَنْهَٰرُ خَٰلِدِينَ فِيهَآ أَبَدًا وَعْدَ ٱللَّهِ حَقًّا وَمَنْ $$

$$ أَصْدَقُ مِنَ ٱللَّهِ قِيلًا ﴿١٢٢﴾ $$

*And (as for) those who believe and do good, We will make them enter into gardens beneath which rivers flow, to abide therein forever; (it is) a promise of God, true (indeed), and who is truer of word than God? (Koran 4:122)*

$$ وَلَهُۥ مَن فِى ٱلسَّمَٰوَٰتِ وَٱلْأَرْضِ وَمَنْ عِندَهُۥ لَا يَسْتَكْبِرُونَ عَنْ عِبَادَتِهِۦ $$

$$ وَلَا يَسْتَحْسِرُونَ ﴿١٩﴾ $$

*And whoever is in the heavens and the earth is His; and those who are with Him are not proud to serve Him, nor do they grow weary. (Koran 21:19)*

187

# PRAYER

The following sequential excerpts from the Old Testament suggest that ancient prayer involved washing of hands and feet before prayer as the Lord commanded Moses (*Exodus 40:30-32*). Later prayer was towards the House of the Lord in Jerusalem (*1Kings 8:29-30*). King Solomon prayed by kneeling on his knees with his hands spread up to heaven (1Kings 8:54). Prayer also involved bowing with the face to the ground (*Nehemiah 8:6*). The Psalms of David again reaffirm the importance of washing (Psalms 26:6) while kneeling is again mentioned in the Book of Daniel (Daniel 6:10).

## Exodus 40

*He placed the basin between the Tent of Meeting and the altar and put water in it for washing, (Exodus 40:30) and Moses and Aaron and his sons used it to **wash their hands and feet**. (Exodus 40:31)*
***They washed** whenever they entered the Tent of Meeting or approached the altar, **as the LORD commanded Moses**. (Exodus 40:32)*

## 1Kings 8

*That thine eyes may be open toward this house night and day, even toward the place of which thou hast said, My name shall be there: that thou mayest hearken unto the **prayer which thy servant shall make toward this place**. (1Kings 8:29)*

*And hearken thou to the supplication of thy servant, and of thy people Israel, when they shall **pray toward this place**: and hear thou in heaven thy dwelling place: and when thou hearest, forgive. (1Kings 8:30)*

*And it was so, that when **Solomon** had made an end of praying all this **prayer** and supplication unto the LORD, he arose from **before the altar of the LORD**, from **kneeling on his knees with his hands spread up to heaven.** (1Kings 8:54)*

**Nehemiah 8**

*Ezra praised the LORD, the great God; and all the people lifted their hands and responded, "Amen! Amen!" Then they bowed down and worshiped the LORD **with their faces to the ground**. (Nehemiah 8:6)*

**Psalm 26**

*I **wash my hands** in innocence, and go about your altar, O LORD. (Psalm 26:6)*

**Daniel 6**

*Now when Daniel knew that the writing was signed, he went into his house; and his windows being open in his chamber **toward Jerusalem, he kneeled upon his knees three times a day,** and prayed, and gave thanks before his God, as he did aforetime. (Daniel 6:10)*

**Zechariah 8**

*Yea, many people and strong nations shall come to **seek the LORD** of hosts **in Jerusalem, and to pray before the LORD** (Zechariah 8:22)*

## JERUSALEM

As just discussed, prayer towards the *"House of the Lord in Jerusalem"* is mentioned in *1Kings 8:29* and *Daniel 6:10*. Prayer is also associated with kneeling and raising one's hands toward heaven *(1Kings 8:54)*. This concept of prayer towards the house of the Lord in Jerusalem and then Mecca is narrated in the Koran and is referred to as the *"qiblah"(Koran 2:143—144* and *2:177)*. Qiblah is the Arabic word for *"the direction of prayer."* The Koran states that the purpose of prayer is for the *"remembrance"* of God *(Koran 20:14)*.

## Psalm 122

*I was glad when they said unto me, Let us go into the house of the LORD. (Psalm 122:1)*

*Our feet shall stand within thy gates, O Jerusalem. (Psalm 122:2)*

*Jerusalem is builded as a city that is compact together: (Psalm 122:3)*

*Whither the tribes go up, the tribes of the LORD, unto the testimony of Israel, to give thanks unto the name of the LORD. (Psalm 122:4)*

*For there are set thrones of judgment, the thrones of the house of David. (Psalm 122:5)*

**Pray for the peace of Jerusalem:** *they shall prosper that love thee. (Psalm 122:6)*

*Peace be within thy walls, and prosperity within thy palaces. (Psalm 122: 7)*

*For my brethren and companions' sakes, I will now say, Peace be within thee. (Psalm 122:8)*

*Because of the* **house of the LORD our God** *I will seek thy good. (Psalm 122:9)*

## 1Kings 5

*And* **Hiram king of Tyre** *sent his servants unto Solomon; for he had heard that they had anointed him king in the room of his father: for Hiram was ever a lover of David. (1Kings 5:1)*

*And Solomon sent to Hiram, saying, (1Kings 5:2)*

*Thou knowest how that David my father could not build an house unto the name of the LORD his God for the wars which were about him on every side, until the LORD put them under the soles of his feet. (1Kings 5:3)*

*And* **Hiram sent to Solomon, saying,** *I have considered the things which thou sentest to me for: and **I will do all thy desire concerning timber of cedar, and concerning timber of fir.** (1Kings 5:8)*

**My servants shall bring them down from Lebanon** *unto the sea: and I will convey them by sea in floats unto the place that thou shalt appoint me, and will cause them to be discharged there, and thou shalt receive them: and thou shalt accomplish my desire, in giving food for my household. (1Kings 5:9 )*

*And **Solomon's builders and Hiram's builders** did hew them, and the stonesquarers: so they **prepared timber and stones to build the house.** (1Kings 5:18)*

## 1Kings 6

*And **the word of the LORD came to Solomon, saying,** (1Kings 6:11) Concerning this house which thou art in building, if thou wilt **walk in my statutes, and execute my judgments, and keep all my commandments** to walk in them; then will I perform my word with thee, which I spake unto David thy father: (1Kings 6:12) And I will dwell among the children of Israel, and will not forsake my people Israel. (1Kings 6:13)*

*And the oracle he prepared **in the house within, to set there the ark of the covenant of the LORD.** (1Kings 6:19)*
## 1Kings 8

*And **king Solomon,** and all the congregation of Israel, that were assembled unto him, were with him before the ark, **sacrificing sheep** and oxen, that could not be told nor numbered for multitude. (1Kings 8:5)*

***There was nothing in the ark save the two tables of stone, which Moses put there** at Horeb, **when the LORD made a covenant with the children of Israel, when they came out of the land of Egypt.** (1Kings 8:9)*

***And it was in the heart of David my father to build an house for the name of the LORD God of Israel.** (1Kings 8:17) **And the LORD said unto David my father, Whereas it was in thine heart to build an house unto my name, thou didst well that it was in thine heart.** (1Kings 8:18) **Nevertheless thou shalt not build the house; but thy son that shall come forth out of thy loins, he shall build the house unto my name.** (1Kings 8:19) And the LORD hath performed his word that he spake, and I am risen up in the room of David my father, and sit on the throne of Israel, as the LORD promised, and have built an house for the name of the LORD God of Israel. (1Kings 8:20)*

*And I have set there a place for the ark, wherein is the covenant of the LORD, which he made with our fathers, when he brought them out of the land of Egypt. (1Kings 8:21)*

**And Solomon stood before the altar of the LORD in the presence of all the congregation** *of Israel, and spread forth his hands toward heaven: (1Kings 8:22)*

*And he said, LORD God of Israel, there is no God like thee, in heaven above, or on earth beneath, who keepest covenant and mercy with thy servants that walk before thee with all their heart: (1Kings 8:23)*

*Who hast kept with thy servant David my father that thou promisedst him: thou spakest also with thy mouth, and hast fulfilled it with thine hand, as it is this day. (1Kings 8:24)*

*Therefore now, LORD God of Israel, keep with thy servant David my father that thou promisedst him, saying, There shall not fail thee a man in my sight to sit on the throne of Israel; so that thy children take heed to their way, that they walk before me as thou hast walked before me. (1Kings 8:25)*

*And now, O God of Israel, let thy word, I pray thee, be verified, which thou spakest unto thy servant David my father. (1Kings 8:26)*

*But will God indeed dwell on the earth? behold, the heaven and heaven of heavens cannot contain thee; how much less this house that I have builded? (1Kings 8:27)*

*Yet have thou respect unto the prayer of thy servant, and to his supplication, O LORD my God, to hearken unto the cry and to the prayer, which thy servant prayeth before thee to day: (1Kings 8:28)*

*That thine eyes may be open toward this house night and day, even toward the place of which thou hast said, My name shall be there: that thou mayest hearken unto the prayer which thy servant shall make **toward** this place. (1Kings 8:29)*

*And hearken thou to the supplication of thy servant, and of thy people Israel, when they shall **pray toward this place:** and hear thou in heaven thy dwelling place: and when thou hearest, forgive. (1Kings 8:30)*

*And it was so, that when Solomon had made an end of praying all this prayer and supplication unto the LORD, he arose from before the altar of the LORD, from **kneeling on his knees** with his hands spread up to heaven. (1Kings 8:54)*

وَكَذَٰلِكَ جَعَلْنَٰكُمْ أُمَّةً وَسَطًا لِّتَكُونُوا شُهَدَآءَ عَلَى ٱلنَّاسِ
وَيَكُونَ ٱلرَّسُولُ عَلَيْكُمْ شَهِيدًا وَمَا جَعَلْنَا ٱلْقِبْلَةَ ٱلَّتِى كُنتَ
عَلَيْهَآ إِلَّا لِنَعْلَمَ مَن يَتَّبِعُ ٱلرَّسُولَ مِمَّن يَنقَلِبُ عَلَىٰ عَقِبَيْهِ وَإِن كَانَتْ
لَكَبِيرَةً إِلَّا عَلَى ٱلَّذِينَ هَدَى ٱللَّهُ وَمَا كَانَ ٱللَّهُ لِيُضِيعَ إِيمَٰنَكُمْ إِنَّ
ٱللَّهَ بِٱلنَّاسِ لَرَءُوفٌ رَّحِيمٌ ﴿١٤٣﴾

*And thus We have made you a medium (just) nation that you may be the bearers of witness against people and (that) the messenger may be a bearer of witness to you; and* **We appointed the qiblah (Jerusalem) which ye formerly observed only that We might know him who followeth the messenger from him who turns back upon his heels** *and this was surely hard except for those whom God has guided aright; and God was not going to make your faith to be in vain; most surely God is Affectionate, Merciful to the people. (Koran 2:143)*

قَدْ نَرَىٰ تَقَلُّبَ وَجْهِكَ فِى ٱلسَّمَآءِ فَلَنُوَلِّيَنَّكَ قِبْلَةً تَرْضَىٰهَا فَوَلِّ وَجْهَكَ
شَطْرَ ٱلْمَسْجِدِ ٱلْحَرَامِ وَحَيْثُ مَا كُنتُمْ فَوَلُّوا وُجُوهَكُمْ شَطْرَهُ وَإِنَّ
ٱلَّذِينَ أُوتُوا ٱلْكِتَٰبَ لَيَعْلَمُونَ أَنَّهُ ٱلْحَقُّ مِن رَّبِّهِمْ وَمَا ٱللَّهُ بِغَٰفِلٍ عَمَّا
يَعْمَلُونَ ﴿١٤٤﴾

*Indeed We see the turning of your face to heaven, so We shall surely turn you to a qiblah which you shall like; turn then your face towards the Sacred Mosque (Kaaba at Mecca), and wherever you are, turn your face towards it, and those who have been given the Book most surely know that it is the truth from their Lord; and God is not at all heedless of what they do. (Koran 2:144)*

۞ لَّيْسَ ٱلْبِرَّ أَن تُوَلُّواْ وُجُوهَكُمْ قِبَلَ ٱلْمَشْرِقِ وَٱلْمَغْرِبِ

وَلَـٰكِنَّ ٱلْبِرَّ مَنْ ءَامَنَ بِٱللَّهِ وَٱلْيَوْمِ ٱلْأَخِرِ وَٱلْمَلَـٰٓئِكَةِ وَٱلْكِتَـٰبِ

وَٱلنَّبِيِّـۧنَ وَءَاتَى ٱلْمَالَ عَلَىٰ حُبِّهِۦ ذَوِى ٱلْقُرْبَىٰ وَٱلْيَتَـٰمَىٰ وَٱلْمَسَـٰكِينَ

وَٱبْنَ ٱلسَّبِيلِ وَٱلسَّآئِلِينَ وَفِى ٱلرِّقَابِ وَأَقَامَ ٱلصَّلَوٰةَ وَءَاتَى ٱلزَّكَوٰةَ

وَٱلْمُوفُونَ بِعَهْدِهِمْ إِذَا عَـٰهَدُواْ وَٱلصَّـٰبِرِينَ فِى ٱلْبَأْسَآءِ وَٱلضَّرَّآءِ

وَحِينَ ٱلْبَأْسِ أُوْلَـٰٓئِكَ ٱلَّذِينَ صَدَقُواْ وَأُوْلَـٰٓئِكَ هُمُ ٱلْمُتَّقُونَ ۱۷۷

*It is not righteousness that you turn your faces towards the East and the West, but righteousness is this that one should believe in God and the last day and the angels and the Book and the prophets, and giveth wealth out of love for Him to the near of kin and the orphans and the needy and the wayfarer and to those who ask, and to set slaves free, and keep up prayer and pay the poor-rate; and the performers of their promise when they make a promise, and the patient in tribulation and adversity and time of stress. Such are they who are sincere. Such are the God-fearing.* (Koran 2:177)

إِنَّنِىٓ أَنَا ٱللَّهُ لَآ إِلَـٰهَ إِلَّآ أَنَا۠ فَٱعْبُدْنِى وَأَقِمِ ٱلصَّلَوٰةَ لِذِكْرِىٓ ۱٤

*Verily, I am God, there is no god but I, therefore serve Me and keep up prayer for My remembrance* (Koran 20:14)

## HAJJ: A SPIRITUAL JOURNEY TO ETERNITY

A Muslim's commitment to Hajj is to acknowledge a Higher Power that is omniscient, omnipotent and omnipresent. Hajj is a desire to obey God's commands and take leave of all worldly concerns and possessions as well as bidding farewell to family, friends, work and domicile. Hajj requires accepting that we will eventually meet our true master the Lord of all lords, who is responsible for giving us life when we knew it not, and then taking it from us again before the final rendezvous when from death life will once again be bestowed. Hajj entails that we believe in the compassion of God who will, in his infinite wisdom and justice, on the day of resurrection punish and reward us then give us the gift of eternal life.

Men, are dressed in two pieces of white cloth, to acknowledge that we are all equal before God, leaving behind status and wealth, and going to an atmosphere of worship. While circulating around the 'House of God' we acknowledge the greatness of God, sustainer of the universe, asking for guidance in this world and forgiveness for our sins. While at Hajj we retrace the footsteps of Hagar, and her infant son Ishmael (in Hebrew means *'God Hears'*), desperately searching for water after being left in the desert by our Patriarch Abraham (in Hebrew means *"Father of many Nations"*). We acknowledge by firm belief that by entrusting our fate with God we will not be deserted in the desert. God against all odds guided Hagar in her moment of need to the spring water of Zamzam—the fountain of life. God's command quenched the thirst of Ishmael and Hagar by providing water—the quintessence of our mortal existence. Drinking from Zamzam, the seemingly eternal well, establishes our connection with God our savior who is truly our sole provider. The ritual stoning of the devil, commemorating the devil's tempting of Abraham in disobeying God's command to sacrifice his son Ishmael, reinforces our resolve to overcome the forces of evil. As Abraham trusted God and was relieved from the seemingly inscrutable decree to sacrifice his beloved son by instead performing a symbolic sacrifice so does a Muslim, on this eternal spiritual journey of life with its challenges and pleasantries, reenact by sacrificing a lamb to feed the poor. To obey God's commandments, even if seemingly inscrutable, resisting all temptations, as Abraham did, is the moral of the story. Hajj, if performed with a sense of purpose and meaning can be a spiritual journey to eternity.

# FASTING

In the Old Testament, as quoted below, we learn that fasting humbles and purifies the soul *(Psalm 35:13 & 69:10)*, may be combined with prayer *(Daniel 9:3)*, and is required by God *(Joel 2:12)*.

*To confirm these days of Purim in their times appointed, according as Mordecai the Jew and Esther the queen had enjoined them, and as they had decreed for themselves and for their seed, the matters of the fastings and their cry. (Esther 9:31)*

*But as for me, when they were sick, my clothing was sackcloth: **I humbled my soul with fasting**; and my prayer returned into mine own bosom. (Psalm 35:13)*

*When I wept, and **chastened my soul with fasting**, that was to my reproach. (Psalm 69:10)*

*And **I set my face unto the Lord God, to seek by prayer and supplication, with fasting**, and sackcloth, and ashes (Daniel 9:3)*

*Therefore also now, **saith the LORD, turn ye even to me with all your heart, and with fasting**, and with weeping, and with mourning: (Joel 2:12)*

# TITHE AND ALMS

### OLD TESTAMENT

*And **all the tithe of the land**, whether of the seed of the land, or of the fruit of the tree, **is the LORD's**: it is holy unto the LORD. (Leviticus 27:30)*

*These are the commandments, which the LORD commanded Moses for the children of Israel in mount Sinai. (Leviticus 27:34)*

*When thou hast made an end of tithing* all the tithes of thine increase the third year, which is the year of tithing, *and hast given it unto* the Levite, *the stranger, the fatherless, and the widow*, that they may eat within thy gates, and be filled; *(Deuteronomy 26:12)*

*Then thou shalt say before the LORD thy God*, I have brought away the hallowed things out of mine house, and also have given them unto the Levite, and unto the stranger, to the fatherless, and to the widow, according to all thy commandments which thou hast commanded me: *I have not transgressed thy commandments, neither have I forgotten them:* *(Deuteronomy 26:13)*

Look down from thy holy habitation, from heaven, and bless thy people Israel, and the land which thou hast given us, as thou swarest unto our fathers, a land that floweth with milk and honey. *(Deuteronomy 26:15)*
*This day the LORD thy God hath commanded thee to do these statutes and judgments: thou shalt therefore keep and do them with all thine heart, and with all thy soul.* *(Deuteronomy 26:16)*

## NEW TESTAMENT

Take heed that ye do not your *alms* before men, to be seen of them: otherwise ye have no reward of your Father which is in heaven. *(Matthew 6:1)*
Therefore when thou doest thine *alms*, do not sound a trumpet before thee, as the hypocrites do in the synagogues and in the streets, that they may have glory of men. Verily I say unto you, They have their reward.*(Matthew 6:2)*

Woe unto you, scribes and Pharisees, hypocrites! for ye pay tithe of mint and anise and cummin, and have omitted the weightier matters of the law, judgment, mercy, and faith: these ought ye to have done, and not to leave the other undone. *(Matthew 23:23)*

*But woe unto you, Pharisees!* for ye tithe mint and rue and all manner of herbs, and *pass over judgment and the love of God*: these ought ye to have done, and not to leave the other undone. *(Luke 11:42)*

Similarly, Islam enjoins believers to pray, fast and give 2.50% of their savings to charity.

# Reflections

لَّا تُدْرِكُهُ ٱلْأَبْصَرُ وَهُوَ يُدْرِكُ ٱلْأَبْصَرَّ وَهُوَ ٱللَّطِيفُ ٱلْخَبِيرُ ﴿١٠٣﴾

*No vision can grasp Him, but His grasp is over all vision: He is above all comprehension, yet is acquainted with all things. (Koran 6:103)*

إِنَّ ٱلَّذِينَ ءَامَنُوا۟ وَٱلَّذِينَ هَادُوا۟ وَٱلنَّصَرَىٰ وَٱلصَّبِئِينَ مَنْ ءَامَنَ بِٱللَّهِ وَٱلْيَوْمِ ٱلْأَخِرِ وَعَمِلَ صَلِحًا فَلَهُمْ أَجْرُهُمْ عِندَ رَبِّهِمْ وَلَا خَوْفٌ عَلَيْهِمْ وَلَا هُمْ يَحْزَنُونَ ﴿٦٢﴾

*Surely, those who believe and those who are Jews and Christians, and Sabians, whoever believes in God and the Last Day and leads a righteous life shall have their recompense from their Lord, they have nothing to fear, nor will they grieve. (Koran 2:62)*

وَأَنزَلْنَا إِلَيْكَ ٱلْكِتَٰبَ بِٱلْحَقِّ مُصَدِّقًا لِّمَا بَيْنَ يَدَيْهِ مِنَ ٱلْكِتَٰبِ وَمُهَيْمِنًا عَلَيْهِ ۖ فَٱحْكُم بَيْنَهُم بِمَا أَنزَلَ ٱللَّهُ ۖ وَلَا تَتَّبِعْ أَهْوَآءَهُمْ عَمَّا جَآءَكَ مِنَ ٱلْحَقِّ ۚ لِكُلٍّ جَعَلْنَا مِنكُمْ شِرْعَةً وَمِنْهَاجًا ۚ وَلَوْ شَآءَ ٱللَّهُ لَجَعَلَكُمْ أُمَّةً وَٰحِدَةً وَلَٰكِن لِّيَبْلُوَكُمْ فِى مَآ ءَاتَىٰكُمْ ۖ فَٱسْتَبِقُوا ٱلْخَيْرَٰتِ ۚ إِلَى ٱللَّهِ مَرْجِعُكُمْ جَمِيعًا فَيُنَبِّئُكُم بِمَا كُنتُمْ فِيهِ تَخْتَلِفُونَ ۝

*And We have sent down to you the Book (this Koran) in truth, confirming the Scripture that came before it and guarding over it. So judge between them by what God has revealed, and follow not their vain desires, diverging away from the truth that has come to you. To each among you, We have prescribed a law and a clear way. **If God willed, He would have made you one nation, but that (He) may test you in what He has given you; so strive as in a race in good deeds. The return of you (all) is to God; then He will inform you about that in which you used to differ.** (Koran 5:48)*

بَلْ نَقْذِفُ بِٱلْحَقِّ عَلَى ٱلْبَٰطِلِ فَيَدْمَغُهُ فَإِذَا هُوَ زَاهِقٌ ۚ وَلَكُمُ ٱلْوَيْلُ مِمَّا تَصِفُونَ ۝

*Nay, We hurl the Truth against falsehood, and it knocks out its brain, and behold, falsehood doth perish! Ah! woe be to you for the (false) things ye ascribe (to Us). (Koran 21:18)*

لَآ إِكْرَاهَ فِى ٱلدِّينِ قَد تَّبَيَّنَ ٱلرُّشْدُ مِنَ ٱلْغَىِّ فَمَن يَكْفُرْ بِٱلطَّٰغُوتِ وَيُؤْمِنۢ بِٱللَّهِ فَقَدِ ٱسْتَمْسَكَ بِٱلْعُرْوَةِ ٱلْوُثْقَىٰ لَا ٱنفِصَامَ لَهَا وَٱللَّهُ سَمِيعٌ عَلِيمٌ ﴿٢٥٦﴾

**There is no compulsion in religion.** Verily, the Right Path has become distinct from the wrong path; therefore, whoever disbelieves in the Satan and believes in God he indeed has laid hold on the firmest handle, which shall not break off, and God is Hearing, Knowing. *(Koran 2:256)*

سَأَصْرِفُ عَنْ ءَايَٰتِىَ ٱلَّذِينَ يَتَكَبَّرُونَ فِى ٱلْأَرْضِ بِغَيْرِ ٱلْحَقِّ وَإِن يَرَوْاْ كُلَّ ءَايَةٍ لَّا يُؤْمِنُواْ بِهَا وَإِن يَرَوْاْ سَبِيلَ ٱلرُّشْدِ لَا يَتَّخِذُوهُ سَبِيلًا وَإِن يَرَوْاْ سَبِيلَ ٱلْغَىِّ يَتَّخِذُوهُ سَبِيلًا ذَٰلِكَ بِأَنَّهُمْ كَذَّبُواْ بِـَٔايَٰتِنَا وَكَانُواْ عَنْهَا غَٰفِلِينَ ﴿١٤٦﴾

**I will divert from My revelations those who are arrogant** on earth, without justification. **Consequently, when they see every kind of proof they will not believe.** And when they see the path of guidance they will not adopt it as their path, but when they see the path of straying they will adopt it as their path. This is the consequence of their rejecting our proofs, and being totally heedless thereof. *(Koran 7:146)*

لَهُۥ مُعَقِّبَـٰتٌ مِّنۢ بَيْنِ يَدَيْهِ وَمِنْ خَلْفِهِۦ يَحْفَظُونَهُۥ مِنْ أَمْرِ ٱللَّهِ إِنَّ ٱللَّهَ لَا يُغَيِّرُ مَا بِقَوْمٍ حَتَّىٰ يُغَيِّرُواْ مَا بِأَنفُسِهِمْ وَإِذَآ أَرَادَ ٱللَّهُ بِقَوْمٍ سُوٓءًا فَلَا مَرَدَّ لَهُۥ وَمَا لَهُم مِّن دُونِهِۦ مِن وَالٍ ۝

For each (such person) there are (angels) in succession, before and behind him: They guard him by command of God. Verily **never will God change the condition of a people until they change what is in themselves.** But when (once) God willeth a people's punishment, there can be no turning it back, nor will they find, besides Him, any to protect. (Koran 13:11)

أَفَلَا يَتَدَبَّرُونَ ٱلْقُرْءَانَ وَلَوْ كَانَ مِنْ عِندِ غَيْرِ ٱللَّهِ لَوَجَدُواْ فِيهِ ٱخْتِلَٰفًا كَثِيرًا ۝

Do they not then consider the Koran carefully? Had it been from other than God, they would surely have found therein many contradictions. (Koran 4:82)

وَمَا كَانَ هَٰذَا ٱلْقُرْءَانُ أَن يُفْتَرَىٰ مِن دُونِ ٱللَّهِ وَلَٰكِن تَصْدِيقَ ٱلَّذِى بَيْنَ يَدَيْهِ وَتَفْصِيلَ ٱلْكِتَٰبِ لَا رَيْبَ فِيهِ مِن رَّبِّ ٱلْعَٰلَمِينَ ۝

This **Koran** is not such as can be produced by other than God; on the contrary it is **a confirmation** of (revelations) that went before it, and a fuller explanation of the Book? wherein there is no doubt—from the Lord of the Worlds. (Koran 10:37)

وَقَالَ ٱلَّذِينَ كَفَرُوٓاْ إِنْ هَـٰذَآ إِلَّآ إِفْكٌ ٱفْتَرَىٰهُ وَأَعَانَهُۥ عَلَيْهِ قَوْمٌ ءَاخَرُونَ فَقَدْ جَآءُو ظُلْمًا وَزُورًا ۝

*"Those who disbelieved. said, "This is no more than a fabrication by him, with the help of other people." Indeed, they uttered a blasphemy; a. falsehood. (Koran 25:4)*

وَقَالَ ٱلَّذِينَ كَفَرُواْ لَوْلَا نُزِّلَ عَلَيْهِ ٱلْقُرْءَانُ جُمْلَةً وَٰحِدَةً كَذَٰلِكَ لِنُثَبِّتَ بِهِۦ فُؤَادَكَ وَرَتَّلْنَـٰهُ تَرْتِيلًا ۝

*And those who disbelieve say: "Why is not the Koran revealed to him all at once?" Thus (it is sent down in parts), that We may strengthen your heart thereby. And We have revealed it to you gradually, in stages. (Koran 25:32)*

وَإِذَا بَدَّلْنَآ ءَايَةً مَّكَانَ ءَايَةٍ وَٱللَّهُ أَعْلَمُ بِمَا يُنَزِّلُ قَالُوٓاْ إِنَّمَآ أَنتَ مُفْتَرٍ بَلْ أَكْثَرُهُمْ لَا يَعْلَمُونَ ۝

*When We substitute one revelation for another,—and God knows best what He reveals (in stages),—they say, "Thou art but a forger": but most of them know not. (Koran 16:101)*

وَمَا كُنتَ تَتْلُواْ مِن قَبْلِهِۦ مِن كِتَـٰبٍ وَلَا تَخُطُّهُۥ بِيَمِينِكَ إِذًا لَّٱرْتَابَ ٱلْمُبْطِلُونَ ۝

*Neither did you (O Muhammad) read any book (scripture) before it, nor did you write with your right hand, for then might those have doubted who follow falsehood' (Koran 29:48).*

وَلَقَدْ صَرَّفْنَا فِى هَٰذَا ٱلْقُرْءَانِ لِلنَّاسِ مِن كُلِّ مَثَلٍ وَكَانَ ٱلْإِنسَٰنُ أَكْثَرَ شَىْءٍ جَدَلًا ۝

*We have explained in detail in this Koran, for the benefit of mankind, every kind of similitude: but man is, in most things, contentious.* (Koran 18:54)

كُلُّ نَفْسٍ ذَآئِقَةُ ٱلْمَوْتِ وَنَبْلُوكُم بِٱلشَّرِّ وَٱلْخَيْرِ فِتْنَةً وَإِلَيْنَا تُرْجَعُونَ ۝

*Everyone is going to taste death, and We shall make a trial of you with evil and with good, and to Us you will be returned.* (Koran 21:35)

قُلْ نَزَّلَهُ رُوحُ ٱلْقُدُسِ مِن رَّبِّكَ بِٱلْحَقِّ لِيُثَبِّتَ ٱلَّذِينَ ءَامَنُوا۟ وَهُدًى وَبُشْرَىٰ لِلْمُسْلِمِينَ ۝

*Say, the Holy Spirit has brought the revelation from thy Lord in Truth,* in order to strengthen those who believe, and as a Guide and Glad Tidings to those who have submitted. (Koran 16:102)

أَفَلَا يَتَدَبَّرُونَ ٱلْقُرْءَانَ أَمْ عَلَىٰ قُلُوبٍ أَقْفَالُهَا ۝

*Do they not then **think deeply about the Koran**, or are their locks on their hearts.* (Koran 47:24)

وَنَضَعُ ٱلْمَوَازِينَ ٱلْقِسْطَ لِيَوْمِ ٱلْقِيَمَةِ فَلَا تُظْلَمُ نَفْسٌ
شَيْـًٔا وَإِن كَانَ مِثْقَالَ حَبَّةٍ مِّنْ خَرْدَلٍ أَتَيْنَا بِهَا وَكَفَىٰ بِنَا
حَسِبِينَ ٤٧

**We shall set up scales of justice for the Day of Judgment,** *so that not a soul will be dealt with unjustly in the least, and if there be (no more than) the weight of a mustard seed, We will bring it (to account): and enough are We to take account. (Koran 21:47)*

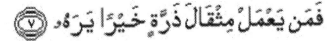

*So **whosoever does good equal to the weight of an atom shall see it.** (Koran 99:7)*

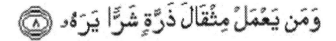

*And **whosoever does evil equal to the weight of an atom shall see it.** (Koran 99:8)*

قُلْ يَجْمَعُ بَيْنَنَا رَبُّنَا ثُمَّ يَفْتَحُ بَيْنَنَا بِٱلْحَقِّ وَهُوَ ٱلْفَتَّاحُ ٱلْعَلِيمُ ٢٦

*Say: "**Our Lord will** gather us together and will in the end **decide the matter between us (and you) in truth and justice:** and He is the One to decide, the One Who knows all."(Koran 34:26)*

وَذَرِ ٱلَّذِينَ ٱتَّخَذُواْ دِينَهُمْ لَعِبًا وَلَهْوًا وَغَرَّتْهُمُ ٱلْحَيَوٰةُ

ٱلدُّنْيَا وَذَكِّرْ بِهِۦٓ أَن تُبْسَلَ نَفْسٌۢ بِمَا كَسَبَتْ لَيْسَ لَهَا مِن دُونِ

ٱللَّهِ وَلِيٌّ وَلَا شَفِيعٌ وَإِن تَعْدِلْ كُلَّ عَدْلٍ لَّا يُؤْخَذْ مِنْهَآ أُوْلَٰٓئِكَ

ٱلَّذِينَ أُبْسِلُواْ بِمَا كَسَبُواْ لَهُمْ شَرَابٌ مِّنْ حَمِيمٍ وَعَذَابٌ أَلِيمٌۢ بِمَا

كَانُواْ يَكْفُرُونَ ۝

And **leave alone those who take their religion as play and amusement,**
and are deceived by the life of this world. But remind (them) with it (the
Koran) lest a person be given up to destruction for that which he has earned,
when he will find for himself no protector or intercessor besides God, and even
if he offers every ransom, it will not be accepted from him. Such are they who
are given up to destruction because of that which they have earned. For them
will be a drink of boiling water and a painful torment because they used to
disbelieve. (Koran 6:70)

أَفَغَيْرَ ٱللَّهِ أَبْتَغِي حَكَمًا وَهُوَ ٱلَّذِىٓ أَنزَلَ إِلَيْكُمُ ٱلْكِتَٰبَ مُفَصَّلًا وَٱلَّذِينَ

ءَاتَيْنَٰهُمُ ٱلْكِتَٰبَ يَعْلَمُونَ أَنَّهُۥ مُنَزَّلٌ مِّن رَّبِّكَ بِٱلْحَقِّ فَلَا تَكُونَنَّ مِنَ

ٱلْمُمْتَرِينَ ۝

**"Shall I seek other than God as a source of law,** when He has revealed this
book fully detailed? Those who received the Scripture know that it is revealed
from your Lord, truthfully. So be not you of those who doubt."(Koran 6:114)

وَإِن تُطِعۡ أَكۡثَرَ مَن فِى ٱلۡأَرۡضِ يُضِلُّوكَ عَن سَبِيلِ ٱللَّهِ إِن يَتَّبِعُونَ إِلَّا ٱلظَّنَّ وَإِنۡ هُمۡ إِلَّا يَخۡرُصُونَ ﴿١١٦﴾

*Wert thou to follow the common run of those on earth, they will lead thee away from the way of God. They follow nothing but conjecture: they do nothing but lie. (Koran 6:116)*

If *"In God We Trust"* then God's infinite wisdom will guide us to a new world order where there will be true peace and prosperity but if we only trust in the selfish and limited logic of mankind then we could be misled into a new world of disorder. The choice is ours. We either submit to God or our own desires. The word Muslim means one who *'submits'* his soul to the will of God. The God of Israel is the God of Arabia and the God of all mankind . . .

# ABRAHAM'S DESCENDANTS

**ABRAHAM**

(Hebrew meaning: *"father of many nations"*)

↓                                                            ↓

**ISHMAEL**                          **ISAAC**

*(Hebrew meaning: "God Hears")*

↓                                                            ↓

**KEDAR & TEMA**                        **JACOB (ISRAEL)**

*(Gen. 25:13-15; Isaiah 21:11-17 & 42:1-11)*        (Father of the 12 tribes)

↓                                                            ↓

↓                                    JOSEPH, JUDAH & 10 brothers

↓                                    ( *Twelve tribes'* settled in Egypt)

↓

↓                                                            ↓

↓                                                            ↓

↓                                                            ↓

↓                                                            ↓

↓                                                            ↓

↓                                                            ↓

↓

↓                                    **MOSES**

↓                                    (Jews left Egypt for the *"promised land"*)

↓                                                            ↓

↓                                    DAVID

↓                                                            ↓

↓                                    SOLOMON

↓                                                            ↓

↓                                    King Nebuchadnezzar of Babylon

↓                                    (Jews taken into captivity)

↓                                                            ↓

↓                                                            ↓

↓                                                            ↓

↓                                                            ↓

↓

↓                                    **JESUS**

**MUHAMMAD**

# TEMA IN ISAIAH'S TIME

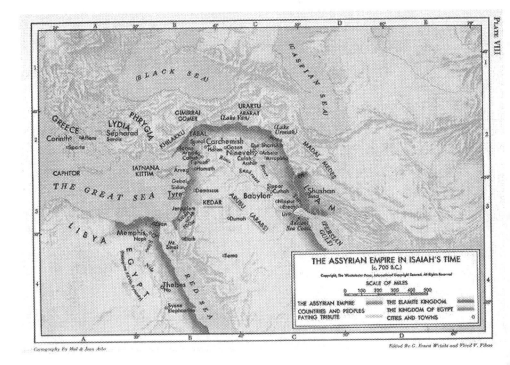

*This ancient map, during Isaiah's time, reveals that Tema is in the heart of Arabia.*

Reproduced from *A New Testament History* by Floyd V. FIlson. ©1964 W.L. Jenkins. Used by permission of Westminster John Knox Press.

# MAP OF ARABIA

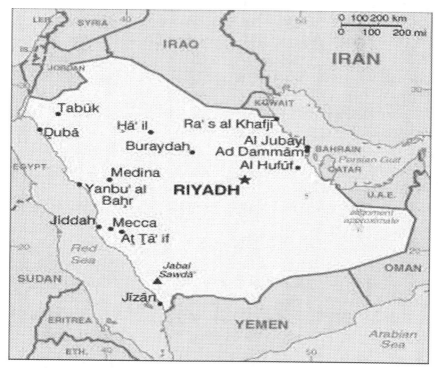

*The World Factbook 2007* (public domain)
(www.cia.gov/cia/publications/factbook/geos/sa.html)

*The relative **proximity of Medina to Tema**, as it pertains to Isaiah's vision is quite striking.*

*The ancient map (on the previous page), during Isaiah's time, reveals that Tema is in the heart of Arabia. Muhammad the prophet of Islam is buried in Medina.*

## About The Author And His Work

The author, a medical doctor, born in England and raised in Canada presently resides in the United States with his wife and three children. Dr. Gad's scientific background as well as knowledge of the Arabic and English languages facilitated the examination of scriptures utilizing both scientific and linguistics methodology to help enhance a better understanding of the message relayed in scriptures. For over twenty-five years the author has been on a personal journey painstakingly analyzing and investigating religious scriptures for irrefutable evidence in support of the existence of Divine Revelation. *In Search of God* is a compilation of different concepts derived from multiple sources. The author synthesizes these ideas in a lucid manner so that the readers may arrive at their own conclusions.

The first section of *In Search of God* begins with discussions supporting the existence of God and refuting Darwin; yet also arguing for the co-existence of evolution and creation. Subsequently, in the second section, the author examines the Koranic claim that the advent of the prophet Muhammad is foretold in the Torah and the Gospel *(Koran 7:157)*. The author studies this Koranic claim in the second major portion of *In Search of God* starting with Ishmael, father of the Arabs, whose Hebrew name means *"God Hears"*. Rabbi Glenn Blank affirms that the translation of Ishmael from the Hebrew is *"God Hears" (http://www.beitsimcha.com/s_ser/s_ser_0012.asp)*. Also, the Bible reveals that Ishmael's descendants were promised a *"Great Nation" (Genesis 17:20, KJV)*. In fulfillment of this promise, Ishmael's sons Kedar and Tema *(Genesis 25:13-15)* are mentioned further, in the Old Testament's Book of Isaiah, as part of Isaiah's prophetic vision *(Isaiah 21:11-17 and 42:1-11)*.

In the third section of *In Search of God* the author examines the difficult yet challenging controversy surrounding the identity of Jesus; the major point of contention between the three major world religions of Judaism, Christianity and Islam. The fourth part of *In Search of God* deals mainly with the revelation of Koranic scientific facts that became common knowledge with recent developments in scientific discoveries. The author's scientific background enables him to examine and present this section in an informative style. Finally, *In Search of God* closes by examining the commonalities, as well as the essence and spirit of revelation, as found in the Old Testament, New Testament and Koranic scriptures.

The information in this publication is condensed yet sufficiently detailed; offering a wealth of information and a knowledge base that will serve as a resource for future reference. *In Search of God* is an intellectual journey that promises to be a challenging endeavor for serious readers of all faiths and backgrounds. The author wishes to thank God for giving him the strength to work laboriously in compiling this material and utmost of all for enlightening him and instilling in him the desire to share the information that he has uncovered. Finally, as all humans have limitations in knowledge, the author wish to acknowledge any shortcomings by quoting old Islamic sages with the words that *"only God knows"*.